EARLY ISLAM

LIFE WORLD LIBRARY

LIFE NATURE LIBRARY

TIME READING PROGRAM

THE LIFE HISTORY OF THE UNITED STATES

LIFE SCIENCE LIBRARY

INTERNATIONAL BOOK SOCIETY

GREAT AGES OF MAN

TIME-LIFE LIBRARY OF ART

TIME-LIFE LIBRARY OF AMERICA

GREAT AGES OF MAN

A History of the World's Cultures

EARLY ISLAM

by

DESMOND STEWART

and

The Editors of TIME-LIFE BOOKS

TIME INCORPORATED, NEW YORK

THE AUTHOR: Desmond Stewart is a British writer who for many years has lived and traveled widely in the Middle East. He completed his studies as a classical scholar at Oxford in 1948; in the same year he received an appointment as Professor of Literature from the Iraqi Ministry of Education, and subsequently taught in Lebanon. He has contributed articles on Middle Eastern affairs to British and American publications and is the author of *The Arab World* and *Turkey* in the LIFE World Library. He has also written a number of novels.

THE CONSULTING EDITOR: Leonard Krieger, University Professor at the University of Chicago, was formerly Professor of History at Yale. Dr. Krieger is the author of *The German Idea of Freedom* and *The Politics of Discretion* and coauthor of *History*, written in collaboration with John Higham and Felix Gilbert.

THE COVER: The title page of *The Quintet*, a collection of Persian poems, shows angels surrounding a medallion in which each poem's title is ornately inscribed.

TIME-LIFE BOOKS

EDITOR
Maitland A. Edey

EXECUTIVE EDITOR
Jerry Korn

TEXT DIRECTOR   ART DIRECTOR
Martin Mann   Sheldon Cotler

CHIEF OF RESEARCH
Beatrice T. Dobie

PICTURE EDITOR
Robert G. Mason

Assistant Text Directors:
Harold C. Field, Ogden Tanner
Assistant Art Director: Arnold C. Holeywell
Assistant Chief of Research: Martha Turner

PUBLISHER
Rhett Austell
General Manager: Joseph C. Hazen Jr.
Circulation Director: Joan D. Manley
Marketing Director: Carter Smith
Business Manager: John D. McSweeney
Publishing Board: Nicholas Benton,
Louis Bronzo, James Wendell Forbes

GREAT AGES OF MAN

SERIES EDITOR: Russell Bourne
Deputy Editor: Carlotta Kerwin
Assistant Editor: Betsy Frankel
Editorial Staff for *Early Islam:*
Text Editor: William Longgood
Picture Editor: Jean Tennant
Designer: Norman Snyder
Assistant Designer: Ladislav Svatos
Staff Writers: Sam Halper, Edmund White
Chief Researcher: Peggy Bushong
Researchers: Jacqueline Boël, Sigrid von Huene,
Alice Baker, Carol Isenberg, James MaHood,
Kaye Neil, Nancy C. Newman, Paula Norworth,
Himilce Novas, Rhea Padis, Arlene Zuckerman
Art Assistant: Anne Landry

EDITORIAL PRODUCTION
Color Director: Robert L. Young
Assistant: James J. Cox
Copy Staff: Marian Gordon Goldman,
Barbara Hults, Dolores A. Littles
Picture Bureau: Margaret K. Goldsmith,
Joan Lynch
Traffic: Douglas B. Graham **245943**

The following individuals and departments of Time Inc. gave valuable aid in the preparation of this book: the Chief of the LIFE Picture Library, Doris O'Neil; the Chief of the Time Inc. Bureau of Editorial Reference, Peter Draz; the Chief of the TIME-LIFE News Service, Richard M. Clurman; and the correspondents Maria Vincenza Aloisi (Paris), Barbara Moir and Margot Hapgood (London), Ann Natanson (Rome), Elizabeth Kraemer and Lexi Blomeyer (Bonn), Traudl Lessing (Vienna), Helga Kohl (Athens), Charles Lanius (Istanbul) and Andrzej Glowacz (Cracow).

Contents

INTRODUCTION   7

1   A Messenger from God   10
        Picture Essay: "THE PROPHET'S PROGRESS"   21

2   Five Pillars of Faith   30
        Picture Essay: DESERT SANCTUARIES   41

3   A Time of Conquest   52
        Picture Essay: REACHES OF EMPIRE   65

4   The Golden Age   78
        Picture Essay: A MUSLIM'S LIFE   89

5   An Art of Many Peoples   100
        Picture Essay: CRAFTSMEN'S TREASURES   111

6   The Scientist-Philosophers   120
        Picture Essay: A PERSIAN BESTIARY   131

7   From Spain to Sumatra   140
        Picture Essay: PATTERNS OF AN ENCHANTED PALACE   149

8   A Durable Religion   162
        Picture Essay: ISLAM'S MAGIC CARPETS   171

Chronologies, 183
Bibliography, acknowledgments, 186
Credits and art notes, 187
Index, 188

Introduction

Islam is a way of life that has religious aspects, political aspects and cultural aspects, and each of the three overlaps and interacts. To do justice to a triple story of this kind presents problems that tax the ingenuity of any author—what to choose from the vast storehouse of the past, how to make it intelligible and meaningful.

Of all religions, Islam is nearest in kin to Judaism and Christianity. In fact the alienation between the Islamic and the Christian worlds is more one of politics and economics than of ideology. Islam the religion is a system of beliefs and practices revealed to Muhammad, enshrined in the Koran and supplemented by a traditional record, the *hadith*, of the things said and done by Muhammad.

In the course of its development, the religious unity of Islam was broken down into a variety of sects. Each added its own accretions to the learned system, mostly in the form of folk beliefs designed to fit Islam to local needs. In all, some 450 million men and women, representing every race and every one of the six continents, today consider themselves followers of the Prophet. Theirs is the dominant faith in a broad swath of land, running from Morocco on the west to Pakistan in the east; and they are also the dominant religious group in Malaysia and Indonesia.

Islam the state was a political entity that based its laws on the canon law of the Koran and on the modifications of that law worked out by Muhammad's successors at various times and in various places. Initially, the state of Islam grew at the expense of the Byzantine and Persian empires, the two greatest forces in the Middle East during Islam's period of expansion, and this is still the heartland of Islam. At its height, however, the Muslim empire extended from Spain to India, exceeding even the Roman empire in its prime.

Islam the culture, unlike the religion and government of Islam, is not essentially an Arabian invention. Except for the Arabic language through which it was disseminated, the Arabians contributed almost nothing. Islamic culture is a compound of other cultures—ancient Semitic, Classical Greek, medieval Indo-Persian. It was formulated for Islam largely by the peoples it conquered, the neo-Muslims. For a period of about 400 years, from midway through the Eighth Century to the 12th Century, the achievements of this synthesized culture were perhaps unsurpassed. In fact much of the science and literature of the European Renaissance was inspired by Islamic models.

Desmond Stewart, the author of this book, has done a thoroughly commendable job of putting together this vast and sprawling story. His narrative is vivid, his illustrations add authenticity, and his documentary evidence will, I hope, whet the appetites of some of his readers to further study.

PHILIP K. HITTI
Professor Emeritus of Semitic Literature
Princeton University

SPAIN

• Cordoba

• Palermo

Qayrawan •

• Tripoli

Danube R.

Konya •

Aleppo •

SYRIA

Damascus •

Jerusalem •

Alexandria •

• Cairo

EGYPT

Nile R.

*A
View of the
Islamic World
632-1258*

Murray Tinkelman

1
A MESSENGER FROM GOD

The Koran, a book of about the same length as the New Testament, is one of the most remarkable scriptures in history; it has molded the lives of millions of people and given birth to a powerful and enduring religion known as Islam, which has helped shape the modern world. Unlike the holy books of the Jews and Christians, which are collections of religious narratives, laws, poems, proverbs, prophecies and prayers, dating from different periods and written by different men, every word in the Koran was delivered to the world through the lips of a single man, the Prophet Muhammad, over a 22-year period in the early Seventh Century.

Some of the Koran's chapters, or *suras*, are short and fiery warnings of doom, proclaiming a Day of Judgment and demanding the worship of one God. Others discuss the Biblical prophets and the lessons of their lives; still others lay down detailed regulations concerning the family, property and justice. All are phrased in a hypnotic Arabic that helped convince the Koran's original hearers—Arab tribesmen who prided themselves on eloquence as much as courage—that this was no human speech but the word of God Himself.

The Koran is the heart of Islam—a word meaning, quite simply, "surrender to God." Islam began as a religious movement in the torrid wastes of Arabia and quickly spread through the Middle East. It encompassed many diverse peoples, who came to call themselves Muslims, or believers, welding them into a vast monotheistic state. In less than 10 years after the Prophet's death, through conquest and conversion, Islam shook the foundations of Byzantium and Persia, the two most powerful civilizations of the era. In less than a century it swept through parts of Asia, Africa and Europe, dominating an area larger than that of the Roman Empire at its peak. Eventually it was to make Arabic the common language of some 90 million people, to dictate a way of life for one out of every seven persons inhabiting the earth, and to exert a powerful influence on the West.

For more than six centuries—from the dawn of Islam, when on horse and camel the new converts surged out of Arabia, until the turning point in its long history, when Mongol nomads sacked the Muslim capital of Baghdad in 1258—Islam was the

A MASSIVE MINARET, *some 175 feet high, spirals skyward above the ruins of Islam's largest mosque, in the Ninth Century capital of Samarra. From atop its ramp, which echoes the stepped forms of ancient Babylonian ziggurats, criers once summoned tens of thousands of worshipers to prayer.*

world's most challenging religion, its strongest political force and its most vital culture. This culture linked, for the first time in history, such varied and distant peoples as Spaniards, black Africans, Persians, Turks, Egyptians and Indians. In this unifying role, Islam served to transmit more than one invention that proved crucial to the development of Western civilization. Muslims learned the technique of making paper from Chinese warriors they had captured in a battle near Samarkand, and eventually relayed the process to Europe. "Arabic" numerals were taken from India and transmitted to the Western world, where they became the standard mathematical symbols. Islam also performed another important service: the heritage of Classical Greece—both scientific and philosophical—which had been lost to the West for centuries, was in large part returned to it through translations undertaken in Islamic lands.

At the same time, the followers of Muhammad created a distinctive and valuable culture of their own. The genius of Islam was its ability to take elements of the various cultures that it embraced, synthesize them and then enlarge upon this amalgam. In medicine, for example, Muslims enhanced Greek theory by practical observation and clinical experience. Significant contributions were also made in chemistry, physics and mathematics; algebra, geometry and particularly trigonometry were largely developed in Islam.

In architecture Islam's most distinctive achievement was the mosque. A popular style of surface decoration used in these buildings was a rich pattern of swirling and interlocking designs; they were widely copied elsewhere and came to be known as arabesques. In such minor arts as carpet making, pottery, bookmaking, calligraphy, ivory and wood carving, Islamic craftsmen created exquisite works. In literature Islam produced famous works such as *The Arabian Nights*, which some scholars consider

an ancestor of the Western novel, and the classic Persian poem, the *Rubaiyat* of Omar Khayyam.

The religious movement that gave rise to these great cultural and political forces took root in what would seem to be one of the most unlikely places on the globe—a hot, parched wedge of land that spreads over one million square miles between Africa and Asia. In the Seventh Century many of its inhabitants were nomadic Bedouin tribesmen who lived in tents woven of goat's and camel's hair, subsisting on a frugal diet of dates and milk. Often they were engrossed in blood feuds with other tribes; sporadic raiding was a way of life.

The pre-Islamic Bedouins worshiped stones, trees and pieces of wood as the dwelling places of spirits whom they endowed with supernatural powers. The supreme human virtue, in their eyes, was manliness, expressed in the traits of loyalty, generosity and courage. Loyalty, above all, was necessary in the struggle for survival in the harsh desert; no man could live without the protection of his tribe, and the tribe could function only as a unit. Loyalty was the core of *asabiyya*, or clan spirit; a man was expected to be valiant to the point of death in defense of his tribe's rights, which related largely to pasturage and water in an arid wilderness where wells were more precious than gold. Generosity was expressed in the desert concept of hospitality; a well-known Arabic folk tale honors a youth who killed three of his father's camels to feed some passing strangers. Courage demanded the protection of one's women, and the participation in many raids; a great premium was placed on a man's skill in archery and horsemanship.

The eloquence that Arab tribesmen so admired was best expressed in their poetry, a spoken art form ideally suited to people who could carry few possessions because they were frequently on the move. This poetry was their major artistic achievement, and it played an important role in their daily

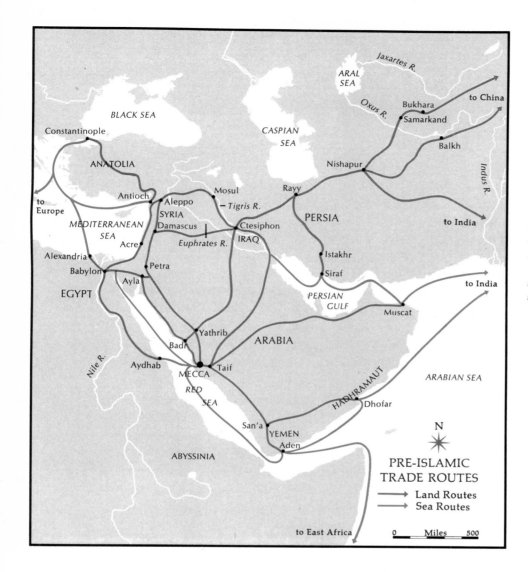

CROSSROADS OF COMMERCE, *Arabia was the ancient trading link between the Mediterranean and the Far East. By the Sixth Century, trouble in the Byzantine and Persian empires had threatened two major trading arteries—the Tigris-Euphrates route to the Persian Gulf and the Nile-Red Sea passage. Wary merchants thereupon turned to the slower land routes through Mecca, which soon became Arabia's greatest center of trade.*

lives. A poet could inspire his tribe's warriors and abash its foes; he also performed many other functions, including that of community spokesman, journalist, hired publicist and historian of his people's valiant deeds.

By the middle of the Sixth Century there were three major towns in northern Arabia. All three were located in a mountainous section called the Hijaz, bordered by the Red Sea on the west and the great desert to the east. In the central section of the Hijaz was Yathrib, a fertile oasis made up of farms and small villages spread over 20 square miles. Some 250 miles south was Taif, a cool summer refuge in the mountains, used by wealthy Arabian families. Immediately northwest of Taif was Mecca,

which lay some 50 miles inland from the Red Sea and was set in a rocky ravine, surrounded by mountains devoid of all vegetation.

Of these three towns, Mecca was by far the most prosperous and important. First, it was at the crossroads of the lucrative caravan trade. Vast camel trains, bearing spices, perfumes, precious metals, ivory and silk, filed through the town, headed north on the way from Yemen and the Hadhramaut to the markets of Syria, and headed east from the Red Sea across the desert to Iraq. Adding to the profits from caravans was a brisk pilgrimage trade, for Mecca was the site of Arabia's holiest pagan shrine. The shrine, located in the center of the town, was a modest cube-shaped building known as the Kaaba. Among its religious objects was a hallowed meteorite known as the Black Stone, embedded in a wall in one corner. The chief deity of Meccans was Allah, the Creator of the universe; He shared His power with some 300 other gods and goddesses whose statues filled the holy place. The people who came on pilgrimages to worship these deities, like the commercial travelers in Mecca, attended big fairs held in the city and left behind a great deal of wealth.

The leading citizens of this commercial and religious center were members of a powerful tribe known as the Quraysh. Through their widespread interests the Quraysh had built up great financial and military strength, and they governed Mecca as an elementary form of "republic," through a council made up of representatives from the city's most influential families.

It was in this bustling city that Muhammad was born, about 570 A.D. In Arabic his name means "highly praised." He never knew his father, a trader named Abdullah, who died shortly before his birth. Although Abdullah had little wealth himself, he did belong to the powerful Quraysh. Following a custom of the Meccan aristocracy, the infant's widowed mother sent him into the desert to be wet-nursed by a Bedouin mother. The desert air was fresher and healthier than the stifling air of Mecca, and it was felt that in this climate a city boy could get a sturdier start in life.

After two or three years in the desert, the fatherless child was brought back to Mecca. When he was six his mother died, and he was placed in the care of his grandfather; but the old man also died soon after. Muhammad's paternal uncle, Abu Talib, then became his adoptive father, and it was he who reared the boy to manhood.

As a young man with no fortune of his own, Muhammad had to work for a living. He did various odd jobs, among them tending sheep, and buying and selling goods in Mecca. Then he went to work as an agent for a woman named Khadija, a widow with considerable business interests. On her behalf he traveled north with one of the caravans to Syria. Syria was then part of the powerful Christian Byzantine empire and Muhammad must have come in contact with many Christians there.

At this time powerful outside religious influences were at work in Arabia. These influences had filtered into the peninsula from Syria and Palestine, as well as from Christian Abyssinia (Ethiopia) just across the Red Sea from southern Arabia. Some Arabians had been converted to Christianity and several oases were partly occupied by tribes of Arabian Jews. A colony of Abyssinian Christians dwelt in Mecca; also in Arabia at this time there were *hanifs*, men dissatisfied with Arabian paganism, who lived ascetic lives and believed in a single god.

From these sources, as well as from his trip to Syria, Muhammad undoubtedly heard tales about Jesus and the Prophets, and about the God worshiped by both Jews and Christians. More and more he must have felt the lack in his own people of a coherent faith. As one who had known poverty and orphanhood, he was particularly distressed by the arrogance of the rich and powerful; these men believed that money and material possessions were everything, and they no longer respected the former desert ethos, under which the rich were expected to share their wealth with the poorer members of their tribe.

Muhammad, known for his thoughtful nature, his gentleness and integrity, was highly regarded in Mecca; he was nicknamed al-Amin—"The Trustworthy." Despite his temperate nature, he is said to have had a forceful personality, and he must have made a striking appearance: handsome and burly, with massive shoulders, large hands and feet and a wide forehead above dark, bushy eyebrows and deep, large black eyes. He was of medium height and walked with his head, which was unusually large, thrust impetuously forward. When spoken to he turned not only his head but his whole frame to face the speaker. When he was angry, a conspicuous vein swelled between his brows.

Khadija was impressed by Muhammad both as a person and for the way he handled her affairs, and when he was about 25 years old she made him an offer of marriage. She had already been married twice before and was some 15 years older than he. Nevertheless, Muhammad accepted Khadija's proposal and was faithful to her for the remaining 25 years of her life. She bore him three sons, all of whom died in childhood, and four daughters. All the girls lived, but only one, Fatima, survived him and bore him descendants. They were to figure in later Islamic history.

His marriage relieved Muhammad of most of his financial cares and gave him considerable time to himself. Often he would escape the bustle of the city by retiring to a cave on the nearby mountain of Hira to meditate; sometimes he went alone, sometimes with his family. Here certain spiritual insights came to him, he was to say later, "like the breaking of dawn."

In the year 610 A.D., when Muhammad was about 40 years old, he had an experience that shattered his tranquil existence and set him on the path that was to transform the lives of millions of people. There are many colorful accounts of this event, based on the various traditions that grew out of his life; all of them, unfortunately, leave many questions unanswered. The account most often quoted is that of Ibn Ishaq, Muhammad's first biographer, who lived in the century following the Prophet's death.

On the eventful day, according to Ibn Ishaq, Muhammad had gone to Hira with his family and was asleep in the cave when an angel appeared. "He came to me," the biographer quotes the Prophet as saying, "with a coverlet of brocade whereon was some writing, and said, 'Read!' I said, 'What shall I read?' He pressed me with it so tightly that I thought it was death; then he let me go and said, 'Read!' . . . He said:

'Read in the name of thy Lord who created,
Who created man of blood coagulated.
Read! Thy Lord is the most beneficent,
Who taught by the pen,
Taught that which they knew not unto men.' "

Muhammad awoke from his sleep in spiritual turmoil. At first he feared that he was possessed by some kind of demon. He was so distraught that he set out to climb the mountain and kill himself. Then, according to the account, he heard a voice from Heaven; looking up he saw "the form of a man with feet astride the horizon, saying, 'O Muhammad! thou art the apostle of God and I am Gabriel.'"

Muhammad returned to Khadija and told her what had happened. She immediately went to a *hanif* kinsman of hers; the holy man heard the story and unhesitatingly pronounced his verdict: Muhammad had been visited by the same heavenly inspiration that had descended to Moses, and he was to be the prophet of his people.

Muhammad, however, did not assume this role at once. For a long time he received no further messages from God, and he suffered fears and self-doubt. He then had a second revelation ordering him to begin his work, to "rise and warn" the people. Muhammad actually began preaching publicly in Mecca in 613 A.D. He taught that Allah was not one god among many but the solitary and eternal Sovereign of the universe, and that men must thank Him for their existence and worship only Him. He preached that all believers were equal before God, and that the rich must share their wealth with the poor. At the same time he warned that man's destiny was in God's hands: there would be a Day of Judgment for all men.

Muhammad thus gave new values to life. Under paganism it was believed that death was the end of all existence. Now, according to Muhammad, every man would be held accountable in an afterworld for his deeds on earth—a stunning concept for a people who had believed that the criterion of success was the wealth a man accumulated during his lifetime. For those who accepted God, and Muhammad as His Messenger, he said, there would be justice in this world and a glorious life after death. But for those who did not submit, there would be hell-fire and terrible tortures.

The Prophet's first convert was his wife Khadija, who was soon followed by three others: Ali, a younger cousin of Muhammad; Zayd, a slave he had freed; and Abu Bakr, a man of substance. Abu Bakr and Ali were to play important roles in the rise of Islam. Many of Muhammad's early followers came from the ranks of the poor and downtrodden, who eagerly seized upon his message of hope in this world and the next. However, most of the aristocratic Quraysh not only refused to accept him as a prophet but greeted him with fierce opposition. They saw a threat to their whole privileged way of life from a faith that made piety rather than position the measure of human worth. They also feared that if Muhammad won large numbers of followers, he could eventually convert his religious power into vast political power and dominate the city. Finally, they saw Muhammad's attack on their pagan gods leading to a loss of profitable trade. The Quraysh ridiculed Muhammad, calling him a liar and a "poet" and suggesting that his revelations were the products of his own imagination. They even subjected some Muslims to stonings and beatings.

After a time this abuse became so severe that Muhammad advised a group of his followers to

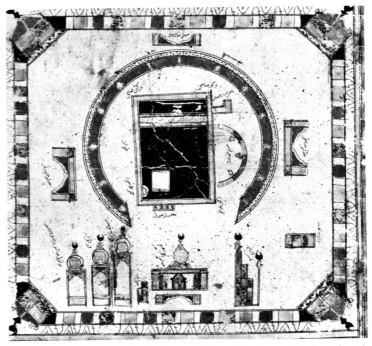

ISLAM'S HOLIEST SHRINE, *the Kaaba, a 50-foot-high stone cube draped with black brocade, is shown on part of a souvenir scroll once owned by a 15th Century pilgrim to Mecca. To the left is its only door and a recess containing the sacred Black Stone that pilgrims kiss. A colonnade, shown in plan view, once circled the Kaaba. This opened onto an array of holy structures, including the domed Zamzam well and two companion store houses (left), a shelter covering the footprints of Abraham (center), and a pulpit (right).*

escape to Christian Abyssinia; some 80 of them went, and were granted refuge there. But a delegation of the Quraysh pursued the fugitives and urged the Negus, the King of Abyssinia, to expel them as people who had slandered his religion. The leaders of the Muslims were called in to refute the Meccans' charges; as proof that Islam did not insult Christianity, they read a passage from the Koran's chapter of Mary. The Koran paid Jesus and His Mother the highest reverence—though it held that Jesus was merely a prophet, not the Son of God. The Negus, finding this view inoffensive, permitted the Muslims to stay.

Meanwhile, Muhammad and his followers in Mecca were being subjected to even more severe attacks. At about this time the Prophet's wife Khadija died; her death was soon followed by that of his uncle, Abu Talib, who had raised him and through whom he had enjoyed clan protection. Muhammad's position in the city was now extremely insecure and he reached a decision to leave.

At first he went to Taif, but he was ridiculed and insulted by the people there, and was forced to return to Mecca. At this point, fate came to Muhammad's rescue. A group of pilgrims from Yathrib, who had heard Muhammad preach and were impressed by him, asked him to come to their city. Yathrib was being torn by a feud between two Arab tribes who lived there, and an arbitrator was needed to bring peace. Muhammad accepted the invitation, and encouraged his followers to go to Yathrib ahead of him. A few weeks later the Prophet himself slipped out of Mecca and joined them. The migration, the famed *Hijra*, or Hegira, took place in September, 622 A.D., and later was designated as the beginning of the Islamic era.

In Yathrib Muhammad began to construct around himself and his followers a larger community of Muslim believers, who were to be the foundation of the Islamic state. Arabs who had been members of feuding tribes gradually submitted to the commands of God, as revealed through His Prophet Muhammad. The substitution of faith for blood ties made it possible to suppress the old tribal rivalries and gave rise to a revolutionary political unity. Yathrib, the heart of the new community of Islam, became known as Madinat al-Nabi, "the city of the Prophet," or simply Medina, "the city," the name it bears in English today.

From this time onward, Muhammad's role changed drastically. While in Mecca he had been merely the religious leader of a small group, somewhat in the tradition of the earlier Hebrew prophets. But once settled in Medina he played a new and more powerful role, with increasing spiritual and political authority. In keeping with his new status, the nature of his continuing revelations changed from being purely religious to having greater legislative and social content.

One of Muhammad's early problems in Medina was with the Jews there. Several Jewish clans controlled the richest agricultural lands, and had made formal alliances with one of two Arab tribes that dominated the oasis. Muhammad, according to Western scholars, expected the Jews to recognize him as a prophet, thus strengthening his position in Medina. In an effort to win their support, he adopted some of their religious practices, among them fasting on the Day of Atonement and the custom of praying toward Jerusalem. A few of the Jews became Muslims, but the majority saw in the growth of Islam a threat to their own political and economic self-interest. Far from accepting Muhammad as a prophet, they rejected his claim and bitterly criticized him, contending that many of his revelations contradicted their scriptures and were therefore false. Muhammad countered by saying that the Jews had distorted their scriptures and only the Koran was the true Word of God. Seeing that he could not win the support of the Jews,

Muhammad now concentrated on building an Islamic community that was, in the beginning, made up primarily of Arabs.

As time passed, the Prophet started giving Islam its own unique religious customs. In place of wooden clappers or ram's horns, used as religious signals by the Christians and Jews, the ringing voice of Bilal, an Abyssinian convert, called the faithful to pray; Bilal was thus the first muezzin, the crier who summons Muslims to prayer at the appointed hours in Islamic communities. The fast of the Day of Atonement was replaced by an entire month of fasting during Ramadan, the ninth month of the Islamic lunar calendar. Instead of praying toward Jerusalem, Muslims were ordered to prostrate themselves toward the Kaaba in Mecca as the shrine of Allah. The kissing of the Black Stone, the venerated meteorite embedded in one of the Kaaba's walls, was authorized.

This period also marked the beginning of a new form of activity against the enemies of the faith in Mecca. Muhammad started leading his followers in raids against Meccan caravans passing through Medinese territory. Some scholars think that the reason for these raids was primarily economic, to help the emigrants acquire food and supplies. But others offer a different explanation. They say that some of Muhammad's followers learned that their families in Mecca were being persecuted and their property confiscated; they demanded revenge against the Meccans, and Muhammad placated them by attacking the caravans.

One of these raids led to the first serious armed clash between the Muslims and the Meccans. Two years after the Muslims had migrated to Medina, Muhammad learned that a richly laden Meccan caravan was about to pass near Medina. He immediately made plans to attack it. But word of this reached the caravan, whose leader promptly changed its route and rushed a messenger to Mecca asking for reinforcements. The caravan subsequently escaped, but the Muslims ran into the reinforcements at Badr, a caravan stop southwest of Medina.

Muhammad had about 300 men, the largest force he had ever assembled, but the Meccans had close to a thousand. The Muslims could not turn back without loss of face. For the Meccans it was an opportunity to teach Muhammad and his followers to leave Mecca and its trade alone. Muhammad directed his followers from a nearby shelter, spending a great deal of time in prayer as the two sides clashed in battle. Surprisingly, the Prophet's small band inflicted a crushing defeat on the proud Quraysh, who had not expected such fierce opposition.

The startling Muslim victory had far-reaching effects. Arabs everywhere looked upon it as a miracle, a sign of God's favor to the Prophet's cause, thus strengthening Muhammad's claim that he was the apostle of God. In addition, the Muslim warriors shared in the booty from the raids, and word soon spread that the cause of God could bring rewards on earth as well as in heaven. Nearby tribes now began to join Islam and to fight under its banner. If victorious they got booty. If killed in battle they were sure of going to heaven, where the Prophet had promised them they would enjoy, without surfeit, the most sensual delights known on earth.

The Quraysh, however, did not accept their defeat at Badr lightly. The following year a force of 3,000 Meccans attacked the Muslims at Medina, inflicting on them a minor defeat; the Prophet himself was wounded in the action. Two years later, in 627 A.D., the Meccans, determined to wipe out Muhammad, mounted a full-scale assault on Medina with 10,000 troops mustered from among their allies, including a powerful front line of 600 horsemen with which they hoped to overwhelm the Muslims. Muhammad, allegedly on the advice of a Persian convert experienced in fortifications, dug a deep dry moat in front of the exposed portion of the city—a novel tactic in desert warfare. The innovation so confused the attackers that it rendered their cavalry useless and halted their charge. Changing tactics, the Meccans camped outside Medina, negotiating with a Jewish clan inside the oasis to attack the Muslims from within. The negotiations broke down, however, and the weather turned cold. After 40 days the Meccans, now demoralized and short of supplies, went home.

Muhammad, who had learned about the Jews' negotiations with the Meccans, dealt harshly with them: he sanctioned the decapitation of all the men —some 600 in number—and the enslavement of their women and children, and he allowed his followers to settle on their land. A modern reader may wonder at such violence in a religious leader. But what surprised the people of Yathrib was Muhammad's total disregard of the long-standing alliance between the Jewish and Arab tribes there—an alliance considered virtually sacred under the Bedouin code. By this dramatic act, the Prophet was not only showing the Jews, and any future enemies of Islam, that opposition would no longer be tolerated. He was also showing his fellow Arabs that their previous tribal loyalties, which for so long had led to feuds that weakened and divided them, were at an end. The only loyalty now recognized was that given to Islam itself.

In 628 Muhammad set out on a pilgrimage to Mecca with 1,400 of his followers. The Meccans, hearing about this force, sent out 200 horsemen to stop it. Fighting threatened, but the two sides agreed upon a treaty that provided for a 10-year truce, and for the Muslims to return to Medina on the condition that they could come back to Mecca on pilgrimage the following year. Both sides saved face, but Muhammad had won a victory by establishing himself as the equal of the Quraysh, as a result of having entered into a treaty with them. Also, by having set out upon a pilgrimage—an old

pagan custom—he had shown Arabs that Islam was a religion with an Arabian character.

The following year Muhammad led 2,000 Muslims on the promised pilgrimage to the Kaaba. But subsequent clashes between Muslims and Meccans ended the truce, and in 630 A.D. Muhammad marched on Mecca to settle the issue with a force of 10,000 men. Mecca, weakened by the loss of many of its leading men in the battles against Muhammad and consequent dissensions over the leadership of the city, fell with little more than a token show of resistance. Muhammad entered the Kaaba in triumph, exclaiming, "Truth has come and falsehood has vanished," and set about the destruction of the pagan idols that filled the holy place. Later a tradition was established forbidding anyone but Muslims to enter the city. The purified Kaaba in Mecca was now the spiritual center of Islam, just as Medina was its political capital.

The Prophet was a lenient and forgiving conqueror, and soon even the Mecca leaders who had opposed him most bitterly became Muslims. At the same time his troops began to strike out farther and farther into Arabia; before long all but a few of the peninsula's tribes had joined Islam, either through new-found fervor or in hopes of material gain. Christians and Jews were permitted to practice their own faith, but were compelled to pay a tax, adding indirectly to Islam's ever-growing might.

In the 22 years of his prophethood, Muhammad had brought about a synthesis of the Judaeo-Christian tradition of a single God and a latent Arabian sense of nationalism, and his people found in this synthesis a cause for which they could unite, fight and win. Yet Muhammad himself remained remarkably unchanged. Throughout his life, even after he had become the absolute ruler of a powerful new state, he retained basically simple tastes; it was said that he even mended his own clothes. As a leader he gave his people a broader concept of humanity by abolishing many social evils. For example, he modified Arabia's widespread slavery; the practice was still permitted but slaves had to be treated humanely. They were now allowed to marry and they could buy their freedom; moreover, the freeing of slaves was regarded as meritorious. Muhammad also outlawed gambling, usury and the drinking of wine as against the rule of God.

To his followers, Muhammad embodied a new human ideal. His idealized figure, in fact, was so embroidered upon by pious admirers that at times it became practically unrecognizable. The Prophet was thought to possess all virtues, particularly those dearest to Arabs. Since virility in a man was highly esteemed, some Arabs pictured Muhammad as a man of immense potency—a portrait that later led to much Western derision and satire. It is true that one tradition about the Prophet quotes him as saying that women were among the three things that he enjoyed the most (the others were pleasant odors and prayer). Whatever sensuality he may have had, however, was tempered by his kindness and loyalty.

For more than two decades Muhammad had been faithful to a woman considerably older than himself. After Khadija's death he took nine wives. (The Koran allowed Muslims to take up to four wives, but an exception was made in the case of the Prophet.) Most of Muhammad's marriages were motivated primarily by political or humane reasons; some of his wives were the widows of his lieutenants killed fighting for Islam, while others were the daughters of important Arab leaders. One of them was A'isha, the daughter of Abu Bakr, the Prophet's dearest friend and closest adviser; he married her when she was less than 10 years old and still playing with her dolls. Muhammad's wives lived in separate rooms around the courtyard of his house, and he took turns staying with them. The Koran gave husbands the right to chastise unruly wives, but Muhammad was an indulgent husband. On one occasion he took A'isha on an expedition with him and she dropped behind to look for a necklace she had lost; later she arrived at Medina with a handsome young tribesman. Some of Muhammad's followers accused her of infidelity, but the Prophet soon had a revelation exonerating his young wife; the Koran ordered that henceforth four witnesses would be required of anyone accusing a woman of adultery, and failure to provide such evidence would bring punishment of 80 lashes.

In his 63rd year, the 10th year of the new era of Islam, Muhammad fell ill. He developed a sudden fever accompanied by violent headaches; he spoke to A'isha of death, but she replied lightheartedly, probably thinking, like many Muslims, that the Prophet of God was immune to death. But the pain increased, and Muhammad asked permission of his other wives to move into the dwelling of A'isha. From there he managed to stagger to the mosque, where he once again told his followers that the faithful would follow him to Paradise, and that the unbelievers would be punished. From his tone his friend Abu Bakr could tell that he was about to die.

For the last time the Prophet returned to A'isha's house. As the death agony came upon him, he muttered, "Nay [I have chosen] the exalted company in heaven." With that, he died in A'isha's arms.

As the word of Muhammad's death spread through Medina, his followers were swept by a shock that verged on panic. In the confusion Abu Bakr kept his head. "Whichever of you worships Muhammad," he shouted to the Prophet's distraught followers, "know that Muhammad is dead. But whichever of you worships God, know that God is alive and does not die." He quoted a verse from the Koran that only then acquired its full significance: "Muhammad is a Prophet only; there have been Prophets before him. If he dies or is slain, will ye turn back?"

THE VEILED PROPHET *prays beside the Kaaba, the ancient religious shrine of Mecca.*

"THE PROPHET'S PROGRESS"

In the Koran a Muslim could read all the revelations the Prophet received from God, but few details concerning Muhammad himself. For a fuller picture of the great man's life the pious had to turn to legends that were often fanciful. Some of these attributed miracles to the Prophet, though he had claimed to possess only ordinary human powers; others disagreed about where or when an event had occurred. To establish a tale's authenticity, the scholars who compiled the stories scrupulously gave each its pedigree ("Yasha ibn Abbad told me that his father Abbad told him that his grandmother Asma said . . .").

If the writers were scrupulous, the artists who illustrated the tales were equally so. They were particularly wary of painting the face of the Prophet or his family, lest the portraits be inaccurate or sacrilegious. Thus, the 16th Century Turkish artists who executed the miniatures for a biography titled *The Progress of the Prophet* veiled Muhammad and surrounded him with a halolike flame (above). Yet for all the documenters' efforts, the *Progress* inevitably intertwines fact and fiction into a highly colored but pious version of the Prophet's life.

Just before Muhammad was born, an Abyssinian army tried to destroy the Kaaba, the pagan shrine in Mecca. The Abyssinian elephants, however, refused to attack the future Prophet's birthplace.

Behind the elephants came a wave of cavalrymen, but they were also stopped from attacking Mecca when a flock of birds dropped stones from their beaks on the invaders. The Abyssinians beat a hasty retreat.

A host of angels visited Muhammad's mother, Amina, in a dream and told her she would soon give birth to the Prophet. The angels instructed her to name him Muhammad, meaning "highly praised."

When the hour of Muhammad's birth at last arrived, angels rushed to see the event. They brought a mattress and a coverlet (top) so that his mother, though poor, might rest in comfort.

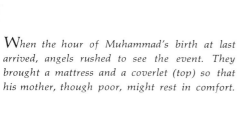

As an infant, the Prophet was visited by more angels bearing a pitcher, a basin and a towel to inaugurate the ritual ablutions Muslims have performed ever since, before offering prayers to God.

the legends say, heaven and earth gave signs of his future greatness

When he reached the age of 25, Muhammad married a wealthy widow named Khadija (at right). She relieved him of financial worries, bore him children and eventually became the first convert to the Prophet's new religion.

While meditating on a mountain near Mecca, Muhammad received a revelation from God through the archangel Gabriel. Dazzled, Muhammad turned away, but no matter where he looked, Gabriel's face appeared.

After his meeting with Gabriel, Muhammad feared he might be possessed by evil spirits. Although the Prophet continued to pray, God did not speak to him again for a time. Then, one day, Gabriel reappeared and said, "Thy Lord hath not forsaken thee, nor is he displeased . . ." and commanded Muhammad to call men to God.

One night angels appeared to Muhammad and prepared him for a night journey through Paradise. Gabriel, some of the legends say, awakened the Prophet, slit his body from his neck to his waist, and removed and washed his heart. As the angel returned Muhammad's heart to his body, he filled his soul with faith and wisdom.

In the dead of the night a

Purified, Muhammad mounted a fabulous creature named Buraq that had a woman's face, a mule's body, a peacock's tail—and the ability to cover, in a single bound, a distance as far as the eye could see. Riding Buraq (who, tradition holds, had borne up other prophets before him), Muhammad passed through seven heavens and enjoyed the rarest privilege of all—seeing God's unveiled face.

magic beast swept Muhammad aloft

During the night journey, Muhammad led patriarchs, Old Testament prophets and angels in prayer in a celestial mosque. While in Paradise, Muhammad met Moses, whom he later described as "a ruddy faced man." Jesus he depicted as freckled and of medium height; of Abraham he said, "Never have I seen a man more like myself."

Rejected by his people, Muhammad endured harsh persecution and fled Mecca

One of Islam's early converts, Abdullah ibn Masud (at right), attempted to recite the Koran in front of the Kaaba, but the idol-worshiping Meccans, outraged by the new religion, beat him severely.

Surrounded by hostile Meccans, the Prophet sought help from desert tribes. Most scorned him, but one tribe was converted when he conjured up a well, where the people could fill their water bags.

When Muhammad brought forth a spring in Mecca, however, the people declared he was an evil sorcerer, not a prophet; some in fact, led by the wicked Abu Jahl (blue turban), plotted his death.

Feeling against Muhammad among the Meccans grew so strong that one day they attempted to stone him; they spared the Prophet only because Abu Bakr (center), a respected merchant and an illustrious convert to Islam, wept and pleaded with them. Muhammad approached foreigners who came as pilgrims to the pagan shrines in Mecca and tried to make arrangements for a new home for Islam in some distant city. Most of them, however, had been warned by the Meccans that Muhammad was a "mad poet," and they refused to listen to him. But finally, delegates arrived from Medina, and invited Muhammad and the faithful of Mecca to their city, some 200 miles away.

In small and large groups the Prophet's converts departed from Mecca and undertook the journey to Medina. In September 622 A.D.—the first year of the Islamic calendar—Muhammad and his friend Abu Bakr mounted camels and headed across the desert. They slept the first night in a cave. Soldiers from Mecca—led by Satan, in a blue robe with a quiver of arrows—pursued them, but they never searched the cave because Allah had caused a spider's web to be spun and a dove's nest to be built at the entrance—proving no one was hiding within.

One Meccan found the fugitives, but when his horse (at right) approached the Prophet, it threw its rider. The Meccan repented and received a written pardon from Muhammad, which is being handed to him above by Abu Bakr (foreground).

One night Muhammad and Abu Bakr found shelter with a poor Bedouin family. The Bedouins were unable to offer their guests any sustenance, as their ewe was dry—until the Prophet made it give milk.

Granted refuge in Medina, the Prophet firmly established the new religion

Awaiting the Prophet's arrival, the Muslims of Medina gathered outside the city every morning. At last Muhammad and Abu Bakr were sighted in the distance on camelback. While crowds of men and women awaited the Prophet, wealthy converts rode out to escort him into town.

So many people in Medina wanted to be the Prophet's host that he decided to stay wherever his camel stopped first. After creating great suspense for the Muslims of the city, the camel chose the humble dwelling of Abu Ayyub, who was so overcome the Prophet had to calm him.

Muhammad's stay with Abu Ayyub was only temporary; soon after arriving he and his followers built a structure that would serve both as his house and as the chief mosque of the city. The Prophet himself helped his followers clear the ground and lay the bricks. As the devout laborers worked they chanted songs in praise of God.

Having completed the mosque (pictured here in the style of later Turkish structures), Muhammad had to announce the hour of prayer. He thought of borrowing the Christians' clapper or the Jews' horn, until Gabriel told him to use the human voice.

After the faithful were called to prayer, Muhammad mounted the pulpit and preached sermons on the new faith. He exhorted his congregation to "Love God with all your hearts, and weary not of the word of God or its mention."

When the Prophet reached the age of 63, the Angel of Death appeared and offered him a choice: he could either live on earth forever or join Allah in Paradise. Muhammad chose Paradise, but his decision left his followers—particularly his devoted daughter Fatima (far right)—deeply bereaved. After the Prophet had distributed his few belongings to the poor and enjoined his congregation to hold to the faith, his soul was borne away by the angel.

2
FIVE PILLARS OF FAITH

Over the centuries, the political state and culture created by Islam have been modified, but the system of religious beliefs, duties and moral values has remained remarkably the same. This system rests securely on a foundation commonly referred to as the "Five Pillars of Islam": faith, prayer, alms giving, fasting and pilgrimage. These pillars comprise the ritual obligations of all Muslims; more than anything else they gave Islam its unique form and helped it to stand firmly since Muhammad first received his revelations and worked out their implications in the Seventh Century.

The first pillar, faith, was based on the *shahada*, the declaration of belief through which a man joined Islam: "There is no god but Allah, and Muhammad is His Prophet." Not only was it one of the tersest religious slogans in history, but one of the most memorable, for in Arabic it had a musical alliterative force: *"La ilaha illa Allah; Muhammad rasul Allah."* A man had only to recite the *shahada*, prefaced by the words, "I testify," in front of any Muslim, and it made him a Muslim, just as it does today. He thus professed his belief in the oneness of God, and Muhammad as His Messenger. By implication, he also accepted three other articles of faith: belief in the Koran as the Word of God, belief in angels as the instruments of God's will and belief in a final Judgment Day for all men. After the profession of faith there could be no turning back; the punishment for apostasy was death.

One of the most powerful attractions of the *shahada* was its remarkable simplicity. No special person was required to administer the rite of entry into the faith; there were no mysterious sacraments, such as baptism or first communion, and no elaborate indoctrination schools. There was not even an organized priesthood, although Islam did develop a formidable army of religious scholars known as the *ulama* (meaning "the learned"). They fulfilled an important role, formulating and interpreting Islamic law; they also acted as judges and were the intellectual and spiritual leaders of the community. Throughout the centuries Islam has retained its basic simplicity, at least outwardly, as shown in a rejection of ceremony and a distaste for luxury and ostentation. Inwardly, however, the faith gave rise to many complex theological questions; Muslim

A GOLDEN LEAF FROM THE KORAN, *Islam's sacred book, is elaborately decorated with Arabic motifs. The verse commands the soldiers of Islam to give one fifth of all plunder seized in battle to the mosque and the state.*

A DESERT NATIVITY

Islamic religious lore, which draws upon Judaeo-Christian tradition, abounds with stories also found in the Bible. With minor modifications, the Koran recounts Jonah's engulfment by a whale, Noah's salvation in the Ark, and a Day of Judgment surpassing even the Christian one in its visions of terror and bliss to come.

Islam honored Christ, as second only to the Prophet himself, and portrayed the events of the New Testament in scenes like the 16th Century Muslim painting shown above. Although this version of Christ's birth is uniquely Islamic—its locale is a desert oasis rather than a village stable—Muslims believed in the miraculous nature of the event itself. The scene pictures Mary making the desert bloom for her newborn Son by touching a withered date palm, causing its branches to bear fruit and its roots to gush water. The infant Jesus' holiness, in the stylistic tradition of Muslim art, is marked not by a halo of light but an aureole of flame.

scholars have argued endlessly over such matters as predestination—whether a man's choices in this life determined his fate after death or whether it was preordained by God.

From the beginning there was one dogma that admitted no argument: belief in the oneness of Allah, or God. Muslims conceived of Him as uncompromisingly transcendent and all-powerful, the unique Creator of the world, the Father of no daughters and no sons. He had no sharers in His power and those who associated other gods with Him were guilty of the supreme sin of *shirk* (literally, "ascribing partners to God"). To this all-powerful Being, the greatest virtue in man was unquestioning obedience to His Word; this was exemplified by Abraham, an earlier prophet to whom God had revealed Himself, and the founder, with Isma'il, of the Kaaba in Mecca. "Abraham," states the Koran, "was neither a Jew nor a Christian; he was an upright man, one who had surrendered himself to Allah. He was no idolater. Surely the men who are nearest to Abraham are those who follow him, this Prophet, and the true believers."

While God's transcendence was emphasized, He was not remote from man; the Koran describes Him as "nearer to man than his neck vein," and many of its poetic passages attest to God's goodness and mercy and the bounty that He bestows upon men. This all-powerful but benevolent God could be described only by certain of his apellations, such as the Merciful, the Generous, the Compassionate; tradition established 99 of these as the finest epithets of praise.

Next to God, as an article of faith, was belief in the prophets and their preachings. In Islamic doctrine there were five major prophets before Muhammad: Adam, Noah, Abraham, Moses and Jesus. Each of these apostles had brought the Word of God in his own lifetime; but men kept straying from it, and a new prophet had to be sent so that men could again find the path to salvation. Muhammad, however, had a special role: he was the last of the prophets, and the Word God sent through him would guide men henceforth until the Day of Judgment.

As the final Word of God, the Koran was believed by Muslims to be infallible. During the two decades that the Prophet received the revelations, his faithful hearers either memorized them or wrote them down; the recitation of these revelations then formed a part of Islamic worship. Some of the most devout Muslims memorized the entire Koran, as many of them still do today—a fantastic feat of piety when it is considered that this holy book, almost as long as the New Testament, contains approximately 78,000 words.

Shortly after the Prophet's death, Muhammad's former companions took steps to preserve his revelations in permanent form. Even then Islam's growing holy wars were beginning to reduce the numbers of those who knew the Koran by heart. Fearing that large portions of the Koran would thus be forever lost, Abu Bakr, Muhammad's immediate successor as the leader of Islam, ordered that the existing fragments be collected from wherever they could be found—from the "ribs of palm-leaves and tablets of white stone and from the breasts of men."

Thus, from various sources the revelations were gathered and a single text was prepared. But there were also in existence different collections gathered by other companions of the Prophet. Inevitably this led to confusion. At that time Arabic was written in a rudimentary form, with no vowels or signs to distinguish certain consonants, and this led to disputes about the reading of some words.

The Prophet's revelations might have suffered the fate of other holy scriptures and become the cause of lasting and bitter controversy but for the resolute action of Uthman, Muhammad's third successor. Uthman had been one of his earliest converts

and married no less than two of his daughters. Almost two decades after Muhammad's death, Uthman formed a committee, headed by one of Muhammad's former scribes, and their efforts led to a standardized copy of the holy book. Uthman then sponsored this as the official version of the Koran, the one that is read today. All other copies were destroyed.

Only part of this traditional account is accepted by modern scholars. They believe that Muhammad himself had large parts of his revelations written down by his scribes, and that this text, along with other versions then in circulation, was examined by the committee Uthman appointed and incorporated into the holy book.

Since no one was completely sure of the order in which the Prophet had received his revelations, the Koran's chapters, or suras, were arranged according to length. The longest ones, which were placed first, were the most legalistic and instructive ones, fundamental to the organization and regulation of Muslim life. After a seven-line introductory sura called "The Opening," which praised God as "Lord of the Universe," came the longest sura, "The Cow." Many of the suras were named after an incident or some striking word in them. "The Cow" took its title from a story about the sacrifice of a yellow heifer. Despite its title, it is devoted primarily to instructions on such diverse matters as the religious duties of Muslims, divorce and warfare. The short, ecstatic suras revealed in the first eruption of Muhammad's inspiration come at the end of the Koran; they are mainly concerned with warnings about Judgment Day and the awesome fate awaiting those who worshiped more than one god.

The fourth article of faith, following belief in God, the prophets and Muhammad's revelations, was belief in angels. Primarily, these celestial attendants were conceived of as God's messengers, but they were also thought to perform other tasks,

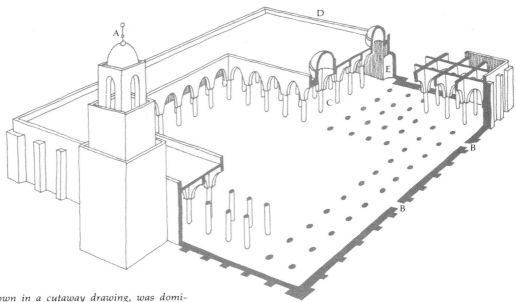

A MEDIEVAL MOSQUE, *shown in a cutaway drawing, was dominated by a minaret (A), from which criers called the hour of prayer. Worshipers entered through doors (B) into the courtyard; they prayed in the sanctuary (C) facing the qibla wall (D), which indicated the direction of Mecca, and its mihrab, or niche (E).*

such as supporting His throne, guarding the gates of Paradise and Hell and interceding with God for men. Only two angels are mentioned by name in the Koran: Gabriel, who delivered the revelations to Muhammad, and Michael, who executed God's commands for the universe, such as sending the winds and rains. But according to tradition there were other angels, among them Israfil, assigned to blow the trumpet on the Day of Judgment, and Is-ra'il, the angel of death, who appeared to dying men to take their last breath.

The final article of faith was the belief that after death there would be a Day of Judgment for all men. At that time those destined for Hell would be separated from the blessed, who would go to Paradise. Only God knew when the world would end, but the Koran warned that the final day would be announced by a shattering trumpet blast, and the dead would be summoned from their graves to be judged by their deeds on earth. Those who were going to heaven would have their "book" (the record of their actions) placed in their right hand, and the damned would have it put in their left hand.

What would befall the wicked and the righteous was graphically portrayed by the Koran. One passage dramatically describes the terrible torments to be inflicted on the guilty soul who, realizing that his power has gone and his wealth has been profitless, hears God command his angel:

> Seize him and bind him
> Then burn him in the fire
> Then in a seventy-cubit chain control him.
> For he disbelieved in God
> And towards feeding the hungry did nothing.

The Koran also painted the exquisite delights that awaited those who had believed in God and treated their fellow men kindly. Heaven was described as a garden of bliss where the faithful reclined on thrones encrusted with jewels, while around them circulated "youths forever young," with goblets "of pure drink," the choicest of foods and "houris (young women), like guarded pearls, a reward for good actions." It is small wonder that the prospect of entering the groves of such a Paradise—so verdant compared with the barren deserts of Arabia—inspired many Muslim warriors with a contempt for death and helped bring them great victories.

The second pillar on which Islam rested was that of prayer. To a Muslim, prayer was the most important duty of his religion; through prayer he paid homage to God, acknowledging that he owed to Him his existence and all that he possessed. Two kinds of prayer were recognized by Muslims: *du'a*, the private or inner prayer, and *salat*, the formal ritual prayer.

Du'a, while not obligatory, was considered meritorious, and a person could use it to communicate with God as often as he chose, even making personal requests. *Salat*, on the other hand, was a precisely defined form of worship required of all believers. Since the early days of Islam, Muslims have performed this essential duty five times daily. The first prayer occurred shortly after dawn, when the faithful were awakened by the muezzin's exhortation that "prayer is better than sleep." The other four prayers took place just after noon, late in the afternoon, immediately after sunset and following nightfall.

At these appointed times the muezzin climbed to the minaret, the tower of the mosque, and called the faithful to prayer, his powerful voice ringing out its summons:

> *God is most great*
> *I testify there is no god but Allah*
> *I testify that Muhammad is the Messenger of Allah*
> *Come to prayer;*
> *Come to salvation,*
> *God is most great!*
> *There is no god but Allah.*

Once a day a Muslim had to perform certain ablutions or his acts of worship were not valid. These ablutions were intended to purify a man's body in the same way that prayers purified his soul, making him both spiritually and physically clean before God. Usually the ritual was performed before morning prayers. The worshiper had to wash his face, hands and arms up to the elbows, his feet up to the ankles, and the hair of his head. Normally water was used for such cleaning, but if none were available, sand or even dust was acceptable. If at any time of the day a Muslim broke his ritual purity, for example, by falling asleep or fainting, he had to repeat his ablutions. If a part of his body or clothing came in contact with "impure" substances like wine, urine or blood, he had to wash this part. If he engaged in a major defilement, such as sexual intercourse, he had to wash his entire body and hair.

Before beginning his prayers, a worshiper removed his shoes and covered his head. He then went through a series of specified movements, known as a *rak'a*, accompanied by prescribed prayers that were said silently or in a low voice. At each hour of prayer a different number of *rak'as* was called for, but sometimes Muslims performed extra ones to win God's favor. Before praying, a Muslim had to state silently that he was going to make the *salat* called for at that time of day, and specify the number of *rak'as* he would do; without this "declaration of intention" his prayers were considered invalid.

The worshiper began his prayers standing upright, with his hands raised beside his head, palms forward, saying *"Allahu Akbar!"* ("Allah is most great!") This phrase was repeated many times during the prayer, but the first time was the most important, as it cut the worshiper off from the profane life about him and devoted him entirely to God. He then bowed and prostrated himself, reciting passages from the Koran, and ended in a sitting or squatting position, in which he recited the *shahada*. His final act was to turn his face to the right and then to the left, each time saying, "Peace be with you and the Mercy of God." According to popular belief, an angel rested on each of his shoulders, and he was thus addressing a greeting to these observers of his piety.

Prayers could be said with equal validity anywhere: at home, in the open air, in a place of work.

Prayer was considered so important that the Koran even provided for it on the battlefield; one group of soldiers was ordered to stand to arms while the others offered their devotions to God. Prayers could be said individually or, preferably, in congregation; but once a week—at noon on Friday—the faithful were enjoined to pray together. Such corporate worship was led by an imam, or prayer leader, and included listening to a sermon in which a preacher, usually the imam, uttered certain formulas praising God and Muhammad, and also talked about matters of public interest.

For these devotions the faithful gathered in a mosque, a building that developed out of the requirements of Muslim worship. Its form was partly an outgrowth of Muhammad's own home in Medina, which consisted of several huts, belonging to the Prophet and his wives, set around a courtyard. This courtyard was the place where the early Muslims had come together for meetings with Muhammad, and for prayer. On the north side some palm trees supported a roof made of palm leaves and mud to shade the faithful from the fierce Arabian sun. Echoing this basic pattern, the mosque consisted of a courtyard, usually surrounded on three sides by shady porticos, leading on the fourth side to an enclosed hall of worship.

Because the prayers had to be made in the direction of the Kaaba in Mecca, a large, decorated niche, or mihrab, was set in one wall, indicating the direction of this holiest of shrines. There was also a raised pulpit, used for the Friday sermons, and a fountain was usually placed in the courtyard to provide water for the ritual ablutions. The mosque was not only a place of worship, but an important educational institution: students were welcome to study there, and scholars often lectured in its tranquil shade, leaning against a favorite pillar with their pupils crowded around them. Mosques sometimes served as courts of law where judges sat to hear cases and give decisions. They were always open to weary travelers, who often refreshed themselves by the fountain, napped in cool corners or slept overnight before continuing their journeys.

The third pillar of Islam was the giving of alms. By donating part of what he owned, a Muslim was believed to purify the rest of his wealth. There were two kinds of alms: the first, sadaqa, was given voluntarily, while the second, zakat, was mandatory. Although the zakat was not considered a tax, but a "loan to God," it was collected by the state and used to meet many of Islam's needs: supporting the poor, widows and orphans, helping slaves to buy their freedom, and equipping volunteers for the holy wars. The zakat was paid in kind, in crops, animals, precious metals or cash, depending on the nature of a man's wealth.

The fourth pillar of Islam was fasting. "O ye who believe! Fasting is prescribed to you," the Koran states, "as it was prescribed to those before you, that ye may ward off evil." The season for fasting was Ramadan, the month in which the Koran was first revealed to Muhammad, and in which the Prophet's followers defeated the Quraysh at Badr, the first major victory over their enemies from Mecca. As a lunar month, Ramadan rotated through all of the seasons of the year, and so Muslims knew the rigors of going hungry and thirsty even in the oppressive heat of summer. The obligation to fast fell on all Muslims except the young, the sick and those on long journeys.

Fasting was observed during the daylight hours of the entire month. Shortly before dawn, sleeping Muslims were routed from their beds by a signal —the beating of a drum, a knock on the door or a melodious call from the minaret—for a last brief meal. From the time when the light made it possible to discern a "white thread from a black one" until sunset, Muslims were commanded to eat nothing, drink nothing and abstain from sexual relations. During the hours of fasting, work continued, and the ordinary business of life was supposed to be conducted in a spirit of restraint and gentleness.

Despite its many injunctions, Ramadan was for Muslims a much-loved month, as it still is. The Prophet had disapproved of extreme asceticism, and fasting was not seen as a punishment of the flesh. Like prayer, it was supposed to bring a person closer to God, reminding him of a spiritual life beyond that sustained by food and drink. By fasting, a Muslim also learned to discipline his body, and to understand the sufferings of the poor, thus enlarging his sympathies. To him, Ramadan was a time of atonement for all of the sins committed during the year.

The restrictions of the daylight hours, however, gave way to gay festivities at night. The moment the day's ordeal was over—signaled by the call of the muezzin, or in later times by the firing of a cannon—a holiday spirit affected everyone, especially the young. The pangs of the fast were first broken with a few dates or a refreshing drink (one popular beverage today is a sherbetlike liquid made from dried apricots, which has the fanciful name of *qamar-al-deen*, or "moon of religion"). After such an appetizer, everyone sat down to the long awaited meal, an "evening breakfast" known as the *iftar*, at which families came together.

When the meal was over few persons slept. All night the markets, streets and lanes were thronged with strollers; children rushed happily through the darkness, carrying little lanterns and begging money from grown-ups for more lights. In the mosques, preachers expounded to large congregations on the significance of the holy month. Outside there were various entertainments: conjurors did tricks, acrobats tumbled, and crowds surrounded poets and storytellers reciting their verses and tales.

The end of Ramadan was observed in a joyous

climax, a feast lasting up to three days, during which new clothes were worn and friends embraced and congratulated one another. Special dishes were made for the occasion, delicacies such as thin little pancakes dipped in powdered sugar, savory buns and dried fruits. The dishes varied with the place and the family's means, but whatever was on the table, it was sure to mark a fitting end of this special month of nearness to God.

The fifth and final pillar of Islam was the all-important pilgrimage to Mecca, a traditional Arab custom adopted by Islam. Once in a lifetime every Muslim capable of undertaking it was obliged to go on this holy journey to the city where the Prophet had his first revelations. It was meritorious to visit Mecca, and the Kaaba, at any season, but the obligatory pilgrimage, known as the *hajj*, took place just once a year, in the month of *Dhu'l Hijja*, two months after Ramadan.

Through the ages the *hajj* became one of Islam's peculiar strengths. It gave Muslims a unique sense of brotherhood, as it brought together thousands of believers from the farthest regions of Islam. All of the pilgrims dressed alike and performed the same devotions, to remind themselves that all men were equal before God. By bringing into contact different people from different lands, these gatherings also led to an exchange of ideas that helped to unify and strengthen the empire.

Nothing was so inspiring to Muslims—even to those who were not making the holy journey—as the departure and return of the pilgrims on *hajj*; in villages and cities all over Islam these memorable occasions were marked by ceremonies and charged with deep emotion. Many Muslims sacrificed and saved money all of their lives to spend on the holy trip. Once he had arrived on the outskirts of Mecca, the pilgrim sanctified himself by washing from head to foot, for during the forthcoming days he would concentrate on the care of his soul rather than on that of his body. From that moment, he was forbidden to shave or cut his hair or nails, or to have sexual relations.

Following the ablutions, male pilgrims replaced their worldly garments with two seamless lengths of white cloth, wrapping one around the waist and the other around the shoulders; women usually wore a long, plain robe. The donning of this special costume was accompanied by specified prayers and the recitation of the *talbiya*, the pilgrim's statement that he had come in answer to the command of God.

Upon entering Mecca, the pilgrim went directly to the Kaaba, where he kissed the Black Stone. He then walked around the holy shrine seven times, reciting different prayers in glorification of God. Next, he ran seven times between two small hills nearby, a custom that had survived since the pilgrimages of pre-Islamic days.

The single most important ceremony of the pilgrimage was held at Arafa, in a valley some nine miles from Mecca, on the ninth day of *Dhu'l Hijja*. After traveling from Mecca by camel, on horseback, or on foot, the pilgrims gathered there in the afternoon, on and around a small hill. In an impressive ceremony, tens of thousands of pilgrims stood erect "before God," praying and listening to a sermon preached by some dignitary. This was the greatest moment in the life of a Muslim, moving him deeply and inspiring him with a powerful sense of his faith.

After sunset the pilgrims turned back toward Mecca, spending the night at Muzdalifa, a village not far from Arafa; the following day they proceeded into Mina, half way between Medina and Arafa, where they threw pebbles at stone pillars that were supposed to symbolize the devil and temptation. In Mina the *hajj* came to a dramatic climax as each pilgrim made a sacrifice to Allah, cutting the throat of a goat, sheep or camel. For Muslims who did not care to perform the blood rite themselves, special butchers were on hand; part of the meat was cooked and eaten by the pilgrims, and the rest was given to the poor. This sacrifice, which took place on the tenth day of *Dhu'l Hijja*, was duplicated by Muslims all over the Islamic world; they celebrated the day as the "Great Festival" with an exchange of presents and the wearing of new clothes.

Following the sacrifice, the pilgrims were allowed to cut their hair and don their normal clothing. The last ceremonies were performed upon returning to Mecca, where the pilgrims made seven final circuits of the Kaaba and ran as many times between the two small hills nearby, thus bringing the *hajj* to an end.

For Muslims who made the pilgrimage, the ceremonies left a lifelong impression. Henceforth they themselves were known as *hajji*, a title of great honor, representing an act of devotion that God would count in their favor on Judgment Day.

The Five Pillars of Islam—faith, prayer, the giving of alms, fasting and pilgrimage—formed an essential part of the complex system of legislation that regulated Muslim behavior. Indeed, this legislation, known as the *shari'a* ("the clear path to be followed"), was perhaps the most distinctive aspect of Islamic life. Unlike Western cultures, in which law and religion were separated, Islam wove these two into a single set of rules that governed a man's relations not only with God, but with his fellow men as well.

The *shari'a* had four primary sources: the Koran, analogy (based on principles underlying previous decisions), consensus (the collective approval of religious scholars representing the entire Muslim community) and the Traditions (various actions and sayings attributed to the Prophet). To Muslims, the Traditions, or *hadith*, had a special meaning, as the goal of every believer was to emulate the Prophet in his daily life. Complex problems often arose with the growth of Islam, and when no solution was found in the Koran it became customary to try to find a guiding principle in the Traditions.

As individual Muslims sought authority to support their actions and decide their quarrels, the manufacture of counterfeit Traditions became almost an industry. One imaginative rogue, who was later executed, confessed to having invented no less than 4,000 Traditions. By the beginning of the third century after the Prophet's death, some 600,-000 Traditions were said to have been in circulation. At this point a group of scholars collected and recorded those that they regarded as reliable. Their criterion was the reputation of the people through whom the incident or quotation could be traced back to a companion of the Prophet; each link in the chain might begin by, "I heard it from . . . who heard it from . . . who heard it from . . ." Of course not even this method was foolproof, relying as it did on the memories of men.

The Traditions, along with the other sources of the *shari'a*, were supposed to guide a Muslim on the road to heaven. As further guidelines, Islamic jurists placed all human acts into five categories: obligatory acts, such as paying *zakat*, or saying prayers; commended acts, such as freeing slaves or giving alms to beggars; morally neutral acts, such as going on a pleasure trip; disapproved acts, such as eating onion or garlic, which could cause bad breath; and forbidden acts, or *haram*, such as murder. The basic morality underlying this classification was similar to that of the Bible, especially the Old Testament; it enjoined Muslims to be patient, chaste and kind to the needy.

In other fields, however, there were significant differences between Christianity and Islam. One of the most marked was in warfare. Christ had taught

FEASTS TO END A FAST

During Ramadan, Islam's holy month of fasting and prayer, the Muslim commandment to give alms and be charitable to the poor took on heightened meaning. At the conclusion of this period of abstinence, princes and rich merchants implemented their faith by holding public feasts for the needy. Great mounds of succulent foods were heaped high on fine ceramic dishes like the Ninth Century Persian platter shown above, which is decorated in stylized Kufic script.

Among the many delicacies served at *Id al-Fitr*, the post-Ramadan festival, was chicken or veal, sautéed with eggplant and onions, then simmered slowly in pomegranate juice and delicately spiced with turmeric and cardamoms.

The climax of the meal often was *kharuf mahshi*, a whole lamb—stuffed with a rich dressing of dried fruits, almonds, pine nuts, cracked wheat and onions, sautéed in clarified butter and seasoned with ginger and coriander. Baked in hot ashes for many hours, the roast was tender enough to be taken apart and eaten with the fingers.

To complete the menu, a variety of rich sugar candies and pastries, flavored with spices or even flower petals, was served. Some of these sweetmeats were taken home to be enjoyed in the days to come.

Christians to forgive their persecutors and turn the other cheek; Muhammad, in contrast, had urged his followers to fight for Islam; in fact, *jihad*, or "holy war," narrowly missed being the sixth pillar of Islam. But even while permitting warfare, the Koran imposed certain limitations before fighting could begin: an enemy had to be given the chance to embrace Islam, or, failing that, to submit to Muslim rule and pay taxes.

In the matter of food, Islam followed a policy more similar to that of Judaism and the older Semitic traditions than to Christianity, which had adopted the revolutionary doctrine that no foods were of themselves taboo. "Forbidden to you," states the Koran, "is that which dies of itself, and blood, and pig meat, and that on which any other name than that of God has been invoked, and that strangled, and that beaten to death, and that killed by a fall, and that killed by goring with the horn, and that which wild beasts have eaten and that which has been immolated unto idols." On the other hand, Muslims could eat fish, game caught by dogs trained for that purpose and the meat of approved animals, such as sheep, goats or camels. In an emergency, to sustain life, anything edible was lawful to eat.

On the question of alcohol, Islam was the severest of the three religions. An early revelation in the Koran forbade the practice of going to prayer while in a state of intoxication. A later verse ruled out the drinking of *khamr*, an intoxicating Arabian drink, and, by extension, proscribed all alcohol. However, this prohibition was widely violated, mostly by the aristocracy, and the joys of drinking wine were sung by Islamic poets.

In its treatment of women, Islam differed from Christianity more than in any other respect. The Koran instructed male Muslims that "men are in charge of women." Nevertheless, in many respects Islam improved the condition of women over what it had been previously. In the past an Arab could marry as many women as he wanted, treat them as he liked and divorce them at will. While the Koran did not end polygamy, it at least limited it; a man was allowed to take no more than four wives, and each of them had to be treated equally and with kindness. The bridal gift, formerly paid to the bride's family or guardian, now became the property of the bride herself. Moreover, the woman could keep this payment even if her husband divorced her.

A man still could divorce a woman without giving his reason, as he had in the past, merely by stating, "Thou art dismissed," three times. But once the divorce was accomplished, he no longer could remarry her immediately; this discouraged a man from divorcing his wife in anger, knowing that he could remarry her the next day. It was still almost impossible for a woman to initiate a divorce, but under certain conditions a woman could buy her freedom by relinquishing to her husband the property she owned. Sexual offenses by either a man or a woman were severely condemned. The Koran specified the punishment: "The adulterer and the adulteress, flog each of them with a hundred stripes."

If at times some of their strictures seemed dogmatic, or even harsh, all of the doctrines governing a Muslim's behavior were integral parts of a uniquely organized system of beliefs—a system that remained constant over the years precisely because it served so well the people for whom it was designed. For millions of individual Muslims Islam provided a total way of life—economic and political as well as spiritual and social—that made it possible for them to live in harmony with their universe and to die at peace with themselves. Just as significantly, this system served Islam as a whole, providing the force that enabled it to burst out of Arabia and transform much of its world.

THE DOME AND MINARET *of the Guyushi Mosque, built in the 11th Century on a bluff above Cairo, are boldly outlined against the eastern skies.*

DESERT SANCTUARIES

Muhammad regarded the mosque simply as a place for congregational prayer, and cared little for architecture. Beyond stipulating that the faithful should be ritually clean, face Mecca and perform an unvarying sequence of motions while praying, he left few instructions for the physical components of worship. ("The most unprofitable thing that eateth up the wealth of the believer," he observed, "is building.") Yet the mosque very early acquired certain distinctive features. Basically, it was a rectangular structure formed by arcaded porticoes opening inward to a central court. One side, facing Mecca, housed the sanctuary; the rest functioned as a community gathering place. Beneath its cool arches teachers conducted classes and scholars argued fine points of Koranic law; in its quiet courtyard merchants strolled and talked away from the teeming life of the bazaar, while veiled women came and went, sometimes filling their water jugs at the mosque well.

Photographs by Roloff Beny

A WHITE-ROBED MUEZZIN *calls the faithful to prayer from the tower of Cairo's ancient Mosque of Ibn Tulun, parts of which were erected more than 1,000 years ago.*

THE SPACIOUS COURTYARD *of Ibn Tulun dwarfs a man standing beside the mosque's dome-covered fountain. The entire mosque covers an area of some six and a half acres.*

A House of Prayer for a Desert Religion

The early mosque was in effect a typical desert dwelling built on a majestic scale and put to religious use. Its great central court was patterned after the courtyard of Muhammad's palm-thatched house at Medina, where the faithful had heard the Prophet preach. From the mosque's tower, or mina-

ret, Muslims were called to prayer, just as they had been called, in the Prophet's time, from the rooftop of a nearby house. As Islam advanced, the mosque acquired a staff: an imam to lead the prayers and a muezzin to issue the call to worship, positions once filled by members of the congregation.

Water for Life and Purification

For the desert-dwelling Arab, water was scarce, sacred and intimately associated with his religion. "Prayer," Muhammad reputedly said, "is like a stream of sweet water that flows past the door of each one of you; into it he plunges five times a day; do you think that anything remains of his uncleanness after that?" One of the holiest places in Islam was a well

AN ELABORATE FILTER *in the center of the marble courtyard of the Great Mosque in Qayrawan, Tunisia, channels rainwater into an underground cistern.*

called Zamzam, in Mecca. Its waters were universally regarded by Muslims as a curative for ills of both the body and the spirit. To dip one's shroud in Zamzam was a blessing, to drink its waters bestowed divine grace; few pilgrims to the Holy City neglected these pious rituals.

Water was also identified with everyday worship. Few mosques were without a fountain for the ritual ablutions that preceded prayer, and often these fountains were also the town's main water supply. So pervasive, in fact, was the concern with water in the arid land where Islam was born that the Prophet, when asked to name the act of greatest merit, is quoted as once replying, "To give people water. . . ."

The cuplike catch-basins trap silt and clarify the water.

A RITUAL CLEANSING *in the fountain of the Mosque of Ibn Tulun prepares a Muslim for his prayers.*

The Sheltering Arcades

The arcades of the mosque, which usually extended around all four sides of the court, offered relief from the blazing sun. In the shade of their arches—round, pointed and horseshoe-shaped—Muslims were free to sleep or talk, read or write, in fact to do anything that did not disturb others. (Among the banned activities were spitting and shouting, and making announcements about lost property.) The arcades on three sides of the court were shallow; those on the side facing Mecca were often several rows deep, forming the sanctuary where the congregation worshiped.

POINTED ARCHES of Cairo's Ibn Tulun Mosque are derived from Syrian designs.

Anderson, Rome

PATTERNS OF OPENINGS, *both rounded and pointed, are echoed across an inner courtyard of the Guyushi Mosque in Cairo.*

A FOREST OF COLUMNS *in the Great Mosque of Cordoba, Spain, supports horseshoe arches of red brick and white stone.*

A OPENWORK WINDOW (left) of fine, hard stucco, carved while wet, decorates the sanctuary of the Ibn Tulun Mosque in Cairo. The vine leaves around the frame are a Persian motif.

ARCHING SHADOWS enclose the high stucco windows of Ibn Tulun's "qibla" wall. At the far end of the wall is the "minbar," the traditional pulpit where prayer leaders deliver Friday sermons.

The Sanctuary, a Cloistered Hall Facing Mecca

The Arabic word for mosque means "place of prostration," and the heart of the mosque was the sanctuary, where Muslims unrolled their prayer rugs and prostrated themselves before God. One wall of the sanctuary, the *qibla* wall, marked the direction of Mecca, and was in a sense a holy wall, although its purpose was purely functional and it had no particular mystical symbolism. Like the rest of the

mosque, the sanctuary, in early times, was traditionally decorated in a simple and austere style, for the Prophet abhorred signs of idolatry. A niche, called the *mihrab*, was the *qibla* wall's only distinguishing feature. Sometimes there was more than one niche: in a wealthy congregation, Muslims endowed the mosque with *mihrabs* much as Christians endow churches with stained-glass windows.

49

A Focal Point
for an Act of Faith

At the beginning of the Eighth Century, when the *mihrab*, the niche indicating the direction of Mecca, was first introduced, certain puritanical followers of Muhammad objected to it. It was, they claimed, too much like the alcoves that held statues of saints in Christian churches. But the niche served so well as a focal point for prayer that it was gradually incorporated into mosques throughout Islam.

The *mihrab* shown at the right, in the Ninth Century Mosque of Qayrawan in Tunisia, is one of the finest surviving from early medieval times. Its carved marble screen and lustrous patterned tiles were imported from Baghdad. The superb carved teak staircase to the right leads to the pulpit where the prayer leader, or imam, delivered the sermon every Friday noon. Behind this pulpit is the *maqsura*, an enclosure in which the ruler customarily worshiped in privacy. The *minbar* and *maqsura* in Qayrawan's Great Mosque are the earliest surviving examples in Islam.

3

A TIME OF CONQUEST

THE WALLS OF UKHAYDIR, *which rise some 55 feet high from the desert south-west of Baghdad, enclose a seven-acre fortress-palace built in the Eighth Century. The turreted and arched limestone fortifications conceal the ruined quarters of an Arabian prince, suites for four wives and a simple mosque.*

Following the death of the Prophet in 632, Islam embarked on an era of change and conquest that was to transform it from a small religious community into a mighty political empire. But even while this new state was expanding with unparalleled speed, it was torn by internal dissension and violence.

During this turbulent period, from the early Seventh to the mid-Eighth Centuries, Islam was governed by a succession of caliphs, or "successors" to Muhammad. Some of its bloodiest battles were fought over the caliphate. Three of the first four caliphs were murdered, and the empire was almost constantly racked by rebellions and civil wars. Two successive dynasties emerged to seize power, shifting Islam's capital, in turn, from Medina to Damascus to Baghdad, and altering its character as well. It was under the second of these dynasties, the Abbasid, that Islam was to reach its pinnacle —a brief period when it was the greatest force on earth, and its capital the fairest and foremost city in the world.

Islam's opportunities, and its difficulties, began immediately after the Prophet's death. Muhammad unwittingly caused many of its problems by neglecting to name a successor or to establish a system for selecting one. While he could not be replaced in his role as Prophet, a temporal leader was urgently needed to guide the Muslim community. In the beginning the problem was resolved by roughly following the method used among Arab tribes in selecting a new chief; a group of senior Muslims simply chose the man they considered best qualified to rule.

Muhammad's authority thus passed, in turn, to four of the most respected Muslims, men who were his closest friends, and who were linked to him by marriage. These men, who continued to govern Islam from the dusty Arabian town of Medina, were later referred to as the "rightly guided" caliphs, because they had known the Prophet and had patterned themselves after him. Like Muhammad, they made all of the major decisions about Islam's destiny, relying on the advice of their most trusted friends, in the manner of tribal sheikhs. They were in close touch with the people, personally leading them in prayer and exercising over them spiritual, political and military authority.

The first caliph was Abu Bakr. He had been one of Muhammad's best friends, as well as the father of A'isha, the Prophet's favorite wife at the time of his death. He was now about 60, and although outwardly unimpressive—stooped and simply dressed, with a dyed red beard (a Muslim custom)—he was highly respected for his gentleness, wisdom, humility and piety. He took the title of *Khalifat Rasul Allah*, meaning "Successor of the Messenger of God."

At the start of his caliphate, Abu Bakr was faced with a major crisis, as many Arab tribes began to withdraw from the Muslim state. They had given their loyalty to Muhammad as an individual and had paid the Islamic tax because of this allegiance; after the Prophet died, many of the tribes felt that loyalty no longer bound them. When Muslim tax collectors visited their desert encampments, they refused to pay. Their rebellions became so widespread and serious that some Muslim leaders doubted if they could be suppressed, even by force. But Abu Bakr, despite his gentle disposition, refused to compromise with the Word of God by permitting this repudiation; he energetically dispatched troops to bring the deserters back. Within two years the rebellions—known as the *ridda* (apostasy) wars—were over and the renegades had been suppressed.

Even while putting down the revolts, Muslim troops began their first great wave of foreign conquests. Shortly before his death, the Prophet himself had expressed a desire to carry the Word of God to the peoples in the north, and preparations were begun for such a campaign. Abu Bakr, faithful to Muhammad's wish, sent Islam's banner into the Byzantine and Persian empires. Bearing the Koran and the sword, Muslim troops soon began to win many territories from the great powers.

Religion provided the initial spark for Islam's expansion, but other forces helped to fan the flame.

Foremost among these was the drought-stricken poverty of Arabia, stemming from its almost total lack of resources. The peninsula had never been able to produce enough food for its population. This chronic scarcity had driven previous generations of Arabians to migrate north into that tantalizing area of green that stretched in a fertile arc from Palestine through northern Syria, and southeast through the valleys of the Euphrates and Tigris to the Persian Gulf.

In this area, several minor Arab kingdoms had been established, and they acted as buffer states between the empires of Byzantium and Persia, which had long been enemies. Both powers trained and subsidized these border Arabs to fight for them as mercenaries, but when their treasuries had been depleted by fighting each other they withdrew the subsidies and imposed taxes on the Arabs to pay for the wars. When Islam finally burst out of its Arabian cocoon, the oppressed border peoples looked to the arriving Muslims more as liberators than as conquerors, and many joined them to fight against their former masters.

A second major factor that helped the Arabs was the enmity between the two empires, ruled by Heraclius in Constantinople and King Yezdegerd in Ctesiphon. For more than two centuries there had been power conflicts between the Christians of Byzantium and the Zoroastrians of Persia; in the early Seventh Century, this friction had developed into a major war. Persia had invaded the Middle East, capturing the "True Cross" in Jerusalem and occupying Egypt; Byzantium had then counterattacked and ousted the Persians. Each of the two rivals was so intent on the threat posed by the other that both were blind to the greater threat of Islam. They were like two feudal horsemen, eye to eye, lance twined with lance, so obsessed with besting each other that they did not see the approaching horseman who would unseat them both.

ATLANTIC OCEAN

SPAIN

Cordoba
Seville • • Granad
• Ceuta

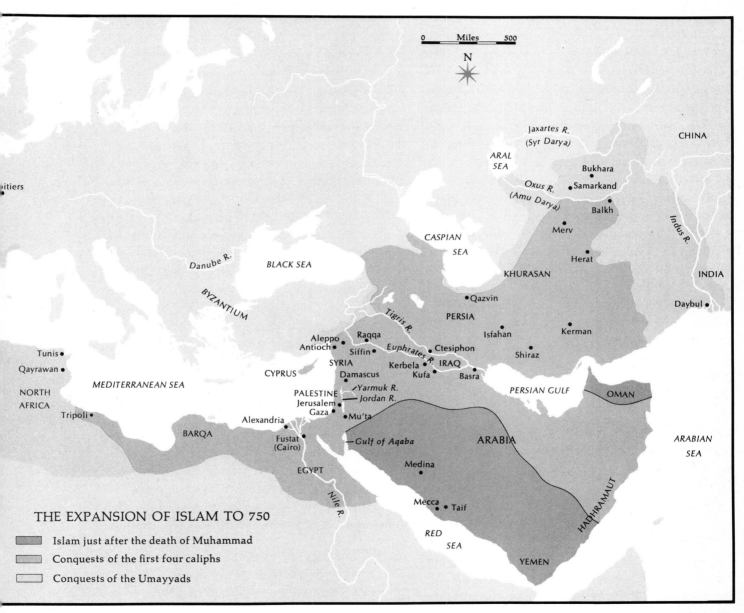

Miles 0 — 500

N

THE EXPANSION OF ISLAM TO 750

Islam just after the death of Muhammad
Conquests of the first four caliphs
Conquests of the Umayyads

Map labels:

CHINA
Jaxartes R. (Syr Darya)
ARAL SEA
Bukhara
Samarkand
Oxus R. (Amu Darya)
Balkh
Merv
CASPIAN SEA
Herat
KHURASAN
INDIA
Indus R.
Qazvin
Daybul
PERSIA
Isfahan
Kerman
Aleppo
Raqqa
Tigris R.
Antioch
Siffin
Euphrates R.
Ctesiphon
SYRIA
Kerbela
Shiraz
Damascus
Kufa
IRAQ
Basra
PALESTINE
Yarmuk R.
Jordan R.
PERSIAN GULF
OMAN
Jerusalem
Gaza
Mu'ta
Alexandria
Gulf of Aqaba
ARABIA
ARABIAN SEA
BARQA
Fustat (Cairo)
EGYPT
Medina
Nile R.
HADHRAMAUT
Mecca
Taif
RED SEA
YEMEN
BYZANTIUM
Danube R.
BLACK SEA
CYPRUS
MEDITERRANEAN SEA
Tunis
Qayrawan
NORTH AFRICA
Tripoli
itiers

AN ISLAMIC EMPIRE, *built on the backbone of the Persian and By-zantine empires, took form in two great waves of Arab expansion. After the death of Muhammad in 632, armies of the first four caliphs burst from the Arabian Peninsula, conquering Palestine, Syria, Egypt, Iraq and most of Persia in less than 20 years. The Umayyads (661-750) broadened Islam's new empire to the borders of India and China in the east and into North Africa and Spain in the west, linking three continents. Not until 732, when the Muslims were defeated near Poitiers by Frankish forces under Charles Martel, was their course of empire stayed.*

In addition to these factors, still another element contributed to Islam's success; the emergence of a number of great Muslim military leaders, men who turned initial raids for booty into sustained campaigns of conquest. One of the most famous was Khalid ibn al-Walid. He had originally fought with the Meccans against Muhammad, and upon converting to Islam had fought for the Prophet himself. As a Muslim he had been among a force of 3,000 warriors who made an unsuccessful raid on Mu'ta in Palestine, a Byzantine border town renowned for its manufacture of fine swords. In this clash, almost unnoticed as the first skirmish between Byzantium and Islam, the Muslim commander was killed. Khalid took charge, and only his great skill enabled the vanquished troops to make an orderly retreat. For his valor and leadership in the raid, Muhammad nicknamed him "the Sword of Islam."

Khalid later became one of Abu Bakr's chief generals and played a key role in Islam's early conquests. He and other commanders molded the disunited tribesmen of Arabia into one of the great fighting machines in history. As warriors they were individualistic; as strategists they inclined to methods of warfare more like those of nautical peoples such as the Vikings than those of land-based powers such as Rome. They used the desert as a sea: an element they knew well, over which they could travel rapidly and from which they could appear unexpectedly to fall on their foes. One Muslim leader, wounded in battle and dying, defined the Arabian battle formula for his successors: "Fight the enemy in the desert. There you will be victorious, or, even if defeated, you will have the friendly and familiar desert at your backs. The [enemy] cannot follow you there, and from there you can return again to the attack."

Indeed it was this flair for attack, based upon surprise and speed, that proved to be the Muslims'

greatest strength in battle. While the Bedouin wars of the past had not been particularly bloody, these skirmishes had taught the Arabian horsemen how to use the horse and camel more skillfully than any other people on earth. Their cavalry advanced, lances at the ready, charging, wheeling and charging again under cover of a hail of arrows fired by the infantry, until the enemy broke ranks.

Islam's zealous warriors pursued their campaigns of conquest almost simultaneously in three main directions: north into Syria and Palestine, east by way of Iraq into Persia—the gateway to Central Asia—and west into Egypt and North Africa. While Khalid was feeling his way on the front with the Persians, he was suddenly ordered by Abu Bakr to throw his forces as fast as he could into the battle in Syria to bolster the troops already there. Khalid made a 200-mile march across the waterless desert. According to legend, he took along a herd of camels gorged with water, slaying the beasts at each stage of the journey and watering his horses with the contents of their stomachs. He joined Islam's Syrian army at Ajnadain, between Jerusalem and Gaza; together they defeated the army of Heraclius and advanced to Damascus, which capitulated in 635, after a six-month siege.

Before entering the city, Khalid imposed remarkably equitable terms of surrender, which were to become a standard for future Islamic conquests:

> In the name of Allah, the compassionate, the merciful, this is what Khalid ibn al-Walid would grant to the inhabitants of Damascus. . . . He promises to give them security for their lives, property and churches. Their city wall shall not be demolished, neither shall any Muslim be quartered in their houses. Thereunto we give to them the pact of Allah and the protection of His Prophet, the Caliphs and the believers. So long as they pay the tax, nothing but good shall befall them.

Only now Heraclius began to take the Muslim threat seriously. He could not passively accept the loss of Damascus, a key city believed to be the oldest in the world. To regain it, he began to muster an army of 50,000 men to drive the Arabs back into the desert. As the huge force formed, the Arabs evacuated Damascus and retreated to the Yarmuk River, at the southern end of the Sea of Galilee. There Khalid camped, with the sanctuary of the desert at his back, and there he awaited the coming battle.

The two armies finally met on a hot summer day in 636. Whether by luck or by Arab strategy, on that particular day the wind was blowing vigorously from the southeast; it swirled dust over the battlefield and into the faces of the Byzantine troops advancing from the north, half blinding them. Despite their superior military training, their heavy armor and the fervid prayers of their priests, the Byzantines could not withstand the Muslims' fierce attacks. Theodorus, the Byzantine commander, was killed, and his huge army was slaughtered. Soon after this stunning loss, all of Syria and Palestine fell into Muslim hands, except for two well-fortified towns, Caesarea, on the northern Palestine coast, and Jerusalem.

Back in Medina, Abu Bakr had not lived to savor this victory; two years earlier he had died of a fever. But he had retained consciousness long enough to indicate that his successor should be Umar, a bald, spare giant of a man who had been one of his, as well as the Prophet's, most valued advisers. In accord with Abu Bakr's wishes, Umar was chosen. At first he called himself the "Successor of the Successor of the Messenger of God," but later used the simpler title "Commander of the Faithful," a designation used by the caliphs who succeeded him.

Umar, who remained in office for a decade, is regarded as one of the greatest of the caliphs, a man who combined energy with modesty, courage with undeviating obedience to the laws of Islam; his moral scruples were so strict, it is said, that he once had his own son flogged for immoral behavior. It was under Umar's leadership that Islam made its greatest conquests.

Following Khalid's defeat of the Byzantines, Jerusalem resisted behind its walls for another year, until 637; then the city's patriarch, Sophronius, offered to surrender the Holy City if the Caliph of the Muslims would take delivery of it in person. Umar accepted this offer and began traveling north along the caravan track from Medina, wearing his usual, much-patched cloak.

On arriving in Jerusalem, Umar treated the city's Christian and Jewish inhabitants with the same restraint and consideration that Khalid had shown to the people of Damascus. While in the city he visited the Church of the Holy Sepulcher, which Christians believed to be the site of Christ's tomb, and while he was there Muslims were called to noonday prayer. But Umar refused to say his prayers in the Christian shrine, fearing that if he did so his enthusiastic followers would insist on turning it into a mosque. Instead, he went outside the church and prostrated himself toward Mecca on the bare ground.

Having at last conquered Palestine and Syria, Muslim armies were freed for new campaigns. In 639, a shrewd and daring Muslim general named Amr ibn al-As began "opening" (the Arabic term for conquering) Egypt, paving the way for the eventual conquest of all North Africa. Egypt, then under Byzantine control, was a threat to the Muslims as a base from which counterattacks could be launched; the fertile Nile Valley also had vast stores of grain that the Muslims needed for food.

Two years later, the city of Babylon, near the site of modern Cairo, surrendered after a seven-month siege; within another year the capital at

Alexandria and the rest of Egypt fell to Muslim troops. While Egypt was thus being "opened," other Muslim troops were advancing into the heart of Persia. By 644 most of the Persian empire, along with its great treasures, had been annexed by Islam, whose expanding realm now reached from the Mediterranean almost to India.

These extensive lands were governed under rules laid down by Umar, who provided the guidelines followed by his successors for many years. Umar's administrative policies were frequently based on the teachings of the Koran, but adapted to the systems already existing in the conquered areas. In the imposition of taxes, for example, the Koran clearly told Muslims their duty: "Fight against those who . . . follow not the religion of truth, until they pay the tribute." Consequently, non-Muslims were required to pay taxes, usually a head tax and a land tax as well.

The Muslims differentiated between territories that submitted peacefully and those that had to be subdued by force. In the former, the people were permitted to retain their lands and were granted protection in exchange for paying taxes; in the latter, the land and property of those who had resisted the Muslim take-over were regarded as spoils of war. The Koran stated that one fifth of the booty should become state property, the rest being divided among the Islamic warriors. Even so, the Muslims usually found it more advantageous to let the conquered people remain on their land, supplying food for the army and paying taxes to finance its campaigns.

Peoples conquered by Islam were not forced to become Muslims, but those who did not were sometimes forbidden to carry on any religious activity outside of their churches or synagogues. They were also prohibited from such religious expressions as the ringing of bells, as well as the building of new houses of worship. Still, the conquered peoples fared better under the Muslim government than they had under their former rulers.

Those who did convert were supposed to receive the same treatment as the Arab Muslims, but often this was not the case. Newcomers to Islam had to be "adopted" by the Arab tribe, and were then known as *mawali*, or "clients," distinguishing them from the Arab ruling class. In the beginning the *mawali* had little significance, but as their numbers increased they caused serious financial difficulties: by paying the lower Muslim taxes, they made less money available for the upkeep of the state itself.

Islam was still struggling with the problems of consolidating and ruling its empire when, in 644, the caliphate again suddenly changed hands. Tragically, Umar was cut off in his vigor when a Christian slave from Persia, nursing a private grievance, stabbed him just as the Caliph was starting to pray in the mosque at dawn. Umar survived long enough to express his satisfaction that the man who had mortally wounded him had been a Christian, not a Muslim.

On Umar's death, the caliphate passed to a pious and lenient Muslim elder named Uthman, a fastidious aristocrat known in his youth for his love of elegant clothing. Uthman had been the only member of the wealthy and powerful Umayyad clan to become Muslim during the early years of Islam. Most of his family had been active persecutors of the Prophet, and only when Islam triumphed had they seen fit to join it. Now, through Uthman, they wished to take over the cause they had once opposed so vigorously, and in large measure they succeeded in this, dominating his actions during his caliphate.

Uthman was caliph for 12 years, and his greatest achievement was the standardization of the Koran. In the beginning his reign was peaceful, but later it was disrupted by many forces that he could not

58

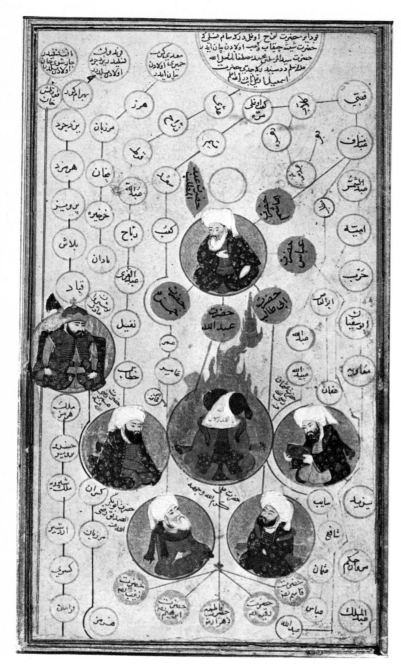

EARLY ISLAMIC DYNASTIES, *stressing Muhammad's lineage, fill a page of a Turkish chronology. The figure nearest the top is the Prophet's grandfather, whose ancestry is traced back through Noah to Adam's son Seth (large block of writing at top). At center below is Muhammad himself, surrounded by the first four caliphs, Umar, Abu Bakr, Ali and Uthman. At left are other Middle Eastern dynasties and a picture of Khosrau I, King of Persia at Muhammad's birth.*

control, among them the Arabs' own fierce resisance to centralized rule. The immediate cause of his undoing, however, was his appointment of many of his relatives and friends to office. The discontent came to a head in Egypt, where he replaced the capable governor with his own cousin, who was better known for his ability to collect taxes than his concern for just government. Eventually a group of 500 dissident Arabs from the army in Egypt went to Medina to protest the appointment of the new governor, and to present other grievances. Uthman promised to consider their complaints, but his family persuaded him to change his mind and to speak out against the rebels in a Friday sermon at the mosque.

The rebels, infuriated by this betrayal, besieged the Caliph's house. A handful eluded the guards posted at the gate and climbed a back wall to gain entry. Uthman was reading the Koran when the murderers broke in and spilled his blood over the book he had served so well. For the first time a caliph had been murdered by his own fellow Muslims, a deed that was to split Islam and bring civil war and further bloodshed.

The new Caliph elected by the elders to replace Uthman was Ali, one of the most respected of all Muslims. He was the son of Muhammad's uncle, Abu Talib, who had raised the Prophet, and the husband of Muhammad's daughter Fatima, who bore him two sons. Ali had been among the very first to accept Muhammad's revelations; he was admired by Arabs for his generosity and eloquence, and, above all, his ability as a soldier. Although by this time he was stout and bald and had a white beard, he was still impressive to his followers. Many Muslims believed that he should have been the first of the caliphs rather than the fourth.

From the beginning of his caliphate Ali was faced with fervent opposition. Among his many enemies were two men who had unsuccessfully sought the caliphate, and A'isha, the influential widow of Muhammad. Some historians say that A'isha's enmity to Ali may have stemmed from the incident many years before when she had arrived tardily at Medina with a young tribesman, after having dropped behind the Prophet's entourage to look for a lost necklace; Ali was among those who had suspected her of infidelity and she had never forgiven him for it.

Whatever the reason for A'isha's dislike of Ali, she joined forces with the two aspirants to the caliphate; they gathered around them a group of followers who staged a rebellion, accusing Ali of not bringing Uthman's murderers to trial. Seeking support, the rebels went to the military town of Basra, in Iraq, near the northern end of the Persian Gulf, where one of the rebel leaders had a following; there they won over the garrison and ousted the governor, who had remained loyal to Ali.

Having no army with which to put down this uprising, Ali gathered a few followers in Medina and headed toward Kufa, another military town some 200 miles northwest of Basra. The two towns were rivals, and Ali capitalized on the fact to win Kufa's support, raising troops there and setting out to suppress the rebels.

The two Muslim armies met at Basra, and their encounter became famous in Islamic history as the Battle of the Camel, because A'isha urged it on from a litter on a camel's back. The clash ended in victory for Ali; one of his two rivals died from a wound suffered in the fighting, and the other was killed by Bedouin raiders soon after. A'isha was escorted back to the city, where she lived out her life in retirement.

Instead of returning to Medina, Ali decided to establish his new headquarters in Kufa, which was more central to his extensive empire than the traditional capital. From there he tried to reconcile matters with his enemies, but soon an even more

formidable crisis developed in Syria. On becoming caliph, Ali had made enemies by replacing some of Uthman's relatives in office; one of these was Mu'awiya, the powerful governor of Syria and a member of the Umayyad family, an influential Meccan clan. But Mu'awiya refused to stand aside for his replacement; instead he accused Ali of complicity in Uthman's murder, and demanded that Ali produce the killers. This demand won great public support, as the Arab law of retaliation required that Mu'awiya revenge his slain kinsman or lose his honor.

Ali either would not or could not produce the assassins. He wavered, doing nothing, and Mu'awiya took advantage of his indecisiveness by claiming that Ali was protecting the culprits. To inflame the people against the Caliph, he displayed in the mosque in Damascus the blood-stained robe that Uthman had been wearing at the time of his assassination. Mu'awiya, an adroit politician as well as a capable administrator, not only had the support of the people of Syria and its well-trained army, but many of the people Ali had alienated also came to his side; among them was the shrewd Amr, who had been dismissed by Ali as the governor of Egypt—an act that was to prove disastrous for the Caliph.

Ultimately, Ali was forced to lead his army against Mu'awiya. His troops met the force from Syria near the ruined Roman town of Siffin, in the upper Euphrates valley in July 657. After a hard fight, Ali was forcing Mu'awiya to retreat when Amr proposed a brilliant ruse. He had the Syrian soldiers attach pages of the Koran to the tips of their lances, and shout a passage adapted from the holy book: "The decision belongs to God alone." Ali saw through the trick, but many of his followers refused to fight an enemy bearing the sacred word of God. The battle stopped, and, much against Ali's wish, the dispute was put to arbitration, which dragged on for six months. From the start, Ali was outmaneuvered: by agreeing to submit to arbitration he virtually conceded that his own caliphate and Mu'awiya's governorship were on the same level, and that both were in dispute. Further, the arbitrator who was chosen by Ali's advisers was no match for the one representing Mu'awiya—the wily and brilliant Amr.

Finally the decision was announced. According to one account, Ali's representative said that he and Amr recommended that both leaders be removed from their offices and a new caliph named. Amr then suddenly caused a furor by saying that he agreed with this—but that Mu'awiya should become the new caliph, filling Ali's vacated office.

Ali, quite understandably, refused to accept this verdict. But he was unable to renew the battle with Mu'awiya, as his ranks were torn by discord and rebellion. Many Muslims believed that by submitting to human arbitration he had violated the will of God. They abandoned his cause in disgust, joining with other dissidents to form an extremist group called the Kharijites, or Seceders.

The Kharijites, who were to play a troublesome role in Islam's future, became such a threat that Ali soon had to confront them too. The two sides met in battle in July 658, just east of the Tigris River in Central Iraq. Ali was victorious, but so weakened by the opposition to his rule and the many factions that split Islam that he still could not challenge Mu'awiya. The Syrian leader continued to rule that country virtually as an independent state within Islam; he added to Ali's humiliation by using Syrian troops to raid Ali's provinces, and even won control over Egypt.

Three years after his victory over the Kharijites, Ali was entering the mosque at Kufa to pray when a Kharijite zealot leaped out from hiding and plunged a dagger into the Caliph, killing him instantly. Ali's dismayed followers then pledged their loyalty to his eldest son Hasan. But after a few months Hasan, who was weak and politically unambitious, surrendered his claim to the caliphate in return for an immense subsidy from Mu'awiya—who was at last generally recognized as caliph.

Islam's focal point now shifted to Damascus, as Mu'awiya established the new Muslim capital in the land he knew and had governed and that was the source of his political and military power. Here he founded a dynasty, having his son Yazid recognized as his heir. From the time Mu'awiya became caliph in 661 until his last descendant in Damascus was overthrown in 750, the 14 caliphs in his line were succeeded in office by their sons or some other member of the Umayyad clan.

The Umayyads made sharp departures from the practices of their predecessors, not only in their dynastic succession, but also in the manner in which they governed the Muslim state. Mu'awiya ruled more like a secular king than a religious leader. He observed many of the egalitarian customs of Arabia; like a sheikh, he surrounded himself with counselors who spoke frankly without danger to themselves, and he remained easily accessible to his followers. Mu'awiya also established a tradition of excellence in administration. He reorganized the system of government that had broken down during the civil upheavals that followed Umar's death, and he and his heirs worked to strengthen and centralize authority in the Caliph's hands. While Mu'awiya ruled largely through persuasion, later Umayyad caliphs became more autocratic, relying on the Syrian army to control the empire.

Under the Umayyads, a distinctive Islamic culture began to take form, influenced largely by their Arab background. Arabic became the official language of the administration, replacing Greek and Persian, which had been used in the conquered territories for keeping records. The first Islamic currency—gold dinars and silver dirhams bearing

Koranic texts—were minted to replace standard Byzantine and Persian coins stamped with images of the emperors. An extensive communications system was established, with horseback postal routes and staging points for official use. Numerous public works projects were undertaken, including the rehabilitation and upkeep of long-neglected irrigation canals. Exquisite mosques were erected, among them the magnificent Great Mosque of Damascus in the capital.

In their private lives, the Umayyads enjoyed the fruits of their empire. They relaxed in lavish desert palaces, where they not only escaped the plagues of urban life but also savored the pleasures of the spirit and the flesh against exotic background murals of birds, beasts and dancing girls. They took great pride in their ancient Arabic poetry, which now flourished as it had not since pre-Islamic times, and in their own Arab lineage.

The Umayyads were also talented military leaders, and under their rule Islam's second great wave of conquests took place during the early part of the Eighth Century. They carried Muslim arms into Central Asia as far as the Indus valley in India, and west, through North Africa and Spain, to the Atlantic. Their bold manner of conquest is suggested by the rallying words of a Muslim leader who, upon landing his troops at Gibraltar in 711, ordered all of his boats burned, shouting to his men: "The sea is behind you, and the enemy is in front of you. By God, there is no escape for you save in valor and determination!"

Within seven years almost the entire Iberian peninsula had fallen into Muslim hands. In the east, hostilities with Byzantium, which had continued intermittently since the conquest of Syria, were pursued with greater intensity; once the Muslim armies advanced as far as Constantinople, and held a strong point just outside the Byzantine capital for seven years before they were forced to retreat.

A CONQUEROR'S COIN, *this Eighth Century silver dirham was minted by the first Umayyad caliph of Spain. The inscriptions read, in part, "There is no god but Allah" and state that the piece —roughly equivalent to a U.S. quarter in size and value—was struck in al-Andalus, as the Arabs called their Spanish domain.*

But, as it had been with the enemies from whom Islam had won its empire, internal weakness and dissension finally led to the Umayyads' collapse. Economic and social injustices perpetrated under their rule brought about deep resentments, and once more Muslims became divided by bitter disputes. One of the largest and most dissatisfied groups was the *mawali*, Islam's converted subjects. The Arabs denied them equality, considering them inferior; to marry a non-Arab convert, for example, was regarded as a social stigma. And although many of these newcomers to Islam fought in its armies, they usually had to fight as foot soldiers rather than in the elite cavalry, and they received less pay. Often non-Muslims were discouraged from converting so that they would have to continue to pay higher taxes. Joining the *mawali* in their dissatisfaction were certain Arabs who, because they were not members of the military aristocracy, did not receive pensions given to the warriors and were obliged to pay the land tax.

Realizing the explosiveness of these inequities, the Umayyads repeatedly tried to institute new measures. The caliph who made the greatest effort in this respect was Umar II, one of the most famous of all the Umayyad rulers; during his reign, from 717 to 720, he called an end to foreign campaigns and devoted himself to tax reforms. One of his most noteworthy achievements was to revive the former rule of exempting all Muslims from all taxes except the compulsory religious tax.

However well intentioned, this had a disastrous effect on Islam's economy. Egypt was so hard hit by the new policy that an official there asked Umar to rescind it, complaining that, "The conversion to Islam has so reduced [the tax revenue] that I have had to borrow 20,000 dinars." But Umar stood firm. Unfortunately, his reforms proved too costly, and his successors also failed to find a solution to the economic problem that was undermining the state.

Disenchanted with their rulers, many people joined anti-Umayyad parties, among them the Kharijites and another militant group called the Shi'a ("the party"), formed by Muslims who felt that the Umayyads had usurped the caliphate from its rightful heirs, Ali and his descendants.

When Mu'awiya died in 680, the Shi'a tried to make Ali's younger son, Husayn, the new Caliph. Accompanied by his family and a small group of his supporters, Husayn set out from Medina for his father's former capital at Kufa, where he expected to be eagerly received as the new caliph. But on the way he was halted by troops of Mu'awiya's son Yazid, who had already succeeded to the caliphate, and ordered to turn back. Husayn's followers persuaded him to refuse. The soldiers seized him and held him captive for ten days; then they killed him and sent his head to Yazid in Damascus. The slaying of the Prophet's grandson shocked all of Islam and made still more enemies for the Umayyads. The anniversary of his death is still observed in parts of the Islamic world as a day of mourning.

To make matters worse for Mu'awiya's heirs, the tribal wars that Muhammad had long ago tried to abolish once more erupted. The Bedouin tribes had never lost their spirit of independence, and resented any form of centralized authority. But now, instead of fighting among themselves in small, isolated units, they organized into two large factions, one claiming ancestry from northern Arabia and the other from the south. These factions, almost constantly at war with one another, became a strong force in Islamic politics, and their support sometimes even influenced the choice of caliph.

While the Umayyads were occupied with these difficulties, there appeared a new revolutionary force that ultimately was to overthrow them. This was the Abbasid party, headed by a ruthless Muslim named Abbas, a descendant of an uncle of the Prophet. The center of the Abbasid movement was in Persia, where there was much ill feeling against the Umayyads; the Persians considered themselves heirs to a higher culture than these haughty Arab conquerors who treated them as inferiors. Exploiting this and other undercurrents of discontent, the Abbasids won not only the support of the Persians, but also that of many Arab Muslims who had various grievances against the Umayyads. To undermine the ruling dynasty, the Abbasids conducted an extensive propaganda campaign; they proclaimed that the Umayyads were not true caliphs, that they lived worldly and decadent lives, and promised that they, the Abbasids, would again make Islam a true theocracy in the tradition of the "rightly guided" caliphs.

In June 747, the Abbasids raised the black banner of revolt that was to become their emblem, overthrew the Umayyad governor in Persia and took power there. Led by a brilliant Persian general, Abu Muslim, they then moved west, overrunning Umayyad armies that opposed them. In 749 Abbas was acclaimed caliph by his followers, although the Umayyads still held Syria. The following year his troops met those of Marwan II, the Umayyad Caliph, in a decisive battle at the Great Zab, a branch of the Tigris in northern Iraq. The Abbasids routed Marwan's army, bringing to an end Umayyad rule. The deposed Caliph fled to Egypt, but was caught there and killed, and his head sent to the new Caliph as a present.

Settling into power, the new rulers of Islam and their allies began wiping out the rest of the Umayyads with systematic thoroughness. At one epic slaughter a Persian general named Abdullah invited 80 of the remaining members of the Umayyad clan to a banquet. At the height of the festivities he had all of them murdered, then ordered the bodies covered while he and his aides resumed their meal. (Only one of the Umayyads escaped, it is said; he was Abd al-Rahman, known as "the Falcon of the Quraysh," who managed to flee to Spain, where he founded a dynasty that flourished for 300 years.) The Abbasids carried their revenge even to Umayyad caliphs who were already dead, exhuming their corpses and desecrating their graves. Only one tomb was not violated—that of Umar II, considered the only pious caliph among all the Umayyad rulers.

In their effort to assure a stable government, the Abbasids tried to eliminate all dissidents who might undermine their rule—even those who had supported them. The Shi'ites soon learned that they had been betrayed; the Abbasids not only failed to help their cause, but persecuted them as well. In their thoroughness, the new rulers also ruthlessly executed the men who had helped them gain office, so that the power of these allies could never be used against them. The victims were often dispatched with ingenious cruelty. Abu Muslim, the general who had led the Abbasid forces against the Umayyads, was hacked to pieces while conferring with the Caliph, and his head was thrown to his followers who waited outside the palace gates; another former supporter was killed and his body hung up to public view. The Persian general who had obligingly slaughtered 80 Umayyads at his banquet later made the mistake of trying for the caliphate, and was promptly imprisoned. After seven years he was taken from prison and led with great pomp into a house built especially for him. But the dwelling, unknown to him, had foundations of salt, which gradually dissolved. At last the house crashed down on the unsuspecting would-be caliph, becoming his tomb.

The Abbasid dynasty lasted for 500 years, but it was during the first century that it reached its apex, under Caliph Harun al-Rashid, who ruled from 786 to 809. From his throne in the new capital city of Baghdad, Harun presided over the world's most vigorous culture, and Islam knew the brief hour of glory that was to be its golden age.

Much booty hath God promised you. And ye shall have it.
THE KORAN

REACHES OF EMPIRE

*As the Byzantine and Persian empires battled each other toward
exhaustion and decay, backward Arabia, lying between the adversaries
but shielded by its aridity and poverty, prepared one of history's great
explosions. In 633 A.D., under the unifying banner of the Prophet,
sinewy Arab warriors burst hungrily out of their hot, dry homeland
and reached for the good life of their neighbors. Behind them was a
peninsula one third immured in sand dunes (above), lacking a single
stream that flowed year round; ahead was an irresistible lure: booty
for those who lived, Paradise for those who died fighting the unbeliever.
Within 100 years, this zealous, individualistic people had carved
out an empire that stretched from Spain to India, and at their peak
of power were deep inside France battering vainly at the gates of Poitiers.*

He it is Who made the earth subservient to you, so go about in

*In Arabia's land of heat and hunger—once described as "an iron wilderness"—to possess dates
and water was all a Bedouin tribesman could hope for. In earlier centuries many Arabs had
fled northward in major migrations; those who stayed sometimes practiced infanticide to
quiet hungry mouths and tribal warfare to gain their neighbors' meager goods. Yet only a few*

the spacious sites thereof and eat of His providence.
THE KORAN

*days' camel ride away—in riverine Iraq, in Syria by the Sea of
Galilee (left), on tree-shaded Lebanese slopes (right)—the grain
grew tall, oranges ripened in January, wild flowers bloomed in
profusion and there were seasons of fleeting clouds and crisp air.*

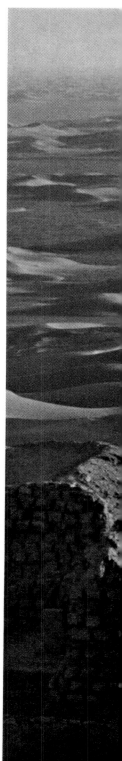

till the going down of the sun. . . . And the fear of the Arabs fell upon all kings.

ARAB HISTORIAN

The Muslims' thrust into the fertile borderlands was made with surprising ease. The Byzantines, who held Syria, fielded an army largely composed of Armenian and Arab subjects, sullenly reluctant to fight; the Persians, in Iraq, were still suffering the effects of four years of anarchy and civil war. The Muslims routed both in the same way. At Yarmuk in Syria, shouting Bedouins attacked out of the desert through a swirling dust storm, overwhelming the half-blinded Byzantines. At Qadasiya in Iraq, less than a year later, the desert-dwellers again materialized out of the blowing sand, and the decimated Persians fled eastward. Almost overnight, ragged Arabs passed from a world of dusty black tents to the mastery of ancient cities like Syria's fortress-crowned Aleppo (far left) and Nippur (left) in Iraq.

To protect newly won Syria against vengeful Byzantine raids from the south and west, an ambitious Arab commander, Amr, led 3,500 cavalrymen into Egypt, from which the Byzantines imported much of their food. Within nine months he had taken a fortress on the site of modern Cairo, swept past the Pyramids (above) and accepted the surrender of the mighty naval base of Alexandria. Then he settled down to enjoy the rich land.

Two decades later, to protect the conquest of Egypt, Amr's nephew Uqba rode farther west, adding Tunisia's pastures to Islam, then all the way to the foothills of the Atlas Mountains, sweeping over farms (right) long fortified against local raiders. Stopped by the Atlantic in 681, he rode impatiently into the surf, exclaiming to Allah: "Were I not hindered by this sea, I would go forward to the unknown kingdoms of the West . . . subduing those nations who worship other gods than Thee!"

with God's blessing and enjoy the land, its milk, its flocks and its herds.
And take good care of your neighbors.
AMR TO HIS VICTORIOUS TROOPS

The Persians, a proud people with their own thousand-year history of empire, proved to be the Arabs' toughest adversary. In 642 Arabs poured onto the Persian plains (right) where herdsmen tended cattle, and at Nehawand won a "victory of victories." But the war continued as the Persian King Yezdegerd fought stubbornly on, until killed by a traitorous subject. Leaderless, Persia slid into the Arabs' empire. But it turned defeat into a kind of victory. Filling the cultural vacuum in the pious but barbaric Arab society, Persian art, literature, philosophy and medicine became major elements of Muslim civilization.

Good news—the Persians have given us the soil of their country.

ARAB EMISSARIES

of landscape it resembles Syria . . . it rivals Egypt in the fertility of its soil.

THE ARAB GOVERNOR MUSA TO HIS CALIPH

From Europe, across the straits, the mist-covered valleys of
Spain (left) beckoned to the Arabs in Morocco. Conquest began
as a gesture; to propitiate his newfound Berber allies, Musa, the
Arab governor of North Africa, authorized a raid in 710. But
when the raiders handily mastered half of Spain within a year,
the temptation to push on proved irresistible; by 718 almost all
of Visigoth Spain had become an Arab province.
At the same time the Prophet's banner was borne eastward
into central Asia over fabled Samarkand, Bukhara and Kandahar
in Afghanistan (one of whose ruined Muslim forts is seen
above). The Arabs' expansion had reached its high-water mark.

In 732 the Arabs stood at the passes of the Hindu Kush (above) and gazed over its snowy peaks to India. Militarily, their strength was ebbing, but now another dream of the Prophet was coming true; Islam had legions of new converts. Turkish and other proselytes moved beyond the Kush and

*G*od hath brought the dream of His Apostle to pass in very truth.

THE KORAN

brought India under Muslim rule. In the West, Berber converts carried
the faith through Spain and halfway into France. People whom Muhammad
had neither seen nor known of were facing Mecca five times a day and
praying: "There is no god but Allah, and Muhammad is His Prophet."

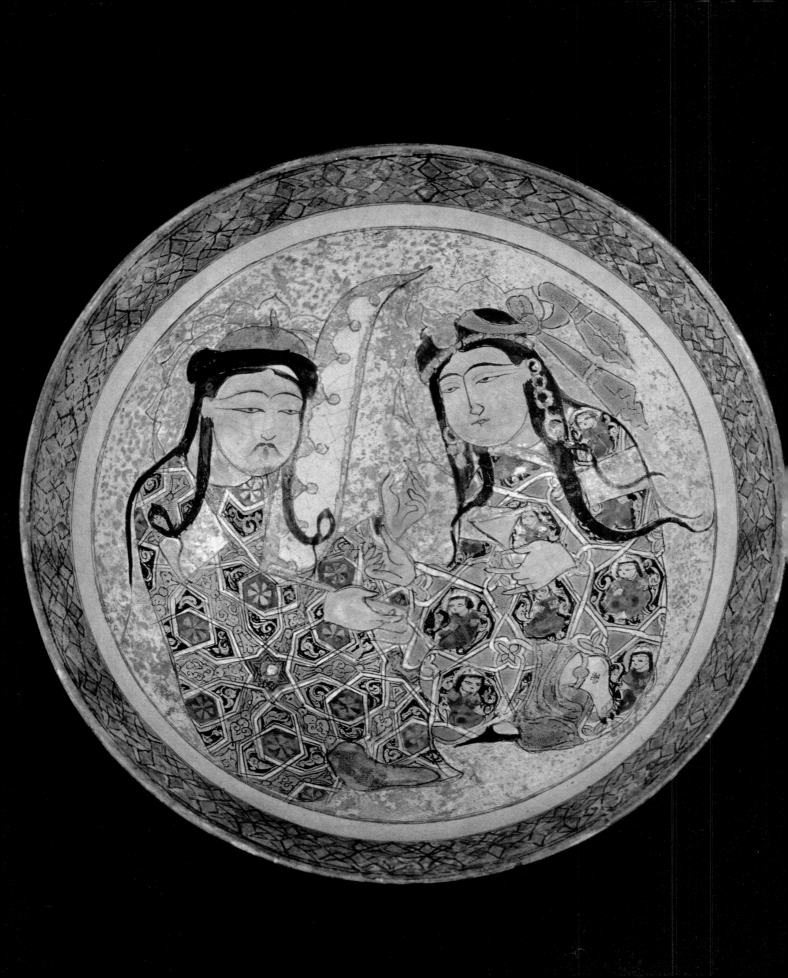

4

THE GOLDEN AGE

Out of the violence that characterized the early days of Abbasid rule, there emerged, at the beginning of the Ninth Century, an Islamic civilization that was both prosperous and culturally well endowed. But the epoch was like a meteor streaking across the night sky; its vitality soon spent itself, and by the middle of the Tenth Century the mighty Abbasid caliphs had faded to little more than shadowy puppets whose strings were manipulated by their own Turkish bodyguards.

At the beginning of their rule, the Abbasids moved their capital from Damascus to the East, heralding the new Eastern influences that were to come in Islam. Abbas, the founder of the dynasty, made his headquarters in Hashimiya, near Kufa, in Iraq, where the Abbasids had received their early support. When he died in 754, cut down by smallpox after only four years in office, he was succeeded by his brother, Mansur. The new Caliph's first years as the ruler of Islam were beset by uprisings, led by rival claimants to the caliphate and by disillusioned Shi'ites who had hoped to see a descendant of Ali on the throne. But Mansur diligently followed his predecessor's example in removing his enemies from the scene, and soon he had suppressed the rebellions and consolidated his power.

At the same time he was looking for a site for a new capital. Abbas' capital in Hashimiya had two major drawbacks: from a military point of view it was not strategically located, and it was too near to Kufa, long a center of rebellion. But Mansur had another motive for establishing a new capital: he wanted it to be a magnificent symbol of Abbasid power. The Caliph is said to have made many journeys through Iraq before finally finding a suitable location. He chose an ancient village named Baghdad, approximately 20 miles northwest of the former Persian capital of Ctesiphon.

From the start Baghdad proved an ideal choice. It lay on the west bank of the Tigris, in the midst of a fertile plain, beside a canal linking the Tigris with the Euphrates; the two rivers bent briefly toward each other at this point so that they were only 20 miles distant. The site was excellently suited to serve commerce, dominating the crossroads of the great trade routes, both land and water, that reached from the Far East to the Mediterranean and even

A POLYCHROMATIC PERSIAN PLATE *of the 13th Century depicts two courtly figures enjoying the pleasures of music, verse and the vine. While the man plucks a harp, the lady sips and listens—and perhaps recites a poem.*

into Europe. Even before Mansur selected it, Baghdad had been, due to its location, a meeting place of merchants and the site of monthly fairs. Because of the two rivers that flanked it, and the irrigation canals that crisscrossed it, the land was rich. Equally important, as a capital city it could be easily defended, since enemies could approach only by ship or bridge.

To Mansur, the new city that would rise in this "island" between the Tigris and the Euphrates would be a "market place for the world." He said, "Praise be to God who preserved it for me and caused all those who came before me to neglect it. By God I shall build it. Then I shall dwell in it as long as I live and my descendants shall dwell in it after me. It will surely be the most flourishing city in the world." Besides being struck by Baghdad's agricultural, commercial and military advantages, the Caliph was said to have been impressed by reports that the region enjoyed two other assets: cool nights and freedom from mosquitoes.

Mansur named his new capital Madinat al-Salam ("The City of Peace"), but the people continued to call it Baghdad. The first stones of the new buildings were laid in August 762, a time picked by the court astrologer as auspicious to begin construction. (Mansur is said to have been the first caliph who kept an astrologer at court.) To help build the new capital, every city in the empire was bidden to send its most skilled craftsmen. Some 100,000 workers were assembled from every corner of Islam—Syria, Egypt, Mesopotamia, Persia—and they worked four years to complete the extraordinary city.

A great citadel of sun-baked bricks, Baghdad was built in the form of a circle nearly two miles across, a shape believed to have been copied from Persian cities of the day; it was referred to as "the round city." Actually it was composed of concentric circles—a deep moat surrounding three huge, sloping walls. Of these three barriers, the middle one was the largest, measuring some 112 feet in height, 164 feet thick at the base and 46 feet wide across the top. It was fortified with lookout towers, and, like the other walls, was pierced at opposite points by four large gates that were guarded by soldiers.

The round city was designed as the administrative center of the empire. The ordinary people of Baghdad lived in houses outside the walls. The space between the outer and middle walls was left clear for purposes of defense. Between the middle and inner walls were the houses of courtiers and army officers. Behind the innermost wall were the residences of the caliph's family and the highest officials, including the commander of the army and the chief of police. At the very hub of the round city was the caliph's palace, a magnificent edifice built of marble and stone said to have been carried from the old Persian capital of Ctesiphon. Next to it was the mosque. Mansur had picked this position for his royal residence, declaring that the caliph should live at the very center of his empire.

The palace had two striking features: a golden gate, and a green dome that rose to a height of 120 feet, covering the caliph's main audience hall. On the summit of the dome, overlooking the city like a sentinel, was an imposing statue of a lancer on horseback; later, legend would hold that this figure swiveled and pointed to any area of the empire where peril threatened.

The round city was divided into four pie-shaped quadrants by two highways that cut across it at right angles to one another, linking the gates and running out through them; these thoroughfares not only afforded good communication but also gave officials firm control of the city, permitting it to be easily patrolled from the center. They also served commerce in Baghdad's early days: between the innermost wall and the middle wall each street was lined with arcades that sheltered all manner of shops, providing four central markets. But suburbs soon grew around Baghdad's walls, and quickly spread to the east bank of the Tigris. In the Tenth Century the capital had an estimated population of one and a half million, and by then the markets had been moved to the outskirts. This move reduced the number of people entering the central city, giving officials more control over who came and went there and adding to its safety.

In many ways Baghdad reflected the changes taking place all over the Islamic empire. Persian influences, which were seen in the city's basic plan, helped reshape Islam's character as well. The brilliant cultural heritage of Persia gradually percolated into Iraq, and from there it filtered out to affect practically every facet of Muslim life.

The empire retained the religion and language brought to it by the Arabs, but in other respects it was no longer dominated by these people. Under Abbasid rule, the state took on an international character it had never known before. With the end of the wars of conquest, the Arab aristocracy had lost its monopoly of high office. The once-privileged Arab warriors, to their chagrin, found themselves replaced by Persian soldiers and consequently had their pensions withdrawn. Officials and administrators were now drawn from the many peoples making up the empire; they achieved social position by their ability and the caliph's favor, rather than by fortune of birth, as in the past. Many of these new officials were Persians, who brought with them their own traditions and ways of thought. Persian and other non-Arab influences also entered Islam through intermarriage within the Abbasid family itself; although the family was originally Arabian, of the 37 caliphs in the dynasty, only a few had Arab mothers.

One result of this was a marked change in the way in which the empire was governed. Even before the Abbasids took control, the Umayyad caliphs had begun to exercise a more autocratic type of rule. This trend was accelerated until, finally, the Abbasid caliphs had absolute power, in the manner of the Persian kings. For centuries, Persian monarchs had reigned not merely as sovereigns, but as semi-divine beings invested with total authority over their subjects. To emphasize the idea of their omnipotence, they had surrounded themselves with elaborate ceremony, shielding their royal personages from the people to create an aura of mystery.

The Abbasid caliphs purposely imitated this example. They screened themselves behind the walls of their palace in the heart of Baghdad, living in awesome splendor. Mansur commanded his family and courtiers never to be seen in public unless they were dressed in costly silken garments and luxuriously perfumed. The caliph himself was inaccessible to all but a privileged few, who had to make their way past a multitude of guards and chamberlains to reach his presence. Upon at last approaching the caliph's throne, concealed by a resplendent curtain, they were obliged to prostrate themselves and kiss the floor—a custom alien to the rude democracy of Arabia.

A more vivid and grisly reminder of the absolute power wielded by the caliph was a leather carpet spread in front of the throne for the use of the executioner; this functionary stood behind the caliph, sword drawn, ready to smite the head from any luckless person who displeased his sovereign.

To further solidify their control over their subjects, the Abbasids emphasized the connection between ruler and religion. In this they could have taken their lead from a Persian saying which held that "Religion and government are twin brothers." As a symbol of the sacred nature of their rule, on important religious occasions the caliphs donned a mantle that the Prophet himself was supposed to have worn. No longer were they merely successors of the Prophet of God; in their new and exalted role they were the deputies of God Himself, calling themselves the "Shadow of God on Earth." In an effort to bring the religious organization of Islam under state control, the caliphs kept religious leaders around them, and tried to exert influence over them. An Arab historian later wrote: "This dynasty ruled with a policy of mingled religion and kingship; the best and most religious of men obeyed them out of religion, and the remainder obeyed them out of fear."

As the caliph withdrew more and more from the day-to-day direction of the state, there developed a new and powerful figure, the vizier, who stood between the ruler and the ruled. The vizier was the caliph's deputy, his chief minister in charge of running the empire. His authority was so great that it was second only to that of the caliph himself.

The role of the vizier was shaped by a remarkable family called the Barmakids, who served the first five Abbasid caliphs as counselors. Abbas brought the Barmakids to prominence when he appointed Khalid ibn Barmak, the son of a Buddhist priest from eastern Persia, as his imperial finance minister. Khalid grew so close to the Caliph's heart that his daughter was nursed by Abbas' wife, while his own wife was the nurse to Abbas' daughter. Khalid rose even higher under Abbas' successor, Mansur, who appointed him to govern various provinces of Persia; in this period Khalid distinguished himself further by crushing a rebellion against Mansur and performing other services for the Caliph. Khalid's son Yahya was schooled to succeed his father as vizier.

A story about Yahya illustrates how closely the Barmakids became involved in the Abbasids' intrigues over the caliphate, even helping to manipulate the line of succession. When Mansur died in 775, on his way back from a pilgrimage to Mecca, he was succeeded by his son, and then by his grandson, Hadi. Hadi's father, while he was the caliph, had ruled that if Hadi died, he should be succeeded by Hadi's younger brother Harun. But Hadi was determined to leave the caliphate to his own son rather than to his brother, and he tried to get Harun to give up his claim, without success. Harun was strengthened in this resolve by Yahya, who had been his tutor and counselor.

Yahya advised his young master to go hunting and stay away as long as he could. For Yahya, so the story goes, knew that the horoscope cast at Hadi's birth foretold that he would die at this time. Hadi learned what Yahya had done and threw him into jail, ordering his execution. The very night that Yahya was to be killed, however, the Caliph fell ill and died. Harun, then 23, was acclaimed the new caliph; he freed the faithful Yahya and made him his vizier, saying to his tutor, "My father, your fortune and your counsel set me in this seat; and now I invest you with all my power." Yahya, with the help of two of his own sons, Fadl and Ja'far, then took control of the affairs of state.

Apparently the Barmakids were excellent administrators, but their rule ultimately came to a tragic and violent end. For 17 years Yahya served Harun as vizier; his sons were tutors to the sons of Harun, and young Ja'far in particular became Harun's most loved companion. Indeed, Harun was so fond of Ja'far that to show his favor he allowed him to marry his favorite sister. He intended it to be a purely nominal match, never to be consummated; however, legend holds that the Caliph's sister gave birth to a son by Ja'far, and that her efforts to conceal it from her brother were unsuccessful. Whether for this reason or, more likely, because the Caliph had begun to fear the growing power of the Barmakids, the ruler suddenly saw a threat in the person of Ja'far. In 803, Harun sent one of his eunuchs to get Ja'far's head. When the head was presented to the Caliph, he is said to have wept and addressed it as if he were speaking to a living person who had wronged him: "O Ja'far! did

A PERSIAN CHESSMAN, *on a headless horse, is an ivory-hewn ancestor of the knight in the modern game. By the Eighth Century, chess, which the Persians had imported from India, had become widely popular in Islam, and caliphs invited champions, including women and slaves, to palace matches.*

I not make thee mine own peer. . . . Ungrateful, insensate fool! Reckless of what must come when thy luck must turn, in the turning of time. . . . Ja'far, my shame! O the sorrow thou hast brought on me, Ja'far! And on thyself!"

Not satisfied with having had his dear friend put to death, Harun had Yahya and the other son, Fadl, cast into prison, where they both died. The vast fortune accumulated by the Barmakids was confiscated and the survivors were ruined, their power at an end.

Despite the intrigues and violence that revolved around the caliphate, the Abbasids helped bring Islam a prosperity that made possible its golden age. The time of conquest was over and the empire was relatively at peace with itself and with its neighbors. Moreover, Islam possessed the immense resources of the conquered lands, and its intention to enjoy them could be seen in the splendor of Baghdad and other flourishing cities of the empire. The Persians introduced to Islam pastimes such as polo, backgammon and chess. From the Far East they brought rag paper and porcelain; their cooks offered exotic new dishes and served them on tables—an innovation to Arabs, who were accustomed to eating cross-legged on the floor. Baghdad's tailors popularized trousers, in place of the

traditional Arab robe. Persia also introduced many new household items: home furnishings such as mattresses and cushions, kitchen utensils—including ovens and frying pans—as well as rich silks and other fabrics.

As these and other imported luxuries stimulated popular demand, local artisans began to manufacture similar items. As the market grew, production increased and commerce expanded. Fabulous fortunes were made out of trade. Mansur's prediction that Baghdad would become the marketplace for the world was dramatically borne out.

Great caravans traveled overland through Central Asia to Baghdad en route to North Africa and Mediterranean ports as far distant as Spain. Ships of the empire plied distant waters carrying merchandise between Far Eastern lands—India, China, Ceylon and the East Indies—and Persian Gulf and Red Sea ports. The vessels arriving at Baghdad's docks brought with them the varied resources of the world. From China came silk, ink, peacocks, porcelain, saddles and spices; from India, rubies, silver, sandalwood, coconuts, ebony and dyes. Other cargoes included grain and linen from Egypt; glass and fruit from Syria; silk and other textiles from Persia; perfumes from Arabia; pearls from the Persian Gulf. Slaves and gold came from Africa;

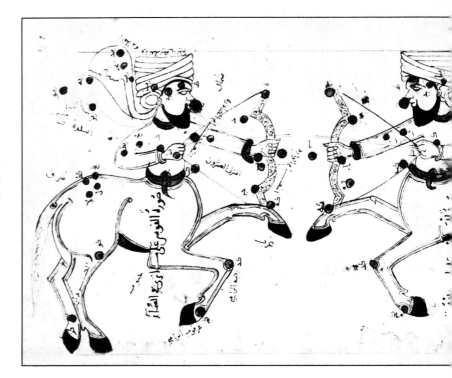

TWO VIEWS OF SAGITTARIUS, *a constellation traditionally pictured as a centaur with drawn bow, are, like much Islamic astronomy, based on the work of Greek scientists. The left view shows the constellation as seen from the earth; at right it is reversed, as pictured on a globe of the heavens.*

drugs, trinkets and slaves from Byzantium; leather from Spain; furs, amber, ivory and swords from as far away as Russia and Scandinavia.

This international traffic in goods, and the payments it entailed, led to a new profession—banking, an enterprise that reached a level of sophistication in Islam that was not to be attained in the West for another three centuries. Banking was a natural outgrowth of the complex monetary system in the Islamic empire. Two kinds of currency were in use: the Persian silver dirham used in the East, and the Byzantine gold denarius in the West. These coins fluctuated in value according to the price of the metal from which they were made, making necessary the presence of money changers in every market to facilitate the exchange of the currencies. Eventually these men became Islam's bankers.

From the financial system they ultimately developed came many of the banking concepts and terms later used in the West, among them the word "check," from the Arabic *sakk.* They had central banks with branch offices, and an elaborate system of checks and letters of credit; it was possible for a check written on a bank in one part of the empire to be cashed in a distant city.

Along with the exchange of goods from all over the world, Islam also prospered from a fresh exchange of ideas. To Ninth Century Baghdad came the most accomplished men of the age: poets, jurists, philosophers, scientists, artists. The lure for them was not merely the celebrated physical attractions of the capital, though they doubtless enjoyed the evenings of food, drink, music and verse that still echo in the pages of *The Arabian Nights.* They were primarily drawn by the pleasures of awakening minds, and the excitement of discussion and debate. Behind the intellectual vigor they displayed lay the rich cultural legacies the Muslims had inherited from the diverse peoples within their empire, particularly the Greeks of late Hellenistic times. Indeed, in the scholarly circles of the empire it was as though the philosophy and science of Greece had been born again.

By an irony of history, this revival of Greek thought owed nothing to the Greek-speaking Byzantines who were neighbors of the Muslims. Proud of their religious orthodoxy, the Christian emperors who ruled Byzantium frowned on pagan knowledge; certainty, not questioning, was what they valued. The men who made possible the intellectual

awakening of Islam were primarily Christians and Jews from Syria. They translated Greek manuscripts into Syriac, and from that tongue into Arabic. Soon, however, as interest grew, translations were made directly from Greek into Arabic.

Although Ninth Century Muslims had a passionate desire to learn what the Greeks had discovered, they were limited by two factors. First, the only manuscripts accessible to them were those that had been preserved by the late Greek schools; thus Homer and Sophocles were not to enter the Islamic heritage, because these Hellenistic schools had shown no concern for drama and poetry. Second, the Muslims' own primary interest was in practical matters, and it was mainly the works of Greek physicians, astronomers, mathematicians and geographers that appeared anew in Arabic dress. Although Greek philosophy had no such practical value, it was related to Greek science, and was therefore translated along with the other works.

Inevitably, this exposure to the Greek way of looking at things had a profound influence on Islamic thought. No longer were Islamic scholars concerned only with the systematization and codification of Muslim theology, based primarily on the revelations of the Koran and the *hadith*, or Traditions. Now they were introduced to Greek speculative philosophy, which grew out of man's ability to reason. One Muslim theologian even went so far as to argue that doubt was the first requirement of knowledge. To some Muslims this verged on heresy. But to many orthodox Muslim intellectuals the logical methods of Greek rationalism were seen as a tool that could be used effectively to clarify Islamic doctrine and to defend their faith against the heretical ideas being introduced by non-Muslims.

The interest in Greek thought, as well as the challenge posed by other foreign ideas such as those of Persia and India, gave rise to a flourishing movement in science, literature, philosophy and theology. These same currents of thought also encouraged a daring theological school known as the Mu'tazilite, which had started about two decades before the coming of the Abbasids. Its viewpoint was expressed by a philosopher named Kindi, who said, "We should not . . . be ashamed to recognize truth and assimilate it, from whatever quarter it may reach us, even though it may come from earlier generations and foreign peoples." The Mu'tazilites began to apply reason and logic to examine concepts previously accepted on faith alone, utilizing the Greek method of argument in advocating their dogmas.

To the horror of the Traditionists, orthodox scholars who accepted the *hadith*, as the basis of belief, the Mu'tazilites' reasoning sometimes led them to startling new conclusions, and bitter public controversy ensued. One issue around which conflict crystallized was the nature of the Koran: Was the Word of God eternal like God Himself, as Muslims traditionally had believed, or had there been a time when it did not exist? The Mu'tazilites shocked Muslim popular belief by arguing that the Koran was not eternal, and used Greek logic to prove it. In essence, they claimed that the traditional concept contradicted the basic principle of the Koran itself that God alone is eternal.

For some 22 years this rationalist approach actually enjoyed the official support of the state. In 827 the Caliph Ma'mun openly espoused the Mu'tazilite position and attempted to impose it on Traditionist theologians; he even established an inquisition to seek out those who adhered to the popular view that the Koran had existed forever. During the two decades that the Mu'tazilite position remained the official doctrine, its opponents were dismissed from public office and, in some cases, suffered physical persecution.

However, the Mu'tazilites' views eventually

were rejected. There were two principal reasons: the people bitterly resented their intolerance and the official attempt to impose their views on all of Islam by force; even more, they rebelled against the Mu'tazilites' insistence on exalting human reason above God's Word. Public opposition became so great that in 849 the Caliph Mutawakkil reversed the official policy, giving victory to the Traditionists. The state thus failed to achieve control of the Islamic religion, which remained in the hands of the community.

Although the Mu'tazilites no longer played a prominent role in Islam, they made a lasting contribution by grafting Greek rationalism onto Muslim thought. The man primarily responsible for this fusion was a famous theologian known as Ash'ari. As his thought developed, he turned away from the Mu'tazilites' conclusions but did not reject the logical methods of Greek philosophy; instead he used these methods to strengthen the Traditionist position. Much as Thomas Aquinas had in the medieval West, Ash'ari asserted the superiority of revelation over reason—but he used the pillars of logic to support the structure of faith.

While philosophers and theologians debated abstract intellectual questions, a mystical movement called Sufism originated among the people. This movement's origins can be traced back to Muslims who, from the beginning of Islam, were drawn by certain mystical elements in the Koran; as early as the second century after the Prophet's death, some pious Muslims had sought salvation through lives of simplicity and poverty in imitation of Christian hermits. As a sign of asceticism, they wore rough, undyed robes of wool (*suf*, in Arabic) from which the name is believed to be derived.

In the Ninth Century, Sufism attracted many devout Muslims and began to take definite shape. In effect, it was a reaction, not only against the rationalists, but against a tyrannical government

A FOLDING KORAN STAND, *with two upper panels that cradled Islam's Holy Book in a 14th Century mosque, is carved with Allah's name, fine arabesques and flowers.*

seemingly supported by orthodox religious leaders, and against the mechanical observance of Muslim rituals by men more interested in worldly wealth and luxury than in a spiritual life. The Sufis, unable to find complete satisfaction either in rationalism or in ritual alone, turned to the cultivation of an inner, spiritual life, through which they tried to achieve union with God and experience Him directly and emotionally. They envisioned God as a Creator who loved His creatures and wished them to draw near Him; they quoted from the Koran, particularly the verse describing God as nearer to man than his neck vein.

Sufism's adherents included many types of individuals, ranging from saints and poets to charlatans. Some Sufis wandered like medieval friars from village to village, living on alms and inflaming listeners with their ecstatic message. Others lived apart, practicing rigorous self-discipline and spending their days in contemplation and other spiritual exercises to bring them into communion with God. The one thing all had in common was fervor for their cause—the love of God. A woman Sufi named Rabi'a, stolen from her family as a child and sold into slavery, was freed because of her incandescent purity and her selfless love of God. "Love of God hath so absorbed me," she exulted, "that neither love nor hate of any other thing remains in my heart." She lived a life of extreme asceticism, rejecting the pursuit of virtue motivated by hope of any reward. "O God," she prayed, "if I worship Thee in fear of Hell, burn me in Hell; and if I worship Thee in hope of Paradise, exclude me from Paradise; but if I worship Thee for Thine own sake, withhold not Thine everlasting beauty."

Many great mystics, like Rabi'a, were venerated as saints by the Sufis. Their passionate attachment to such saints and their tendency to disregard rules incurred the suspicion of orthodox religious leaders. One of the most renowned mystics of the Ninth Century, known as Hallaj ("the wool-carder"), spoke in capricious, troubling riddles, now seeming to remove God from the grasp of mortals, now bringing him blasphemously close. His preaching in Baghdad inspired a cry among the people for moral and political reforms, causing orthodox theologians to demand his death. These religious leaders were further incensed by reports that he had proclaimed, "I am the Truth," by which he was said to have equated himself with God.

Hallaj prudently fled the city, but a few years later was caught and imprisoned. He was freed, but was once more accused by theologians of heretical statements, tried and sentenced to death. Before the 64-year-old mystic was executed he was led out of jail to undergo grisly punishments that included flogging, mutilation, and crucifixion; at last he was decapitated and, finally, cremated. He went to his death, it is said, smiling at his executioners and praising God.

While Hallaj's fate did not prevent the spread of Sufism, it was not until the Twelfth Century that orthodoxy ceased to look upon the movement with suspicion. The change is generally attributed to Ghazali, one of Islam's greatest theologians, who, analyzing various systems of thought and paths to salvation, finally chose Sufism as the one that brought him closest to God. Ghazali did not renounce orthodoxy, but made mysticism a respectable element in orthodox Muslim practice.

While religious and philosophical ferment continued, Islam was beset by deep internal troubles that were to lead to its political disintegration. Almost from the beginning of Abbasid rule, the vast empire had begun to break up into independent or virtually independent local dynasties. As early as 756 Abd al-Rahman had founded an Umayyad line in Spain, and soon thereafter other dynasties began to take control in Morocco and Tunisia. In 820 the Governor of Khurasan in Persia declared his independence from the Abbasids and, although he acknowledged nominal allegiance to the caliph, he and his successors were the actual rulers there. Within the next century all of Persia similarly fell under the control of local rulers.

In the face of this fragmentation of their empire, the Abbasid caliphs at first managed to retain considerable power, primarily through their command of the Persian military forces. But gradually their authority began to diminish, even in the capital itself. It was during the reign of Mu'tasim, a son of Harun, who ruled from 833 to 842, that the Abbasid caliphate began to lose control. Mu'tasim included in his personal bodyguard Turkish slaves from Central Asia, and he made what was to prove a disastrous blunder by placing them in command of the guard. By doing this he hoped to offset any possible disloyalty on the part of his Persian soldiers—who had helped the Abbasids to power but now were open to the influences of political rivalries. As a result of Mu'tasim's action, friction grew between the Turks and the local population. The situation became so acute that in 836 the Caliph moved his capital 60 miles up the Tigris, where he built the new city of Samarra. This remained the administrative headquarters of the empire for the next half century, during the reign of seven caliphs.

Located on the east bank of the Tigris, Samarra was renowned for its palaces and parks. On the west bank of the river Mu'tasim laid out a special pleasure ground, which was connected with the capital by a bridge of boats; there he planted lush gardens with palms from Basra and exotic plants from distant regions of the empire. Samarra's Friday Mosque was the largest ever built, covering some 45,500 square yards (nearly three times the ground area of St. Peter's Church, Rome), and was celebrated for its magnificence: it was paved with marble, its walls were covered with enameled tiles, and the roof was supported by stately marble columns. The spiral-ramped minaret, some 175 feet tall, could be seen for miles.

While in Samarra, the Abbasid caliphs became increasingly dependent on their Turkish guards, until they actually were their pawns. One of Mu'tasim's sons, Mutawakkil, was, in fact, placed on the throne by the guards and was virtually their prisoner. Ultimately Mutawakkil was murdered by the Turks at the instigation of his son, who sought to be the caliph himself—and who was allowed to remain on the throne only six months before he too was removed. From then on the Turkish guards appointed and deposed caliphs at will.

Under these caliphs, who had no real political power, although they retained great religious prestige, the provinces of the empire continued to break away from centralized control. In 868 Ibn Tulun, a Turk who was appointed to govern Egypt, made himself a virtually independent ruler there, founding the Tulunid dynasty. Nine years later Ibn Tulun annexed Syria. This encouraged various Arab tribes to seize lands in Mesopotamia and parts of Syria, where they established a number of short-lived Bedouin dynasties.

In 892 the caliphate was returned to Baghdad by the Caliph Mu'tadid in an attempt to reassert authority over the world of Islam. But despite this last desperate move, the Abbasids could not regain control over their disintegrating realm. In 945 the Buyids, a Persian family that had taken control of western Persia, entered Baghdad, and the Turkish guards fled. The Buyids dominated the Abbasid caliphs until they, in turn, were ousted in 1055 by the Seljuk Turks—a powerful people who had entered the empire from Turkestan, east of the Caspian Sea, in the late Tenth Century. Under the Seljuks Islam was to enter a new era that was marked by conquest and relative unity.

HURRYING HOME *for the birth of his son, a wealthy merchant and his friend are met by his anxious servants.*

a muslim's life

From the Eighth to the 13th Centuries, the Islamic empire was at the height of its prosperity, and a Muslim of good birth or enterprise lacked neither luxuries nor leisure. Such a man's way of life, from cradle to grave, can be glimpsed in the illustrations done in 1237 by the artist Yahya al-Wasiti for the *Maqamat*, a classic series of Arabian tales. His birth, which may have taken place in an elaborate mansion like the one above, was a joyful event celebrated by a week of feasting and offerings. The first words that the child heard, whispered ritually into each ear, were those of the sacred Muslim oath: "There is no god but Allah, and Muhammad is His Prophet." They were also the last words murmured at his grave.

the litany of learning

At the age of seven a Muslim boy left the exclusive society of the women who raised him and began his education as a man. His father entered him in a mosque school where he learned to write by scratching passages from the Koran, dictated by the teacher, over and over again onto a tablet. In the schoolroom shown below, one boy recites for the teacher while another boy takes his turn pulling the ceiling fan. These formal studies were supplemented at home; under his father's tutelage, the boy learned the manners of a Muslim gentleman—not to eat, or talk, too much, not to spit in public, not to speak ill of one man to another.

The mosque school was open to all boys whose fathers could afford the trifling tuition, but only the sons of the well-to-do moved on from literacy to training in the niceties of literary style. In the book-lined library of the mosque *(right)*, young men destined for positions of wealth and privilege attended seminars, in which they listened to men of letters discuss poetry and the classics. Sufficient knowledge to quote a favorite poet, and even to do a bit of original versifying, was considered essential to a Muslim who moved about in respectable society.

domestic life

For every male Muslim, marriage was not only a custom but a duty. "When a servant [of God] marries, verily he perfects half his religion," the Prophet had said. Usually a man took his first wife at the age of 20, and was permitted to take three more—but only if he could provide each wife with her own quarters, her own conveniences for cooking and sleeping, and her own household slaves.

Slaves were an integral part of Muslim life. They served as soldiers, servants, clerks and concubines. In the typical slave market seen at right, a Muslim gentleman makes a choice from a group of black and white slaves, while a dealer transacts a sale on the platform above. Like all good merchants he weighs his gold dinars to make sure that no one has lessened their value by clipping the edge.

A number of formalities preceded a Muslim marriage, but the girl was never a direct party to these, nor did the marriage need her consent. The preliminary arrangements were made by the respective mothers; then the suitor approached the girl's father, as in the scene above. Finally, a contract was drawn up, affirming the girl's age (usually 12 to 20) and her virginity, as well as the purchase price that the man paid to his bride, and which remained hers in the event of divorce.

Good women are obedient," said the Prophet, who believed that Allah had made men to excel. "As for those from whom you fear rebellion," he ordained, "admonish them and banish them to separate beds, and scourge them." Should a man and wife nevertheless fail to get along, they could appeal to a *qadi*, or judge, empowered to arbitrate domestic disputes.

In the illustration below, a *qadi* listens to the complaints of a husband *(center)*, while his unrepentant wife *(left)*, backed up by two friends, points an accusing finger at her spouse. If the *qadi*'s conciliation failed, the husband could divorce his wife simply by repeating three times, "I dismiss thee"; he had to wait three months, however, before the divorce became final.

pleasure in a man's world

A Muslim had few major holidays, but he generally made the most of them. The biggest one was the Great Festival, a four-day period of feasting and gift-giving that marked the final days of the annual pilgrimage to Mecca. Below, mounted musicians prepare for one of this festival's parades, raising brilliant flags, blowing a lusty fanfare on their trumpets and thumping a pair of drums. Two of the banners in the background proclaim: "There is no god but Allah."

Muslim society was a man's world. While his women stayed behind closed doors, the man of the house spent most of his nonworking hours on the town—gossiping, bathing, playing chess (which the Arabs introduced to Europe), meeting at the local tavern. Although Muhammad had forbidden the consumption of wine, the Prophet himself had drunk *nabidh*, a mild fermented beverage made from raisins or dates mixed with water and allowed to sit in earthenware jugs. (Legal *nabidh* was two days old; illegal *nabidh* was a good deal older and stronger.)

In the tavern scene above, a servant passes up an order for two customers in the balcony, while a man below talks to a friend and sips his drink to the strumming of a lute; in one hand he holds an embroidered napkin, a requirement for polite wine-drinking. At the far right, a slave makes *nabidh* by crushing the fruit with her feet; a servant strains the juice through a cloth suspended over a bowl.

a desert businessman

The great wealth of Islam at the height of empire rested mainly on its far-flung commerce. Into the bazaars of Baghdad, the capital, flowed porcelain, silk, paper and ink from China; spices and dyes from India; rubies and lapis lazuli from Central Asia; furs, falcons and armor from Scandinavia; ivory, gold and slaves from Africa. Outward from the empire streamed Egypt's rice, grains and linen; Syria's glass and metal, Iraq's paper; Arabia's leather and pearls; Persia's silk and vegetables.

For a shrewd merchant, the best business of all to be in was the long but lucrative treks of the camel caravans. In this illustration a merchant prepares to take off on one of these great overland journeys. As his camel kneels to let him mount, his associates bid him good luck. Most desert travelers needed it: brigands lay in wait, and so did thirst. Grouped together for protection and led by a professional guide, the travelers rose before dawn and moved at a steady pace of three miles an hour for as long as 12 hours a day, and woe to the man or camel that fell behind. At rare intervals nightfall found the weary merchant at a caravanserai, a sort of primitive motel where he found rooms for himself and his cameleers and a resting place for his animals; otherwise, he slept under the stars. But the trip, when it was over, was usually well worth it. Profits, according to one account, were never less than 50 per cent.

preparations for paradise

At least once before he died, every Muslim able to do so had to make the pilgrimage to Mecca, the birthplace of Muhammad; it was one of the prerequisites for entering Heaven. Above, a party of joyous pilgrims sets out for the holy city; one of their number is a wealthy lady, riding discreetly in a tentlike litter.

When death at last overtook a Muslim gentleman, his funeral followed a carefully prescribed ritual that included the lamentations of women and readings from the Koran. Washed and wrapped in a seamless white shroud (dipped, during his pilgrimage, in the waters of Mecca's sacred Zamzam well), his body was laid to rest on its side, facing the holy city. In the entombment scene at right, relatives of the deceased wear thin bands of mourning around their heads. The domed structures in the background are the tombs of other wealthy Muslims.

5

AN ART OF MANY PEOPLES

Islam's contributions to the arts were generous, distinctive and lasting. Muslim art blended the beautiful with the functional, the human with the abstract, and this fusion gave it a character uniquely its own. Its major achievements were in architecture, an art that made religious worship decorous and personal life pleasant, and in literature, which embodied man's attitude toward life and death. Yet even in the so-called minor arts—those that made a man's house more beautiful, his body more strikingly clad, his food and drink more elegantly served —Islam created works of great beauty: brilliant textiles, including world-renowned "oriental" carpets; fine ceramics, glassware and metalwork, all enriched by the decorative ornamentation characteristic of Muslim style.

Most of these artistic expressions represented a synthesis of the many elements and peoples that made up the Islamic state. For the Arabs to have a material culture at all, it was necessary for them to borrow from the people they conquered. Pre-Islamic Arabia had been culturally barren, except for its lyrical poetry, which emerged from the spirit of the desert itself. But through the Muslim conquest of Byzantium and Persia, and the establishment of a new Islamic capital, first in Damascus and then in Baghdad, the Arabs became the cultural heirs of those highly civilized states.

Islam did not merely copy the arts created by the cultures it embraced; rather, it carefully selected those elements that pleased the discriminating Muslim eye and purpose, assembling them in a new organization typically and uniquely Islamic. As in virtually every other aspect of Islamic life, religion played a dominant role in Muslim art, largely determining its expression, both in form and content.

It was in architecture that the religious influence was most clearly seen, primarily in the development of the mosque, which was designed to meet the requirements of Muslim faith. As the Arabs began to assimilate the more advanced civilizations they had conquered, their mosques became increasingly large and decorative. But the basic, simple form never changed; throughout Islamic history it has retained the same open courtyard and enclosed prayer halls that made up the Prophet's simple home in Medina in the Seventh Century.

A HANDSOME BRONZE GRIFFIN, *standing more than 40 inches high, probably decorated the home of an 11th Century Muslim nobleman in Egypt. Profuse Kufic inscriptions on its chest and sides wish its owner health and fortune.*

In evolving their architectural forms, the Muslims had no real tradition on which to build; Arabia, the birthplace of Islam, had no public buildings worthy of the name. The only building of importance was the Kaaba in Mecca; at the beginning of the Seventh Century, this rudimentary structure of stone and wood stood only some 27 feet high and consisted simply of four walls and two rows of pillars that held up the roof. The Prophet is said to have discouraged more elaborate buildings, believing that they consumed the wealth of believers to no profitable end.

Not until more than half a century after the Prophet's death did Islam show any real interest in a more advanced architecture. The first four caliphs after Muhammad largely adhered to the simplicity he had advocated. During their rule, as Islam expanded into Byzantium and Persia, Muslims occasionally worshiped in the holy places of the conquered peoples; upon taking over those edifices they merely faced the wall in the direction of Mecca so that their prayers could be properly oriented.

With the establishment of the Umayyad caliphate in Damascus, however, Islam entered a new architectural stage with a tendency toward luxury and ostentation unknown to the Muslims' desert forebears. The conquering Arabs were not only struck by the older and more sophisticated Byzantine culture of Syria; they also knew that the Syrians, used to the opulence of their former masters, would not be impressed by the rustic Arab style of life. Soon the Muslims were building elaborate mosques that rivaled even the Christians' noblest churches.

To give the new capital a more lavish appearance, the Umayyad caliphs took advantage of both the human and material resources of Islam's vast new empire. From every part of their dominion —and even beyond—they summoned artists and craftsmen: sculptors from Syria, stucco workers from Iraq, wood carvers from Egypt, mosaicists

from Constantinople. Working under Syrian and Persian architects, these artisans created the unified and harmonious patterns that eventually became typical of the Islamic style. There were now abundant and varied building materials on which to draw, including Syrian limestone, which acquired a rich amber tint upon long exposure to the weather, and Lebanese cedar wood, which was both decorative and enduring.

Arabs, long used to the primitive simplicity of desert life, gradually found themselves surrounded by beautiful buildings that reflected their own new view of life. In place of the mud enclosures in which earlier Muslims had worshiped, there now appeared resplendent mosques with stately marble columns, wooden gabled roofs and delicately colored glass mosaics. One of the most celebrated of these structures was the Dome of the Rock in Jerusalem, the oldest surviving Islamic monument. Built and decorated in the ornate Byzantine tradition, the mosque is surmounted by a gilded dome that shimmers in the sun, among the hills in which it rests, like a crown of burnished gold.

To Muslims this splendid structure, built in 691, had both religious and political importance. The building was set over a rock that was considered holy by both Muslims and Jews. To Muslims it was the spot from which the Prophet allegedly took off on his ascension to Heaven—a mystical night journey described in many Traditions. To Jews it was the spot where Abraham was preparing to sacrifice his son Isaac when an angel of the Lord stayed his hand. Thus, by building what they intended to be the most magnificent shrine in Jerusalem over this hallowed rock, the Muslims honored God and the Prophet; and by putting an Islamic shrine on a spot holy to the Jews, they demonstrated their political and spiritual superiority over non-Muslims.

As more mosques were built throughout the

empire, new features were gradually added. One of the most distinctive of these was the minaret, the tower from which the muezzin called the faithful to prayer. In the days of the Prophet, the muezzin had merely climbed to the top of a high roof near the mosque to cry out his summons, but now a tower was made especially for his use. How these structures began is not known, but one theory holds that they were inspired by the great lighthouse of Alexandria, the Pharos, which was still standing when the Muslims conquered Egypt in 642; the Arabic word *manara*, from which "minaret" is derived, means "a place of flames."

Another theory about the origin of minarets is that they started in Syria, by chance. Beautiful Christian churches abounded there when the Muslims annexed the territory. These edifices were said to be "so enchantingly fair and so renowned for their splendor" that the Caliph Walid built the Great Mosque of Damascus in 705 to keep Muslims from being bedazzled and distracted from their own faith. It was the most remarkable structure built by the Umayyads, and was considered by Muslims as one of the seven wonders of the world. Rising on the site of some former sacred buildings, it utilized four existing outer walls; at each corner stood a square tower, in the Byzantine manner, and these were retained and were conveniently adopted for the call to prayer.

After the Abbasids moved Islam's capital to Iraq, bricks replaced stone as the chief building material; they were cheaper and easy to make, and could be quickly put in place by unskilled workmen. Unfortunately, they were less durable than the stones of the Umayyads, so fewer Abbasid buildings withstood the erosion of the years and plunder by subsequent builders. Nothing remains of Mansur's original round city of Baghdad, owing to repeated rebuilding and enlargements over the centuries. The short-lived Abbasid capital of Samarra, some

60 miles to the north, lies in ruins, with only crumbling walls and broken foundations of two huge buildings to attest to its former glory.

The most striking structure that remains from Abbasid times is not in Iraq but in Egypt—a mosque erected by Ibn Tulun, the son of a Turkish slave who was raised at the Abbasid court in Samarra. Ultimately he was made the governor of Egypt, where he set up a semi-independent dynasty. During his rule he enlarged the Egyptian capital of Fustat, building many monuments there. The mosque, which still bears his name, is the largest place of worship in Cairo.

Ibn Tulun displays the marriage of delicacy with strength that became typical of Islamic architecture. Its basic plan is that of earlier mosques, but its materials and decoration reflect later Persian influences. Its wide, pointed arches rest on great brick piers, forming the arcades and sanctuary. Both the arches and their supports are covered with stucco and decorated with graceful bands of carved patterns. Just below the massive ceiling beams is an inscription in wood that stretches around the perimeter of the mosque, emblazoned in a stately Arabic calligraphy with whole sections of the Koran. One of the most striking features is the windows; there are 128, each in the shape of a pointed arch resting on a pair of small columns topped with stucco capitals, and each window is bordered with stucco ornament.

As the medieval mosque evolved toward its final form, it incorporated various Persian elements. The most dramatic of these, introduced in the late 11th Century, was a high, domed structure set in front of the *mihrab*, possibly inspired by pre-Islamic temples in which Persians kept sacred fires burning. Another new feature was the *iwan*, a high, vaulted open hall adopted from the *madrasa*, a building that housed an institution of higher religious learning. The *madrasa*, like the mosque, consisted of a courtyard bordered by four arcades; in the *madrasa*, however, the arcades were divided into cells where the students lived and studied, and each arcade had at its center a large *iwan*, which served as a meeting place and classroom. Gradually this ground plan was adopted in the mosque itself, and became typical of most Persian mosques from the 12th Century on. In the new plan, one *iwan* served as the main entrance to the mosque courtyard from the outside. Across the court, another led into the sanctuary; the *iwans* on either side of the court were used as halls and gathering places.

As Muslim rulers developed increasingly impressive mosques for communal worship they also built huge fortress-like palaces to live in themselves. The Umayyad caliphs constructed many of their massive dwellings at the edge of the deserts of Syria and Jordan. They chose these isolated locations because they were still emotionally attached to the desert environment from which they had come, and they could also hunt gazelles and other game. Most of the palaces were inspired by the plan of Roman frontier forts in Syria—an enclosed courtyard fortified with towers along the walls and entered through a single gate. Around the courtyard were arranged various facilities: a throne room, a reception room, living quarters, a prayer hall, a guardhouse and storerooms.

These castles were built on large estates that sometimes included large bathhouses, which were often beautifully decorated. One such building had an exquisite stone-mosaic floor showing a tree in many shades of color, with two gazelles grazing beneath it and a third being attacked by a lion. There were also isolated hunting lodges; in one of these the walls were covered with mural paintings of everything from scenes of daily life to nude women and signs of the zodiac.

The Abbasids followed the basic architectural schemes of the Umayyads, but, lacking good building stone, they constructed their palaces of mud brick covered with carved panels of plaster. These structures, erected at the whim of rulers, were given monumental proportions and vast audience halls in keeping with the court ceremonials that now surrounded the caliphs.

Some of the most beautiful of these palaces were in Samarra—and behind this was a curious reason: after the caliphs became virtual prisoners of their Turkish guards, they found time heavy on their hands, and occupied themselves laying out parks and gardens and designing magnificent state buildings and palaces. One of the most famous of all the structures in Samarra was the so-called Jawsaq palace, built during the caliphate of Mu'tasim, who reigned from 833 to 842. This huge complex of buildings covered 432 acres and comprised every kind of oriental splendor, including stately vaulted reception halls and private living quarters, enclosing large harems, that adjoined cool courtyards with pools, gardens and fountains.

Unlike the Umayyads, the more urbane Abbasids built palaces in cities, with private dwelling houses clustered around them. These houses were very large, sometimes consisting of as many as 50 rooms, with lavish baths, pillared halls and underground rooms to keep the occupants cool in the torrid heat of summer.

Despite the impressive buildings they erected, Muslims were generally less interested in structural form than they were in surface decoration. They had a passion for covering every possible surface with some kind of ornamentation: tiles, glass, mosaics, glazed brick, wall paintings, wood paneling. They carved countless low-relief patterns in plaster and stucco, taking advantage of the brilliant sunshine of their latitudes to accentuate vivid contrasts of light and shadow.

The most striking aspect of Islamic religious

decoration was that its designs were abstract rather than representational. In this the Arabs were undoubtedly influenced by their love of the geometrical abstractions of mathematics and astronomy. But the tendency was accelerated in the Eighth Century when all human and animal figures were banned from religious art, in accord with a deep-seated fear of idolatry.

This prohibition on figural representation is believed to stem back to the Prophet himself. Although no verse in the Koran specifically forbade Muslims to depict living figures, the injunction was voiced in a tradition attributed to his young wife, A'isha. Muhammad is said to have found her making a pillow with a picture on it, and he remonstrated, "Don't you know that angels refuse to enter a house in which there is a picture? On the Last Day makers of pictures will be punished, for God will say to them: 'Give life to that which you have created.'"

With this restriction imposed on them, Muslim artists turned instead toward decorative designs. Among the forms from which abstract patterns evolved were Byzantine motifs such as plants and trees. The Persians, on the other hand, had been especially fond of depicting animals: birds, peacocks, lions, antelopes, gazelles, hunting dogs and fantastic creatures such as griffins and dragons. Out of these forms, Muslims developed intricate imaginative patterns that sometimes bordered on the bizarre, as when plant motifs were interwoven with animal bodies.

Perhaps the best-known design was the arabesque. From Byzantium the Muslims had inherited the classical ornament of the acanthus plant's curving leaf but, characteristically, they stylized it until they achieved a purely abstract design. It appeared in an endless variety of shapes and forms; sometimes the emphasis was on the stalk, sometimes on the leaf, the line bending in undulating

A PREDATORY HAWK *attacks a duck in a handsome stucco relief from Persia. Despite the Muslim ban on figural representation, Persian artists who embraced Islam continued their long tradition of depicting animals.*

movements or curving in spirals. But whatever aspect it took the distinguishing characteristic was the constant repetition of the basic pattern. Adaptable to any surface, the arabesque ornamented everything from small objects, like metal boxes, to friezes, borders and even entire walls. The frequency with which it appeared indicates that it must have been highly pleasing to Muslims, both esthetically and emotionally.

Less well known in the West than the arabesque, but even more esteemed by Muslims, was calligraphy, the art of elegant writing. The calligrapher was honored above other artists, as nothing could be worthier than to write the Word of God. And since Arabic was the sacred language—the one in which God had revealed His message to Muhammad—the writing of the Word in Arabic was considered the highest form of decoration. Verses of the Koran, rendered in magnificent script, adorned the walls of mosques; secular objects, including textiles, ceramics and metal works, also bore inscriptions of worldly wisdom, Koranic phrases and words of praise in honor of the person for whom the object was made.

While arabesques and calligraphy were extensively used on religious buildings, other forms of ornamentation were found in secular structures. Despite the religious ban on figural representation, paintings of both humans and animals were popular; generally they appeared in private places like bathhouses, the harems where the women lived, and the living quarters of the ruling classes. Figural designs were also incorporated into carpets and pillows; here they were generally acceptable because of their less honored position, as these articles were stepped or leaned upon.

In the Umayyad era most of this representational painting was naturalistic, due to a lingering Hellenistic influence, and depicted various subjects of court life, animals in combat and hunting scenes.

But under the Abbasids, painting was influenced primarily by the formal style that had developed in pre-Islamic Persia; this tended toward the stylized and symbolic rather than the realistic. The physical type of figures represented in these paintings clearly reflected an Eastern influence: the face was characteristically round, with thick features and enormous, slanting eyes; the hair was black and straight, falling to the shoulders, and the body was fleshy.

In their homes, Muslims considered decoration more important than furnishings. Most dwellings, in fact, had virtually no furniture as we know it. In Arab style, the people walked on floors ornamented with mosaics, and sat and ate on beautifully woven carpets, leaning against pillows. The only breaks in the richly patterned walls were niches used for holding books and treasured possessions.

Among the most varied and versatile objects

A GOLD-EMBROIDERED CAPE, *showing lions attacking camels, was worn by a Norman, Roger II, when he was crowned King of Sicily. It was made at Palermo's Muslim textile works, which flourished long after the Normans wrested the isle from Islam in 1091.*

found in Islamic homes were ceramics, an art form in which Muslims achieved particular excellence. At first these were simple and merely functional vessels, but in the Ninth Century exquisite Chinese pottery was imported into Baghdad, inspiring the Muslims to equal it. Lacking the right kind of clay, the Muslims never discovered the secret of the Chinese porcelain makers, but they did produce ceramics of great beauty. Designed for practical purposes, these objects were made in many forms —plates, vases, jugs, candlesticks—and decorated with stylized human and animal figures, inscriptions and other motifs.

In ceramics, Islam gained its greatest fame from its distinctive luster-painted ware, made by a secret process believed to have been developed in Iraq in the Ninth Century. An object was first shaped, glazed and fired, then coated with metal oxides that after a second firing assumed a soft, metallic sheen.

Eventually this highly valued technique was passed to the West through Muslim Spain.

Luster finish was used extensively on tiles, another popular form of Muslim ornamentation. Tiles were especially favored by the Seljuk Turks, who first used them to decorate the lower portion of walls in mosques, and later to cover entire walls and ceilings. These tiles had many exquisite patterns painted on them—scrolls, leaves, flowers, arabesques and lettering; at times they appeared in gold luster against a white background, occasionally they were outlined in dark blue or turquoise.

Among other so-called minor arts, Muslim glass was especially renowned for its elaborately cut surface designs, animal figures and lettering. Rock crystal, a Muslim specialty, was carved into perfume vials, beakers and even ewers; handsome chessmen were also made of rock crystal and ivory. In metalwork, Muslim craftsmen produced elaborate boxes, basins, bowls, jugs and incense burners covered with arabesques, inscriptions and figures; these artisans specialized in brass and bronze, luxuriously inlaid with gold, silver and copper. Also famous throughout the world were Islamic textiles, especially silks; these rich fabrics were celebrated for their texture, colors and patterns, which included calligraphy and, to a lesser extent, human, animal and mythical figures.

Such figures were also found in manuscript illuminations, one of the best-known forms of Muslim art. These charming miniatures were used only to illustrate secular manuscripts. The earlier illuminations accompanied translations of Greek scientific works into Arabic; one medical book shows pictures of plants, as well as teachers and students discussing the merits of herbs they are seen holding. Other illuminations, found in books of fables, portray jackals, lions and ravens. These miniatures were painted in brilliant colors, sometimes against backgrounds of gold. From the comparative simplicity of these earlier Arabic manuscripts, miniature painting in Persia ultimately developed into a very sophisticated art in which figures in court scenes, hunts and battles move against ornate, panoramic backgrounds.

Although its achievements in architecture and other visual arts were notable, Islam's most original creative expression was in literature. In other cultural areas it synthesized many elements foreign to its primitive origins, but in poetry and prose it grafted new elements onto a sturdy Arabian root.

Islamic literature began with the Bedouin poets who developed the Arabic language into a supple and expressive literary instrument. To these early Arabs, poetry consisted of measured speech in which meter and identical rhyme were vital. Along with this restriction in form, the poet was restricted in content. The *qasida*, or ode, was primarily designed to praise the poet himself, his patron or tribe, and to satirize opponents. But it could also treat other subjects, such as moral and ethical themes, or vivid descriptions of nature.

With the spread of Islam beyond Arabia, poetry reflected the transformation of the society. The transition from a nomadic life to an urban existence is vividly evoked in plaintive lines attributed to Maysun, the Bedouin wife of Mu'awiya, the first of the Umayyad caliphs:

> *Breeze-flowing tents I prefer*
> *to ponderous halls*
> *And desert dress*
> *to diaphanous veils.*
> *A crust I'd eat in the awning's shade,*
> *not rolls,*
> *And watched by a dog that barks*
> *not a cat that smiles,*
> *I'd sleep to the wind's tune,*
> *not to the tambourine.*

> *A youth's impetuous sword,*
> *not a husband's wiles,*
> *Uncouth slim tribesmen I love,*
> *not corpulent men.*

For a while poets living in cities were haunted by the nostalgia of desert life, but eventually Arab poetry broke with many of its former traditions and their limitations. During the Abbasid reign in Baghdad, poetry, like art and architecture, came in contact with the products of ancient civilizations whose thought and culture permeated the Near East—Greek rationalism, Indian philosophy, Persian court literature. All of these influences helped widen the poet's range. Verses of wit and pleasure became popular at the caliph's court, and a poet's skill brought him vast rewards in gold and praise.

Two poets recognized as technically outstanding during the Abbasid reign were Abu Nuwas, who lived in the Ninth Century, and Mutanabbi, who lived in the Tenth Century. The former is best known for poems of love and verses singing the praises of wine, in which he is brilliantly witty and cynical as he portrays the manners and mores of the court. Mutanabbi, though he earned his livelihood by praising the virtues of his patrons, is also renowned for stinging, satirical poems directed at his enemies. The following lines he loosed against the Abyssinian who ruled Egypt:

> *I saw what I hoped never to see alive,*
> *The dog that fouled me pampered and well fed,*
> *The black king in plumes, the good men dead.*

In style, the content of Islamic poetry was subordinate to form; the poet was supposed to be a brilliant technician, preoccupied with the beauty of his verse. Moral values, sincerity or consistency were not required; indeed, a noted Ninth Century critic named Qudama saw nothing amiss in a poet contradicting himself in two different works, as

THE CHANGING ART OF WRITING *is revealed in three fragments from rare manuscripts of the Koran. The characters at top, written in the Eighth Century, illustrate the early, formal script known as Kufic, whose simple forms were easily drawn on parchment or inscribed in stone. The middle panel is a more condensed Ninth Century style known as "gliding Kufic." The bottom one, done in the 14th Century, displays the flowery, cursive style called "thuluth"; it is more easily done with pen on paper, and so closely resembles today's printed style that any literate Arab can read it.*

long as he achieved perfection of form in each. ("On the contrary," he stated, "this better displays the poet's mastery of his art.")

Further, overall construction was considered less important than the perfection of the single line, which was supposed to stand independently, as if isolated from the rest of the poem. Such a limited view of perfection, it might be supposed, could easily lead to an obsession with how things were said rather than what was said. Nevertheless, at its best Arabic poetry produced fusions of content and form that gave it intellectual as well as esthetic distinction.

Among Islam's most brilliant poets was Ma'arri, one of the few of medieval times to speak without reference to religious dogma. Jailed, as he said, in the triple prison of blindness, "confinement to my house, and this vile body for my spirit's dwelling," he expressed a profound pessimism. He believed in God but not in the resurrection of the soul; thus, he proclaimed, death was the end, bringing deliverance from the miseries of the world. Because of this philosophy, he believed that giving life to a child was a sin, and consequently he never married; he alluded to this in a couplet that he asked to have engraved on his tomb.

> This wrong was by my father done
> To me, but ne'er by me to one.

He also expressed the same bleak attitude toward life and death in the following morbid passage:

> This world resembles a cadaver,
>   and we around it dogs that bark;
> And he who eats from it is the loser;
>   he who abstains takes the better part.
> And certain is a dawn disaster
>   to him unwaylaid in the dark.

Whereas poetry had begun with the pre-Islamic Arabs, prose had its beginning with the Koran. Through this greatest—and inimitable—work, the

Arabic language developed into a powerful and effective mode of expression. Because of the wide range of subjects covered, the Koran was obliged to free itself from the rigid rules that governed poetry; content was more important than form. With the spread of Islam, and the dissemination of the Koran as the Word of God, Arabic became the official language of the empire—not only of religion and government but of literature as well.

At first Arabic prose writers were limited in their work to translations of Persian court literature, primarily treatises on manners—manuals containing information a polished gentleman might need—but they soon developed their own prose style of writing. Not until the Ninth Century, however, did the language attain precision of expression, becoming a smooth and flexible instrument for the discussion of varied subjects such as ethics, politics and history. Because of this wide range of interests and its greater flexibility, prose replaced poetry in recording the history and traditions of the people. From the Tenth Century on, poetry was limited to an esthetic role.

In the field of pure literature, there appeared a new form in the late Tenth Century—the *Maqamat*, a collection of anecdotes usually centered on the person of a witty vagabond who wandered from place to place, earning his living by performing for appreciative people. These narratives had historical as well as literary importance, leaving posterity an invaluable social document of life in medieval Islam. But in pure prose, as in poetry, the major concern was for technical excellence, often at the cost of content. In the *Maqamat*, the subject matter was considered less important than the treatment; content here was, again, secondary to form.

Most of the literature of Islam had been in Arabic, but in the 11th Century there was an awakening of interest in the Persian language. Persian authors developed traditional themes in wine and love songs, but they enriched them with their own repertory of evocative images. One of the most famous of these was the *Rubaiyat* of Omar Khayyam, well known to the West through Edward Fitzgerald's brilliant adaptation.

The Persians also introduced new forms into Islamic literature, among them the epic poem. But they reached their height of excellence in mystical poetry, especially that of the Sufis. The greatest Sufi poet was Jalal al-Din Rumi, who founded the monastic order of the Mevlevi, or Whirling Dervishes, who through ecstatic dances hoped to reach communication with God. Rumi's monumental religious poem, the *Masnavi*, a work dealing with Sufi mysticism, fills six volumes and is considered by some Persians as "the Persian Koran."

The Muslim literary work that had the widest and most lasting influence outside of Islam itself was *Alf Layla wa Layla*, or *A Thousand and One Nights*, often known as *The Arabian Nights*. The technical perfection of form sought by Islamic purists is absent from the prose and poetry in which this great popular work is written. Yet its brisk, colloquial language is used to tell stories with a narrative skill that any novelist might envy. The stories of *The Arabian Nights* evoke better than any other record life as it was lived in cities such as Baghdad, Basra and Cairo between the Ninth and 16th Centuries. No one author wrote this great work; the tales represented a variety of origins and types, among them Indian and Persian fairy tales, Arab legends and romances, Egyptian love stories and anecdotes. Through centuries of repetition and compilation, however, all of these facets eventually merged to reflect Muslim values and ideals.

This famous book is, in a sense, representative of all Muslim art—an art that gathered and blended existing patterns into new forms, glowing colors and exquisite shapes, emerging from its synthesis as a unique expression of the Islamic world.

A BRONZE DOOR KNOCKER, *in the form of two writhing dragons, probably graced a palace gate in Iraq.*

CRAFTSMEN'S TREASURES

Muslim theologians regarded the representation of humans or animals as a grave sin. The artist who pictured a living creature, they declared, was vying with God as a creator of actual beings. Although many Islamic artists ignored the ban and depicted animals, men and even the Prophet himself, especially in later centuries, most turned their talents instead to pure decoration and to fashioning functional objects for daily use. Craftsmen created bowls, boxes, pitchers, vases and lamps, working in traditional forms with only slight changes over the centuries. Often these objects were so treasured that they were not used at all, but were displayed in wall niches. They were also given as presents on special occasions, sometimes inscribed by the donor with good wishes or with phrases from the Koran. Though some pieces commanded small fortunes, the wares of the empire were not limited to the wealthy, but were sold in great profusion in Islam's bazaars.

Practical pottery and civilized refinements

A STORAGE JAR, *made in 11th or 12th Century Syria to hold dried fruit, grain or pickled foods, is the sort of everyday piece that was produced in great quantities and sold from stalls in bazaars.*

A ROSE-WATER SPRINKLER *of Persian design harks back to the days when etiquette required men to scent their beards before dining. The rose was the Muslims' favorite flower, and rose water was also used to perfume clothes and carpets and even to flavor foods.*

A GILDED BRONZE PLAQUE *is adorned with a stylized figure resembling a griffin or a winged horse. The piece may once have been used as a buckle or a decorative fitting for a harness or storage trunk.*

AN INCENSE BURNER, *in the shape of a bird with a turquoise eye, was pierced with holes in its breast and its head to release the pleasant fumes of aloe or sandalwood.*

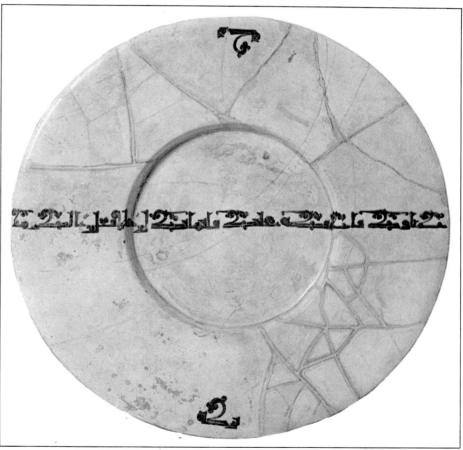

A PERSIAN DISH *of the 10th Century bears a proverb that reads in part: "Only modesty points out the action of a noble man." Many households had whole sets of such dishes, each with a different saying.*

A GOLD PENDANT *made in Egypt (right), the center-piece of a necklace, is bordered by stylized snakes. Such necklaces were often given as marriage gifts.*

AN IVORY BOX, *made in Moorish Spain in the 11th Century, is intricately carved with animals, script and foliage. The inscription around the lid wishes its owner peace, prosperity, health and good luck.*

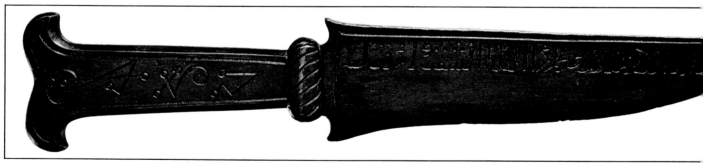

A BRONZE KNIFE *used in Egypt is adorned with magic symbols on the handle. The blade, inscribed with a verse from the Koran, was placed against the afflicted part of a sick person to make him well.*

A GOLD BRACELET *from Persia is studded with cones of twisted wire. Women could wear such jewelry without risk of public censure, but the strictest Muslim traditions forbade men to bedeck themselves in gold because the Prophet disapproved of the metal.*

Objects to cure the afflicted and to delight the rich

AN ORNATE BOWL *made in 13th Century Persia depicts a prince seated on a throne surrounded by nobles. A ceramic piece like this might be the result of the combined efforts of a potter and a painter. Extremely expensive, it was probably made for an aristocrat or wealthy merchant and was intended only for display.*

AN IRIDESCENT BOTTLE *from Persia (right) displays the hues it acquired from centuries of burial in corrosive soil before it was excavated. Originally it was more translucent and may have been used as a flower vase or a candlestick.*

A BOWL FROM KASHAN, *Persia's greatest ceramic center, is decorated with flowers and cursive script in pie-shaped sections (right). Kashan potters constantly sought to emulate fine porcelain that was imported from China but they lacked the essential kaolin clay.*

A BRONZE EWER *has a spout in the shape of a crowing rooster. Since Arabs ate with their fingers—properly the thumb and first two fingers of the right hand—they used such a pitcher and a basin to wash before and after meals.*

Elegant utensils for the rituals of Muslim life

A CEREMONIAL OBJECT, *which is more than a foot long, has a horselike animal for a handle and the phrase "The Kingdom belongs to Allah" inscribed in Arabic on its blade.*

A BRASS INKPOT *was part of a scribe's writing equipment. Muslims regarded calligraphy as the highest art and lavished great care on all writing articles.*

A secret strongbox, a graceful lantern and a key to a sacred mosque

A COMBINATION SAFE, *this small bronze coffer, which was made in Persia in the 12th Century, was opened by turning the four dials on its lid to the correct positions. Three small figures guard the front of the coffer.*

A SYRIAN GLASS LAMP *(left) is adorned with a picture of a mounted falconer. Lamps like this were often filled halfway with water, on which oil and a wick were floated. To keep the wick from drifting, it was secured in the center of the lamp by a small holder.*

A PERSIAN EWER *from Kashan is encased in an elaborate perforated shell that depicts couples conversing. The cobalt that gives the ewer its blue color was worth its weight in gold, and the royal treasury doled it out in tiny quantities to potters.*

A KEY TO THE HOLY OF HOLIES, *this instrument once locked the Great Mosque at Mecca, which surrounds Islam's most sacred shrine, the Kaaba. The legend begs God to have mercy on Sultan Faraj, the ruler who rebuilt the mosque in 1405.*

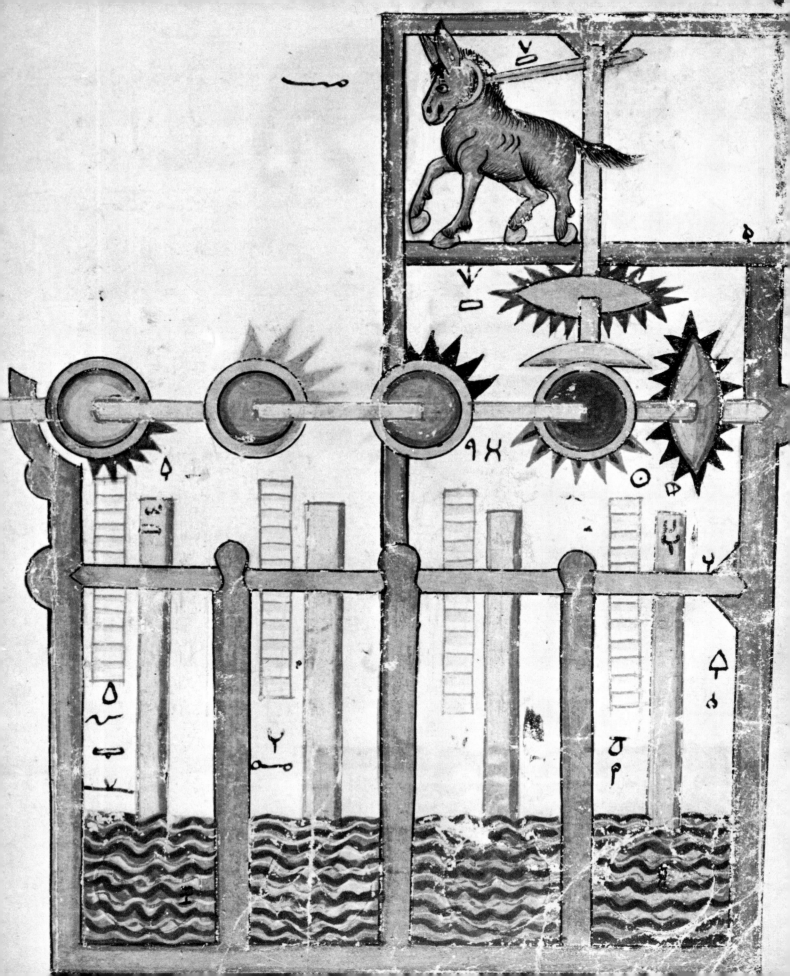

6

THE SCIENTIST-PHILOSOPHERS

A PLAN FOR AN IRRIGATOR, *similar to machines actually used in Iraq, was devised in the 13th Century by the Arab engineer Jazari. The donkey turned an upright pole, which was connected to a series of geared wheels; the wheels were linked to four water scoops (shown submerged) that, rising in succession, emptied their contents into a canal in a continuous flow.*

Modern man—dependent as he is on the drugs of the chemist and the skills of the physician, on the reckoning of the computer and the predictions of the economic planner—owes more of a debt than he might suspect to the Islamic scientists of the Middle Ages. Between the Ninth and 14th Centuries, Muslim chemists, physicians, astronomers, mathematicians, geographers and others not only kept alive the disciplines of Greek science, but extended their range, laying and strengthening the foundations on which much of modern science is built. Many scientific terms with Arabic roots, from "algebra" to "zenith," reflect to this day Islam's activity in fields where knowledge was widened and human suffering decreased.

Islamic science did not concern itself only with man's physical environment, but included a penetrating analysis of man as a spiritual being and of the society in which he dwelt. Its fame was so widespread that everyone in the West who had any thirst for enlightenment turned to Islam, where the spirit of inquiry was flourishing.

In the beginning the main magnet that drew these scholars was the capital city of Baghdad. There the Caliph Ma'mun, who ruled the empire from 813 to 833, created the "House of Wisdom," a famous center of learning that included a library, a translation bureau and a school. According to legend, Ma'mun was at first hesitant about building the center; like many of his contemporaries, he was uneasy about applying reason to God's universe. But, so the story goes, one night the Caliph had a dream in which the ghost of Aristotle appeared to him and assured him that there was no conflict between reason and religion; with this reassurance he ordered the center to be built.

Within 75 years after the establishment of the House of Wisdom, the greatest thoughts of the Greeks and other early peoples had been translated into Arabic, among them the chief philosophical books of Aristotle, some important works of Plato, and major studies by Euclid, Ptolemy, Archimedes, and the celebrated Greek physicians, Hippocrates, Dioscorides and Galen, as well as many important Persian and Indian scientific works. Some of these manuscripts were part of the booty seized by the Muslims when they conquered

Byzantium and Persia. Others were purposely sought out later. Ma'mun is said to have sent emissaries as far as Constantinople to find Greek works and bring them to Baghdad for rendering into Arabic.

From the House of Wisdom, zealous scholars turned out a torrent of translations, inaugurating their age's great voyage of intellectual discovery. One of the foremost of these scholars was Hunayn ibn Ishaq, known primarily as the translator of Galen's works. Born in the town of Hira in western Persia, Hunayn studied medicine in Baghdad under a physician who had trained at the famous Persian medical school in Jundishapur which was to have a profound influence on the development of Islamic medicine. One day, however, the eager youth asked his master more questions than he cared to answer, and the physician expelled him, saying, "What have the people of Hira to do with medicine? Go and change money in the streets."

Hunayn departed in tears, but resolved more than ever to pursue knowledge. He continued his medical studies with other teachers, learned Greek and was employed by scholars to seek out Greek manuscripts. Once he was ordered to find a lost work of Galen; his tenacity was so great that he pursued the manuscript into Mesopotamia, Palestine, Egypt and Syria. "Yet I was not able to find aught save half of it at Damascus," he lamented.

Eventually Hunayn was made assistant to the Caliph's personal physician, and from this post he was placed in charge of the House of Wisdom; there he supervised all translations, assisted by his son, his nephew and some 90 other disciples. He and his disciples went to extraordinary lengths to produce reliable manuscripts. In some cases these works were first translated from Greek into Syriac, in which Hunayn was most proficient, and then rendered into Arabic by one of his assistants who was especially gifted in that language; by this painstaking procedure they attempted to produce a final manuscript that would have the greatest possible accuracy. Hunayn's work was so highly esteemed that he was said to have been paid by the Caliph a sum of gold equal to the weight of the books he translated, indicating the value then placed on scholarship. In addition to his translations, Hunayn also produced a large number of medical works of his own, among them the earliest known textbook on ophthalmology. The great compilation and translation of knowledge accomplished by Hunayn and his colleagues did much to lay the groundwork of modern science, particularly in the field of medicine, as the works of these men were later translated into Latin and made their way into the West, primarily through Sicily and Spain.

The basis of all Islamic science was the Greek belief that underlying the apparent chaos in the universe was a fundamental order. This order was said to be governed by universal laws that could be understood by human reason; once these laws were comprehended, all phenomena, no matter how unrelated they seemed, could readily be grasped. For example, in astronomy, if one knew the laws that maintain the heavenly bodies in their positions, one could predict where any given star or planet would be many years in the future.

In Arabic, knowledge of the universe was called *falsafa*, a word based on the Greek *philosophia*, literally, "love of knowledge." *Falsafa* was indeed a lofty conception of the world; like the Greek definition of the term, it embraced all knowledge within the grasp of man, theoretical and practical alike. In its total approach to the world, *falsafa* included as objects of study not only the physical and natural sciences but philosophy and many other non-religious disciplines as well.

Thus, in an effort to understand the true nature of the universe, scholars pursued more than one branch of learning. The scientist-philosopher was not a narrow specialist, but was expert in such varied fields as medicine, chemistry, astronomy, mathematics, logic, metaphysics and even music and poetry. Such men were relatively few in number, and usually had to depend on the patronage of a court or some rich person to carry on their endless studies, but their learned activity stimulated an intellectual ferment in the cities of the Muslim world. As their fame spread, students traveled from all over the empire to study under them and absorb their vast knowledge.

While learning was pursued for its own exalted sake, its fruits often had practical applications in daily life. Mathematics, for example, not only could be used to work out complex problems of the cosmos, but also served the more ordinary needs of commerce and surveying. By the same token, astronomy was important to religion; it enabled Muslims to know such vital things as the hours of prayer, the direction of Mecca, the moment of the first appearance of the moon of Ramadan; in addition it helped guide travelers on land and sea.

Although the Muslims excelled in many branches of science, some of their most significant contributions were in medicine. Before the great intellectual awakening, Arab medical knowledge had been largely limited to desert superstitions, including the discerning use of magic, talismans and protective prayers, and a few primitive remedies. Among the latter was henna (a red dye still used for coloring hair), commonly taken as a remedy for gout. Honey was used for headaches and fever, and the ashes of burned weeds were applied to wounds to stop bleeding.

Starting in the Eighth Century, the Muslims gradually developed a more sophisticated approach to medicine. The main impetus came from the Persian medical school at Jundishapur, whose teachings were based primarily on the Greek practice of treating disease by rational methods. According to tradition, the contact between Jundishapur and

A HERITAGE OF WORDS

Emerging from the desert with little but keen curiosity, the Arabs quickly adopted ideas and techniques from older societies, and developed many of their own. Today, the West is indebted to Islam for many scientific terms, among them:

ALCHEMY—*AL-KIMIYA*
The medieval predecessor of chemical science

ALCOHOL—*AL-KUHL*
A finely ground cosmetic powder, later a term for any highly refined or distilled substance

ALEMBIC—*AL-INBIQ*
Literally, "the still"; a vessel used by alchemists —and today by chemists—for distilling liquids

ALGEBRA—*AL-JABR*
The binding together of disorganized parts

ALKALI—*AL-QILI*
Saltwort ashes, used in making lye, soap, water

AMALGAM—*AL-MALGHAM*
The various alloys of mercury, applied to alchemy and to the refining of silver and gold

AZIMUTH—*AL-SUMUT*
An arc of the horizon used to reckon position

BORAX—*BURAQ*
A white, powdery mineral used since early times in soldering, cleaning and the making of glass

CAMPHOR—*KAFUR*
An aromatic tree gum often used in liniments

CIPHER—*SIFR*
Literally, "empty"; hence, nothingness or zero

ELIXIR—*AL-IKSIR*
Agent for changing metals to gold; a cure-all

NADIR—*NAZIR*
Opposite of zenith, that is, the lowest point

ZENITH—*SAMT*
The upward direction; figuratively, the acme

the rulers of Islam began in 765, not out of the search for universal truth, and the immutable laws that would explain the mysteries of life, but due to a more urgent and personal reason—a chronic indigestion that plagued Mansur, the founder of Baghdad. The Caliph's own physicians had not been able to cure him; in despair, he invited the chief physician of Jundishapur to come to Baghdad and treat him. The physician, a Christian named Jurjis ibn Bakhtishu', succeeded in returning the ruler to health where the others had failed, and as a reward, he was appointed court physician. The grateful Caliph also invited Jurjis to embrace Islam and thus assure himself of going to Paradise. But the physician refused, saying that when he died he preferred the company of his Christian fathers—be they in Heaven or Hell.

Like Jurjis, most of Islam's early medical practitioners were Persian-born, but they spoke and wrote Arabic, the language of scholarship during the Middle Ages. One of the most celebrated of these Eastern physicians was Razi, who lived from 865 to 925. His stature was so great that his colleagues called him "The Experienced." The finest clinician of the age, he has been compared to Hippocrates for his originality in describing disease.

Razi, known in Europe by his Latin name, Rhazes, is said to have written more than 200 books, ranging in subject matter from medicine and alchemy to theology and astronomy. About half the books are on medicine, and include a well-known treatise on smallpox. In his discussion of smallpox, Razi was the first to differentiate a specific disease from among many eruptive fevers that assailed man. By giving the clinical symptoms of smallpox, he enabled doctors to diagnose it correctly and to predict the course of the disease. He also recommended a treatment for the ailment that has been little improved on since his time. He urged gentle therapy—good diet and good nursing care, which

meant about what it does today: rest, clean surroundings and keeping the patient comfortable.

While Razi knew nothing about bacteria, the theory of which was not to be discovered until the early 17th Century, he had an intuitive sense of hygienic principles far ahead of medieval standards. To appreciate his insight, it must be remembered that he lived in a world where contamination and filth were so common as to go almost unnoticed, and infections and contagious diseases cut down millions. Against this unsanitary background, he was once asked to choose the site for a new hospital in Baghdad. To do so, he suspended pieces of meat at various points around the city, and at the location where the meat putrefied most slowly, he recommended building the hospital.

The crowning work of Razi's career was a monumental encyclopedia in which he compiled Greek, Syrian, Persian, Hindu and early Arabic knowledge, as well as personal observations based on his own extensive clinical experience. This book offered striking insights for its time and had a wide influence in shaping European medicine.

Great as Razi was, he was at least equaled in stature by another Arabic-speaking Persian Muslim, Ibn Sina, better known in the West by his Latin name, Avicenna. Called "The Prince of Philosophers" by his contemporaries, he is still recognized as one of the great minds of all time. He lived from 980 to 1037, and wrote some 170 books on philosophy, medicine, mathematics and astronomy, as well as poems and religious works. He is said to have memorized the entire Koran when he was only 10 years old, and at 18 he was personal physician to the Sultan of Bukhara, in Turkestan.

Avicenna's most renowned achievement was the *Canon of Medicine*, an encyclopedia that dealt with virtually every phase of the treatment of disease. Probably no other medieval work of its kind was so widely studied; from the 12th to the 17th

Centuries it served as the chief guide to medical science in European universities. Consisting of five books, the work was so comprehensive in describing the discoveries of others that the originality of some of the author's own incisive observations were often overlooked.

Ibn Sina is now credited with such personal contributions as recognizing the contagious nature of tuberculosis and describing certain skin diseases and psychological disorders. Among the latter was love sickness, the effects of which were described as loss of weight and strength, fever and various chronic ailments. The cure was quite simple, once the diagnosis was made—to have the sufferer united with the one he or she was pining for. Ibn Sina also observed that certain diseases can be spread by water and soil, an advanced view for his time. Outside the realm of pure medicine, he invented a scalelike precision device that helped to improve the accuracy of instruments used for measuring angles and short lengths. He also made many investigations in the realm of physics, helping to lay the foundations of the experimental science that was to develop in the 16th and 17th Centuries. Ibn Sina died at 58, after treating himself unsuccessfully for an illness; his enemies, jealous of his vast knowledge and great fame, maliciously observed that his medicine could not save his body, nor his metaphysics his soul.

While scholars like Ibn Sina and Razi furthered Islamic medicine in the East, other great physician-philosophers arose in the Western reaches of the empire. Among them was the brilliant Spanish physician, Ibn Rushd, also known by his Latin name, Averroes. A man of broad interests like his fellow scientists, Ibn Rushd studied and wrote on medicine, philosophy, law and astronomy. His talents were varied enough so that he was not only chief physician to Abu Yaqub Yusuf, a Berber who ruled Spain from 1163 to 1184, but also served as a judge in Seville and Cordoba. In addition, Ibn Rushd is known as one of the foremost interpreters of Aristotle; his commentaries on the Greek thinker brought Aristotle to the attention of the West, helping shape European philosophic thought.

Another Spanish-born physician who influenced Western ways was Ibn Maymun, a Jew known as Maimonides who served as court physician to Saladin, the Sultan of Egypt and Syria in the 12th Century. Maimonides—who wrote on medicine, theology, philosophy and astronomy—was as celebrated for his wisdom and humanity as for his vast scholarship. He wrote the famous—and still widely read—*Guide for the Perplexed*, a philosophical study that harmonized religious thought with Aristotle's scientific teachings. Included in his medical works are commentaries on Galen and Hippocrates, as well as his own observations, primarily related to diet and personal hygiene.

Islamic physicians also helped develop the science of surgery, although it was considered a minor branch of medicine. This art had been largely neglected until the Spanish-born physician Abulcasis wrote about it in the 10th Century. Most of his work was based on that of the Greek, Paul of Aegina, and contained illustrations of various surgical instruments and procedures.

Muslim physicians performed many remarkably complex operations for their time, including cranial and vascular surgery and operations for cancer. Avicenna gave them advice on the treatment of the latter disease that would still be timely today—to minister to it in its earliest stage, and to remove all of the diseased tissue as the only hope of cure. Other operations included delicate abdominal surgery, involving the use of drainage tubes, and the amputation of diseased arms and legs.

For these operations various anesthetics were administered to render patients unconscious; among them was opium, which was sometimes made more potent by mixing it with wine. Other strong drugs are also believed to have been used, but their exact nature and method of use is uncertain. One alchemist claimed that he had invented an anesthetic that knocked a patient out for seven days; he considered it so dangerous that he took its secret with him to the grave.

Before a man could practice surgery, he had to have special training and pass tests on his knowledge of anatomy and Galen's writings. In addition, specialists were required to have extensive information about the particular area in which they practiced. Ophthalmologists, for example, had to undergo an examination about their detailed knowledge of the eye, as well as be able to mix certain compounds to treat various eye ailments. Islamic physicians were especially skilled in treating eye diseases, perhaps because such ailments were so widespread in the Middle East. They wrote textbooks on ophthalmology, and invented an ingenious method of operating on soft cataract of the eye, using a tube to suck out the fluid that filled the capsule of the eye lens; this method was used for several centuries before it was replaced by more modern techniques.

In the treatment of other sickness with drugs, the Muslims were equally progressive. Most Islamic physicians prepared their own compounds, but Baghdad had pharmacies that filled prescriptions much as present-day drugstores do. These pharmacies sold a wide range of remedies made from animal and plant products and even more sophisticated inorganic compounds like copper sulphate, which acted as a styptic to help heal open lesions by drawing the tissues together.

Drugs were considered so important—and often so dangerous—that they were carefully supervised by an inspector; this official kept a wary eye on the medicines and how they were mixed, even making sure that the jars in which they were stored

TOOL OF SCIENTIST AND SEER, *this 13th Century Yemeni astrolabe was used primarily to study movements of the planets, essential to casting the horoscopes consulted by camel drivers and caliphs alike. By aligning a pointer on the instrument with the sun, the user could measure latitude or tell the time of day.*

were kept clean. A druggist could never be sure when the inspector might drop in unexpectedly; he was as likely to do so unannounced at night as during the day. Despite this supervision, there was considerable fraud in the preparation and sales of drugs; cheap, ineffective remedies were often substituted for expensive products, or drugs were made impotent by dilution with worthless compounds. When the inspector caught a druggist committing such offenses, the penalties were stiff, ranging from heavy fines to more drastic punishments, such as beating the soles of the unscrupulous pharmacist's feet.

Islamic rulers also required that physicians be licensed in order to practice. In 931 a luckless citizen of Baghdad died after a doctor made a mistake in treating him, and the Caliph Muqtadir ordered that all practitioners of medicine be examined by his court physician, Sinan ibn Thabit. In the first year some 860 physicians took the test. However, the standards apparently were not too strict: one old man pleaded to be allowed to keep practicing to earn a living, although he freely admitted his lack of professional training. Sinan felt sorry for the old fellow and granted him permission to continue, as long as he did not prescribe bloodletting or harsh purgative drugs.

Doctors who were found qualified to practice treated many of their patients in hospitals much as modern physicians do. As early as the start of the Ninth Century, Baghdad had its first hospital, probably copied from the one connected with the medical school at Jundishapur. Soon other hospitals began to spring up, and before long records indicate that there were 34 throughout the Muslim world. Some of these hospitals must have been surprisingly modern; in the larger cities they had different wards for the treatment of different illnesses, and special quarters for the insane. They also had outpatient departments for the immediate treatment of minor injuries, while patients with more serious complaints were admitted to a ward.

One of the most important parts of an Islamic hospital was its dispensary, which provided virtually every kind of remedy then known. Hospitals also had their own medical libraries for the use of doctors and their students. Physicians visited their patients and prescribed medications. In the 11th Century, traveling clinics appeared, to serve areas beyond the hospitals' reach. These were moved from place to place on the backs of camels, and were generally run by one or more doctors. When they stopped in a village or remote spot, they erected a tent, examined the sick and dispensed the necessary medications. These mobile clinics were also used in time of epidemics when hospitals were filled to overflowing.

While Islamic scholars made major contributions in medicine, they also made brilliant progress in laying the foundations on which modern chemistry arose. Many laboratory terms and techniques grew out of the medieval passion for alchemy, the eternal quest to change base metals into gold, which inflamed some of the finest minds of the day. The most famous early Muslim practitioner was Jabir ibn Hayyan, court alchemist to the Caliph Harun. He believed, in effect, that all compounds were basically composed of mercury combined with sulphur, differing only in their "varieties of sulphur . . . caused by a variation in the soils and in their situations with regard to the heat of the sun."

Like their medieval contemporaries in Europe, Jabir and other alchemists searched constantly for the so-called "philosopher's stone," the substance believed capable of transmuting one metal into another—meaning into gold and silver. The theories they proposed dominated men's hopes for centuries and consumed innumerable hours of talent and labor. Many years after Jabir's death, according to legend, a lump of real gold was found lying in a mortar in the ruins of his laboratory in Kufa, keeping alive the wistful dream that men could manufacture the precious metal.

Along with his efforts to produce gold, Jabir conducted many other investigations that helped bring about an understanding of how substances combine to form compounds. He discovered new techniques for refining metals, preparing steel, dyeing cloth and leather, distilling vinegar to form acetic acid, and using manganese dioxide in the manufacture of glass. Jabir was also able to crystallize some compounds, thereby obtaining them in pure form; this made possible more effective chemical investigation, which depends on the purity of the compounds. Along with the techniques he developed, many terms passed from Jabir's Arabic into European languages, among them alkali and antimony, alembic and aludel.

After Jabir's death, other Muslim scientists carried his investigations forward, often making contributions of their own. One of his noted followers was the great physician Razi, who was as famous for his achievements in alchemy as in medicine. Of the 12 books Razi wrote on alchemy, the best known is *The Book of the Secret of Secrets*. Despite its provocative title, with the implied promise of unraveling the mysteries of the universe, it is primarily a straightforward exposition of the chemical composition of many mineral substances.

Razi not only outlined the chemicals and equipment needed in a medieval alchemy laboratory, but in an orderly and rational manner categorized substances under the major headings of animal, mineral or vegetable, a classification still in use today. The typical chemical apparatus used and described by Razi—including beakers, flasks, vials and glass crystallization dishes—continued to be standard equipment for centuries and, with some improvements, is found in chemical laboratories today.

Along with its contributions in chemistry and medicine, the Islamic world did much to advance the science of mathematics. In this discipline, as in others, Muslims displayed their genius for borrowing ideas, particularly from India and Greece, and developing and refining them before passing them along to the West. From the Hindus they took three of mathematics' most basic tools: the so-called "Arabic" numerals, which they popularized, the decimal system and the concept of zero. Among other things, these innovations made it possible to deal in large numbers in an efficient way, far more so than with the cumbersome methods that they replaced; previously numbers had been expressed either with full words or alphabetical letters.

In the modern world it is hard to imagine a number system without zero. Lacking it, the entire concept of abstract mathematics would be impossible, as it enables us to express the difference between two equal quantities, as $2 - 2 = 0$; it is also essential to many other sciences, including physics, chemistry and astronomy. Islamic scholars represented the concept of zero with a dot, or a small circle. Their word for this circle was *sifr*, meaning an empty object. When translated into Latin it became *zephyrum*, and later, in Italian, *zero*. The English language retained it as zero, and also kept the original Arabic word *sifr*, as "cipher."

Islamic scholars were so intrigued with numbers that they spent hours trying to stump one another with difficult mathematical puzzles, some of which are still worked by mathematicians today. For their amusement, they also contrived "magic boxes," grids containing numbers that added up to the same sum horizontally, vertically and diagonally.

With their love of numbers and abstractions, it was almost inevitable that Islamic scholars would be attracted to the serious study of more advanced mathematics. And, indeed, they took the elementary algebra of the Greeks and Hindus and developed it to a high level of sophistication. Algebra was especially fascinating to Khwarizmi, Islam's most outstanding mathematician; early in the Ninth Century he wrote the first readily understandable textbook on the subject. He called his work *Hisab al-Jabr wa'l-Muqabala*, meaning, roughly, "the art of bringing together unknowns to match a known quantity." The modern term algebra comes directly from *al-jabr*, whose literal translation is "the bringing together of separate parts" (to the Muslims it also meant a bonesetter, one who brought together broken bones). Khwarizmi's book was translated into Latin in the 12th Century, introducing algebra into Europe and serving as the principal mathematics textbook there until the 16th Century.

Muslims also helped to develop and transmit to Europe other complex mathematical forms, including plane geometry and plane and spherical trigonometry, whose concepts they also are believed to have taken from the Greeks. These studies enabled them to solve intricate equations and were equally useful in simple daily tasks; they were applied to such varied functions as computing the distance of a star or the speed of a falling body, to measuring a field or how much corn a granary would hold.

One field in which mathematics played a prominent role was optics. The master of this branch of science was Alhazen, a Persian who lived in the 10th Century. Until his time it was commonly believed that the eyes emitted rays that struck on objects, enabling people to see. But his researches, which made use of the geometry of his day, proved that vision results from rays passing from objects into the eye. This is the principle on which the modern science of optics is based, and Alhazen is known as its father.

Probably Islam's most significant application of mathematics was in astronomy. The Arabs had taken a keen interest in the planets and stars since their desert days. Like many primitive peoples they had given the heavenly bodies names, using them to guide their steps on journeys across the sandy wastes; some of these star names are still in use today, among them "Algol," "Betelgeuse" and "Vega." But it was not until the beginning of the Eighth Century that the Muslims had any scientific understanding of the heavens. Their interest was aroused when the Caliph Harun al-Rashid had the Greek astronomer Ptolemy's great work, the *Almagest*, translated. In 830 the Caliph Ma'mun had an observatory built in Baghdad in association with the House of Wisdom. There Islamic scholars made observations, verifying many of Ptolemy's findings and discovering new stars on their own.

Probably the most important instrument Muslim astronomers used was the astrolabe, a device they borrowed from the Greeks. Known to them as "the mathematical jewel," it was essentially a flat disc, usually made of brass, and came in various sizes from portable models some two inches in diameter to large stationary models a foot or more across. Regardless of size, the circumference was marked off in degrees, and swinging on a pivot from the center was a pointer called an alidad. The astrolabe was suspended by a tiny ring at the top and the pointer was aimed at a distant object, such as a star. The pointer thus formed an angle with a horizontal line on the astrolabe, and by measuring the number of degrees in the angle it was possible to determine the height of the star or other object being measured. Astrolabes were also used in computing the position of stars and the movement of the planets as well as to tell time. Like so many other Greek inventions, the astrolabe was introduced into Europe by the Muslims, although it was eventually discarded because of its lack of precision and replaced by the quadrant and the sextant.

Despite the astrolabe's limitations, Muslim scientists obtained some remarkably accurate readings with it, even managing to measure the size of the earth. Like all learned men of their time, Muslim scholars generally believed that the world was a sphere; by measuring a terrestrial degree they deduced a fair approximation of the circumference and diameter of the earth. A few scholars, far ahead of their time, even postulated what then seemed the highly unlikely theory that the earth rotated on its own axis, although more conservative scientists rejected this concept.

As astronomers charted the stars to gain new knowledge about the universe, other scholars began to map earthly landmarks to guide man's steps. Because the Islamic empire was so vast, the government compiled guide books that contained a listing of roads and the names and locations of towns and the distances between them. Knowledge grew rapidly as the reports of merchants returning from journeys aroused interest in distant lands and peoples. The earliest Islamic description of China and India appeared in 851; the first Muslim travelers went to Russia in 921 and wrote colorful reports of their experiences. One of the most gifted observers was the scientist Biruni, who went to India in the 11th Century and wrote a monumental book about that country, describing in detail everything from its terrain to "Siamese" twins he had seen there. Other Muslim geographers worked with astronomers to execute a composite map of the skies and the earth, which was to help convince educated Europeans that the world was round.

While Muslim scholarship had an impact on virtually every field of science, it probably reached a climax in the work of a single historian, Ibn Khaldun, who was the first to examine society scientifically. Ibn Khaldun is considered the greatest historical philosopher that Islam produced, and, indeed, one of the greatest of all time. He did not merely document the events of the past, as his predecessors had done, but gave history a new dimension by trying to find rational laws to explain it and the human behavior that shaped it.

Ibn Khaldun's fame rests on his classic *Muqaddima*, the introduction to a comprehensive history he wrote about the Arabs. In it he presented the first theory of historical development to take cognizance of the many factors that influence human events—the relentless physical facts of climate, geography and economy, as well as the moral and spiritual forces that guide man's destiny. Like other great Muslim thinkers, Ibn Khaldun combined his scholarship with political activity. He traveled widely, acting as secretary to several princes and serving as an ambassador at courts in Spain and Africa. His participation in the turbulent politics of these regions helped prepare him for the penetrating observations that mark his classic work.

Seeing the gradual and painful decline of the Islamic world in the 14th Century, he raised with personal urgency the disturbing question of what strengthens and what weakens human societies. One of his theses was that when human beings have group loyalties, a strong state can be built. This form of loyalty, he wrote, is in one sense akin to patriotism but can equally be the bond of an idea or an ideal; when intense it could enable a state to become strong and creative but usually it was eroded by second or third generation selfishness and a liking for luxury. Such a state, having lost its vital group loyalty and cohesion, was then overthrown by some new, external force that possessed a greater solidarity.

Although the *Muqaddima* was rooted in the experience of a Muslim living in the medieval world, Ibn Khaldun filled his masterpiece with insights relevant not only to his own time but to later times as well. What gave it a sad irony was that its author was diagnosing, with scholarly detachment and brilliant clarity, the decline of his own society's culture—a culture that was soon to collapse—while setting a standard of scholarship that was to be part of Islam's legacy to the West.

The Simurgh, found in inaccessible islands and near the equator, is fearless beyond all other animals. He can carry off exceedingly large animals like the elephant and the rhinoceros and when he does, rocks quake and tremble. He builds his nest upon large trees.

A PERSIAN BESTIARY

In medieval days, encyclopedic accounts of the beasts, called bestiaries, were as popular in the Islamic world as they were in Europe. Of the many such illuminated manuscripts, one of the most engaging is the *Manafi' al-Hayawan* ("The Uses of Animals") now in New York's Morgan Library, an account of many beasts and the medicines that could be extracted from them; it was compiled in the 11th Century by Ibn Bakhtishu', a physician to the Caliph in Baghdad, and two centuries later was translated from Arabic into Persian and illustrated with 94 charming miniatures. The drawings and the text (translated freely here), combine fact with folklore; the home remedies are hardly recommended, and a few of the animals are fanciful. The "rhinoceros" *(page 139),* includes elements of zebra and gnu, and, unhappily, no Simurgh *(above)* exists.

W

olves go about singly because they are ferocious and do not trust one another. For sleeping, they lay themselves in a circle facing each other. A wolf cannot stand hunger. The female is more wicked, more searching and courageous. She howls until the shepherd's dog hears; then she goes toward the barking of the dog. As the dog comes nearer, she turns away and howls from another direction, so that the dog is misled; then she attacks the flock and snatches away a sheep.

The flesh of a wolf, beaten in a mortar, and cooked in the juice of celery and honey, then mixed with saffron, galangale and white pepper, a little bit of each, and taken with the juice of mouse ear, is good for fever. A wolf's right eye, carried as a charm, will protect a person against the evil eye and spells.

Of all wild animals the lion is the strongest. Fearing no other animal, he travels alone and not in groups. He does not attack women or children; he flees from nothing as he does from a little ant. He is afraid of a white rooster and does no harm to a caravan in which a rooster

is found. He is quieted by hearing a sweet musical voice; when he bathes himself he becomes so gentle that a child might sit on him and lead him everywhere. The bone of his neck and spine is one solid piece; for this reason he cannot turn his neck. His bones contain no marrow. By rubbing or striking them together, one can produce fire. When the lion scents the hunter he effaces his footprints behind him with the end of his tail. Lion's flesh produces bad humors but it is good for paralysis. A lion's tooth tied on a child makes teething easier.

An elephant lives three or four hundred years; the animals with the longer tusks have a longer life. The elephant is afraid of a young pig and a horned ram but he is annoyed most of all by the gnat and the mouse. When an elephant is tired, people rub his feet with oil and

warm water and he gets well. One dram of his ivory is good for leprosy; a piece of an elephant's skin tied on the body stops the ague; his fat relieves headaches when it is burned and the patient sits on the fumes.

The leopard is a fierce enemy of man, unmanageable and ferocious. He eats only of his own game. When satiated, he sleeps for three days and three nights in succession; on the fourth day he wakes up with such a loud roar that other animals are attracted to him. A sick leopard gets well by eating mice. His skin is tender and if he is wounded it breaks with a slight stroke.

The flesh and fat of a leopard, boiled in the juice of olives, serve as a good salve for the sores, abcesses and pimples that break out on the body; his blood is a preventive liniment for all skin diseases. Three carats of leopard gall, mixed with liquid pitch and drunk in hot water, cure the spleen disease and the yellowness of jaundice.

The bear eats like beasts of prey and grazes like cattle; he climbs trees backward and likes to be concealed and live in caves. During the cold weather and winter he stays in his den and never eats, but licks the palms of his hands and feet until the weather grows warm; by that time he has grown so fat that he can hardly come out of his hole.

The female keeps her young outdoors until they are strong enough, then she carries them on her back up the big trees to feed them with fruit. The bear is very annoying to the honey bees; he throws the hive into the water, so as to drown the bees and eat the honey. When sick he eats ants and becomes well.

When struggling with an ox, the bear jumps on the back of the ox, holds his horns with his paws, and bites his shoulders until the ox falls. He fights with many other animals.

Bear bile with ground pepper restores the hair; with honey it is serviceable for asthma, chills, liver and spleen troubles, and will improve the sight. If a man puts the hair of the tail of a bear upon his ear, however much wine he drinks, he will never be intoxicated so long as he keeps it there. If his right eye is dried and tied on a child, the child will not be afraid in a dream; the left eye, tied to the arm, cures malaria. His tooth tied on a child makes teething easier.

*C*amels are revengeful and of a good memory; whenever they are beaten they seek an opportunity to avenge themselves. They can see well in the night, and live nearly 80 years, sometimes more. The camel does not like the company of a horse, as they always fight. His flesh is tough; it cannot be easily digested and produces melancholia.

The brain of a female camel, dried and liquefied with vinegar, is good for epilepsy resulting from melancholia. The hump of a camel, taken internally, is good for dysentery; and the milk is useful for dropsy and for trouble of the liver and spleen. The shin bone, pounded small and with an admixture of water, exterminates mice when placed in their holes; the melted marrow, taken with date wine four times, will help epilepsy and cure diphtheria; the saliva, in vinegar, is given to an insane man who is as violent as an infuriated camel.

One of the wonderful traits of the mountain goat is that he leaps down from places that are at a height of about a hundred spears, and stands on his horns. Another wonder is the peculiarly perforated horn through which he breathes; if the hole is stopped up, so as not to let the air enter, he dies shortly thereafter. The number of the joints of his horns corresponds to the number of the years of his age.

If one half dram of the goat's bile is taken in the juice of wild lettuce by a person when the sun is in the sign of Aries, he will have no fear and apprehension for one year, until the sun again reaches the sign of Aries. The dung, burned and applied to baldness, restores the hair; it is also good for burns, mange and the sores and accidental swellings that appear at the root of the ear; applied to the eye, it removes cataracts. When the fat is applied to the body, the sting of the scorpion and the bee do not cause any pain; the scorpion dies of its smell. If the hair is set on fire, insects and reptiles run away. Allah knows best.

The rhinoceros is the rarest of all the animals of his kind, as the female bears only one offspring during her lifetime. The rhinoceros hates the elephant and is not afraid of him. As soon as he sees an elephant he runs toward him and, standing on his hind feet, he raises his forefeet and strikes at the shoulder of the elephant with the horn, which he cannot pull out, and so he remains hanging to the elephant until they both perish. The horn is about a cubit long, but stronger than the tusks of the elephant, more pointed and harder, hence the blow is very effective. The usefulness of a rhinoceros is in his horn and gall; if they are set on fire, the spell and evil eye are offset. He is fierce in reedy places but timorous elsewhere.

7

FROM SPAIN TO SUMATRA

The civilization of Islam profoundly affected the states and peoples that touched upon its borders. Some were drawn by Islam's Five Pillars of religious wisdom, some by its window on the lost world of Hellenic thought, some by its customs and attitudes, as richly and intricately patterned as a Persian prayer rug. The influence of Islam took many forms because Islam was many things—a religion, a culture, a political system. Each of its neighbors absorbed what it needed or was attracted to, depending upon the conditions of its geography or national character.

To the west, Islam influenced Europe through three main areas of collision or contact. One was in Spain, one in Sicily, and one in the Levant—where Christianity's Holy Places were for almost 200 years the targets of the Crusades. To the east, Islam converted millions of Turkish-speaking tribesmen wandering between the Caucasus and the Great Wall of China, and through them eventually affected the destinies of lands as distant from each other as India and the Balkans. In Africa, Muslim caravans penetrated the Dark Continent deeply enough to establish a thriving Muslim university in the city of Timbuktu by the 15th Century. Meanwhile, Muslims engaged in seagoing trade carried Islamic customs across the Indian Ocean to Java and Malaya and even to the Philippines.

The channels through which Islam reached its neighbors were sometimes peaceful, but just as often its influence was a by-product of war. For every scholar or merchant who planted the seeds of Islamic civilization by precept and example, there was a soldier for whom Islam was a call to battle. Defensive warfare was explicitly enjoined on the faithful by the Koran, and aggressive warfare was popularly believed to be equally justified. Just as Christians of the Middle Ages took up arms to advance the religion of Christ, so Muslims took up arms to advance the religion of the Prophet.

Modern men, guided by enlightened principles, choose to believe that war never benefits its victims, but in fact this is not always true. History contains many examples of marauding armies that enriched the culture of those they attacked. A case in point is Alexander the Great, who introduced Hellenic art to Buddhist sculptors in the course of invading the

PRAYING ANGELS, *who stand and bow in the ritual required of all believers, reflect expanding Islam's absorption of varied cultures. The concept of angels is Judaeo-Christian, the custom of crowning them Central Asian; they are pictured in a Turkish translation of an Arab work on metaphysical theory.*

Indus valley, and thus laid the groundwork for a whole new school of Indian art. Today Ghandara sculpture is considered to be one of Buddhist India's greatest artistic accomplishments.

Similarly, the armies of Islam turned a swift military foray into Spain into a cultural conquest that transformed Spanish history. Although Spain was not to remain permanently Muslim, its cities, under Muslim rule, glittered with a brilliance that lasted for centuries. In receding from Spain, Islam left behind a legacy of astonishing palaces and mosques, and certain modes of thought that were to become permanent possessions of the Spanish people.

The conquest of Spain, launched in 711, was the last great feat of the Umayyad dynasty. It was initiated by the Arab governor of North Africa, Musa ibn Nusayr, but the actual invasion force was composed entirely of Berbers. This indigenous North African people, fierce and proud and never quite happy with their Arab rulers, had nevertheless accepted Islam. They did so for much the same reasons as Islam's earlier non-Arab converts: to be Muslim was, among other things, to avoid taxes. Despite such materialistic motives, the Berbers were dedicated Muslims and in less than five years they had added most of Spain to Islam.

Like earlier Islamic invasions of other lands, this one was helped by conditions in the country under attack. Spain was a divided nation. Its native peasantry was oppressed by an alien aristocracy, the Visigoths, and its sizable Jewish population was oppressed by the Church. Together these two factions made things easier for the Berbers. Toledo fell to the Muslims with almost no opposition, thanks to the disaffection of its Jewish inhabitants, and Cordoba was captured through the help of a Spanish shepherd who showed the invaders a breach in the city wall. By 716, when Seville fell to the forces of Islam, the conquest was virtually complete. Thereafter, until 1492, when the last

Muslim ruler was ousted from Spain, a brilliant Arabic-speaking society flourished on Spanish soil. It was a society many layers deep, for Muslim domination brought prosperity to many levels of Spanish life.

At the top of this Islamic Spanish society were, of course, its Muslim rulers. More often than not these were Berbers, but Spain's most spectacular Islamic dynasty was founded by an Arab, the last of the Umayyads, Abd al-Rahman. Fleeing across Africa to escape the Abbasids when they seized power, Abd al-Rahman finally came to the city of Cordoba. There he established an Umayyad state that resolutely refused to recognize Abbasid authority. In fact, his descendants proclaimed Cordoba to be a separate and independent caliphate.

Below the Muslim rulers in the hierarchy of Spanish society were the Spaniards who accepted the religion of Islam and became Muslim converts. Next came a much more numerous group, the Spaniards who kept their Christian faith but adopted Islam's manners and mores. The fourth element in Islamic Spain was the Jews. Finding the Crescent to be far more tolerant of the Synagogue than the Cross had been, they readily accepted Arabic culture. Underneath them all, submerged but still alive, was the Catholic Church. Embittered by its losses, the Church worked ceaselessly among its Spanish sons to fan the flames of vengeance.

For those who did not become embroiled in court intrigue or in the Catholic counter-offensive, life in al-Andalus—Islam's name for its Spanish possession —was highly agreeable. While Europe north of the Pyrenees wallowed in the brutish conditions of the Dark Ages, Cordoba's citizens were enjoying public plumbing and illuminated streets. The city's half-million inhabitants worshiped in 3,000 mosques, bathed in 300 *hammams*, and enjoyed all the feast days of Christianity and Islam combined. Cordoba, and also Granada and Seville, boasted institutions of higher learning where philosophy, law, literature, mathematics, medicine, astronomy, history and geography were taught, and the status symbol for a wealthy man was a well-stocked library.

In this sunlit civilization, Christians imitated Muslims by establishing harems and adopting Muslim literature and music as their own. So extensive was this cultural assimilation that a certain Bishop Alvaro composed an angry broadside: "My fellow Christians delight in the poems and romances of the Arabs; they study the works of Muhammadan theologians and philosophers, not in order to refute them, but to acquire a correct and elegant Arabic style. Where today can a layman be found who reads the Latin commentaries on the Holy Scriptures? Alas! the young Christians who are most conspicuous for their talents have no knowledge of any literature of language save Arabic: they read and study avidly Arabic books; they amass whole libraries of them at vast cost, and they everywhere sing the praises of Arabic lore."

Far from coming to terms with Islam, Alvaro and other Churchmen like him looked upon any compromise with the Muslims as a victory for the Anti-Christ. They encouraged their followers to seek martyrdom by blaspheming the Prophet and welcoming the punishment that followed. Often the Muslim judges of these frenzied wrongdoers were reluctant to grant their wishes—a reluctance not shared by Christian judges when, after seven centuries of Muslim rule, the roles were reversed. After the 11th Century, Spain's Christian princes, in one province after another, gradually reclaimed their lost lands, a process that reached its height in 1248, with the reconquest of Seville. The resurgent Christians turned on their Muslim subjects and persecuted them without mercy. They forced them to deny their faith, drove them from the country, and took drastic steps to uproot every trace of Spanish-Muslim culture. In 1499 Cardinal Ximenes ordered 80,000 Arabic books to be publicly burned in Granada, and denounced Arabic as "the language of a heretical and despised race."

In attacking the people it considered its arch-enemies, Christianity did not even hesitate to distort history. A classic case is the saga of the *Song of Roland*. The real Roland, a soldier in Charlemagne's army, was killed by a band of marauding Basques as Charlemagne was returning home from an expedition in northern Spain. But the Roland of legend was killed by Muslims. As the hero of the troubadours' *Chanson de Roland*, he became one of the great rallying figures of the Crusades. Centuries later, in Ariosto's epic poem *Orlando Furioso*, he was still providing propaganda for the Church's anti-Muslim position during the Renaissance.

And yet, despite the Church's official attitude, the ordinary Christians of Spain—those who had accepted Muslim culture while retaining their own faith—remained permanently affected by their Islamic experience. Hundreds of Arabic words passed into their daily speech, ranging from place names to humble turns of phrase. Spain's longest river, the Guadalquivir, takes its name from the Arabic *wadi al-kabir*, "long valley," while the *hasta* of *hasta mañana* comes from the Arabic word for "until," *hatta*. In dozens of Spanish cities the Muslim mosque became, with a few architectural modifications, the Christian church or cathedral. Similarly, Muslim mysticism passed directly or indirectly into the very fiber of the Spanish Christian tradition. St. Teresa of Avila and St. John of the Cross might never have written as they did if they had not been exposed to such Sufi doctrines as the concept of God as the Beloved and Friend, and the belief that God could be known only through renunciation of the world.

Even Spain's concept of the ideal man owes something to Islam. The *hidalgo*, or Spanish gentleman, one of the world's great patterns of human perfection, has many of the qualities of the wandering

Muslim holy man, the *fakir*. Both regard nobility as a matter of spirit rather than of birth, and believe that a man arrayed in beggar's rags can still have the bearing of a prince. One of the supreme portraits of the *hidalgo* carries the similarity even further. Don Quixote, Cervantes' tragic and ridiculous knight, longs to be noble with an intensity that blinds him to reality; his life, like the *fakirs'*, is completely internal; the real world does not exist.

The *hidalgo*, as an ideal, never ventured much beyond Spain. But in other ways Spain's contact with Islam profoundly affected Europe. Scholars in universities north of the Pyrenees fought to obtain Arabic manuscripts from Spain, valuing both those that were original and those that were translations from the ancient Greek. One of the most respected thinkers in all of medieval Europe was a Spaniard named Ibn Rushd, or—more familiarly, Averroes. Through a series of penetrating commentaries on Aristotle's philosophy, Averroes reintroduced Europe to the true nature of Aristotle's ideas. Indeed, he laid the groundwork for one of the great intellectual triumphs of the Middle Ages: St. Thomas Aquinas' *Summa Theologica*.

Arabic Spain also inspired poets north of the Pyrenees. In Provence, troubadours sang the praises of their mistresses in a rhymed stanza that had been invented by Muslim poets in Spain, and spoke of love in the Platonic terms much favored by the cultured aristocrats of al-Andalus. Indeed, chivalry may have originated in Muslim Cordoba, where the voices of court poets were constantly raised in praise of the delights of spiritual love. One of the most exhaustive treatises on this subject was composed, oddly enough, by a rigorous theologian. His name was Ibn Hazm, and his book, *The Ring of the Dove*, was a product of his youth. It explores all the nuances of desire, and concludes that the noblest of loves is arrived at through patience, restraint and chastity. Such a love, said Ibn Hazm,

was a union of souls, "a sublime bliss . . . a lofty rank . . . a permanent joy, and a great mercy of God"—sentiments later to be echoed in many a medieval romance.

Even the greatest poet of the age may have been influenced by a Spanish Muslim. Although Dante Alighieri, fervent Christian that he was, put Muhammad in Hell alongside religious schismatics, the plot of his *Divine Comedy*, a visit to the world of the hereafter, has many affinities with the Prophet's night journey through the seven heavens to the throne of God. Also, more specifically, Dante's descriptions of man's ascension through the infernal regions to heavenly bliss owe much to the allegorical writings of a Spanish mystic, Ibn Arabi. In Ibn Arabi's account of man's spiritual passage from ignorance to knowledge, the delights of Heaven and the tortures of Hell have many of the physical attributes of Dante's Heaven and Hell—and there is even an intermediate stage comparable to Purgatory.

The second bridge between Islam and Europe lay across Sicily—and Sicily, unlike Spain, offered Islamic ideas a much smoother passage. Possibly because it was ruled by Muslims for a much shorter time and reconquered with much greater ease, Sicily never tried to wipe out the traces of its Muslim occupation. On the contrary, its Norman kings became ardent Arabophiles.

The island was seized for Islam in 827 by a dynasty of Tunisian Arabs, the Aghlabids. It reverted to Christian hands two and a half centuries later when young Roger de Hauteville of Normandy occupied it and became its first Norman ruler. Under Muslim rule, Roger's new domain had been thoroughly Islamized. Its administrative system was Arabian in concept, and Palermo, its capital city, was a center of Arabic art and learning. The cultivation of sugar cane, flax and olives had been introduced, and the royal palace at Palermo contained a thriving silk-weaving establishment.

Roger, a rude Frankish knight, was fascinated and awed by his new possession. He permitted his Muslim subjects to practice their own religion, recruited Muslim soldiers into his army and welcomed Muslim scholars at his court. Roger II, his son, carried a liking for Muslim ways even further. Although technically a Christian, Roger II was called Roger the Pagan. His coronation robe was decorated with a border of Arabic inscriptions and dated according to the Muslim year. The most illustrious member of his court was a Spanish Arab cartographer, Idrisi, whose greatest work was done under the Sicilian King's patronage. More than three centuries before Columbus made the idea famous, Idrisi was suggesting that the earth might possibly be round—and presented his royal patron with a circular map, engraved on silver.

By the time Frederick II ascended the throne of Sicily in 1197, to rule as king (and later as Holy Roman Emperor), the royal court at Palermo was more Eastern than Western. Frederick dressed in Muslim clothes, kept a harem and was on the best of terms with the ruling Sultan in Cairo. The royal entourage included a falconer, imported from Syria, and Frederick himself was the author of a treatise on falconry—the first natural history to be published in Europe. Arab scholars graced his table. Arab administrators ran his government, and Arabic was one of the kingdom's four official languages: Sicilian coins and documents appeared in Arabic, as well as in Latin, Hebrew and Greek. In 1224 Frederick founded the first chartered university in Europe, the University of Naples, and gave it his own collection of Arabic manuscripts; one of the men who studied there was St. Thomas Aquinas.

It was an accident of history that Sicily's Christian reconquerors happened to be tolerant of Islam, disposed to accept the best it had to offer. It was also an accident of history that the reconquest touched off a series of military aggressions against Islam in which all of Europe soon joined. Ironically, the Crusades not only failed in their objective but also accelerated the flow of Eastern ideas to the West. To Europe, the Crusades were an event of epochal importance. To Islam, they were as routine as the border wars that periodically engaged their forces on the frontiers of the empire. One scholar has described them as being to Islam like the tick on a camel's back, which lodges for a while and then falls off—scarcely noticed by the camel.

The ostensible purpose of the Crusades was to assure Christian pilgrims access to the shrines of the Holy Land. Permission to enter Palestine had been guaranteed the West by the Abbasids, but the country was now under the control of the Fatimid dynasty in Cairo—and the Fatimids did not seem disposed to honor the guarantee. This threat became much more real after one mad Fatimid Caliph, Hakim, ordered the destruction of Jerusalem's Church of the Holy Sepulcher in 1009. But Pope Urban II, in proclaiming the first Crusade in 1095, may also have had other motives in mind. The Crusades held out the promise of reuniting the Eastern and Western branches of the Church, bringing back into the fold of Rome the schismatic sects that had formed their own Church in Byzantium 86 years before. The crusades also offered an alternative for the constant feudal warfare that troubled the peace of Europe. Instead of turning their swords inward upon each other, Christians could now turn them outward upon Islam.

As for the men who joined the Crusades, they too had other motives. Younger sons of feudal families, deprived of any hope of patrimony at home, saw in the Crusades a chance to carve out for themselves estates in the Middle East. Merchants from Genoa and Venice saw an opportunity for great profits to be made from trading outposts established in the Levant. Artisans and peasants and shopkeepers saw an escape from the restrictions of their daily lives—

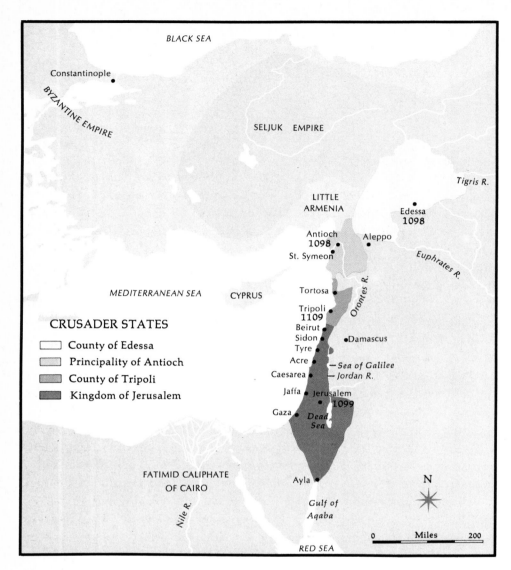

BLACK SEA

Constantinople

BYZANTINE EMPIRE

SELJUK EMPIRE

Tigris R.

LITTLE
ARMENIA

Edessa
1098

Antioch
1098
St. Symeon

Aleppo

Euphrates R.

MEDITERRANEAN SEA

CYPRUS

Tortosa

Orontes R.

Tripoli
1109
Beirut
Sidon
Tyre
Acre
Caesarea

•Damascus

—Sea of Galilee
—Jordan R.

Jaffa

Gaza

Jerusalem
1099

Dead
Sea

CRUSADER STATES

☐ County of Edessa
▨ Principality of Antioch
▩ County of Tripoli
▦ Kingdom of Jerusalem

FATIMID CALIPHATE
OF CAIRO

Nile R.

Ayla

Gulf of
Aqaba

N

0   Miles   200

RED SEA

POCKETS OF CHRISTIANITY, *lining the east-ern Mediterranean, were established in Islam's empire by the First Crusaders. After conquering Edessa and Antioch in 1098, the Christians routed the Saracen and Turkish defenders of Jerusalem, the main objective of the Crusade, and mas-sacred thousands of Muslims and Jews after the city fell in 1099. On Christ-mas Day, two years later, a Frank, Bald-win of Boulogne, was crowned King of Jerusalem. Tripoli was added in 1109. The Crusaders held sway from Little Armenia to the Gulf of Aqaba until the Turks retook Edessa for Islam in 1144.*

as well as the promise of indulgences to be gained from fighting for the Cross.

For a brief period during the Crusades, Europe succeeded in establishing a handful of Christian statelets in Palestine, but it did not re-Christianize the Middle East. On the contrary, it may have un-wittingly helped the counterwave that eventually carried Islam deep into Europe. Two hundred years of almost continuous warfare so weakened the Cru-saders' Byzantine allies that Byzantium was power-less to withstand the armies of the invading Turks —and the Turks subsequently used Byzantium as a base for attacking Europe.

The Crusades were important not for what they attempted to accomplish, but for results that were never planned. They forced Europe from the isola-tion of the Dark Ages and showed new horizons to its sons. Christian warriors learned new military skills, some of them of their own devising, some borrowed from their Muslim foes. Siege tactics de-veloped rapidly under the pressure of necessity, and the Muslims, skilled trainers of birds, intro-duced the Christians to the use of carrier pigeons. Similarly, the Muslim warriors' martial games and armorial bearings were to be echoed later on in the tournaments and heraldic devices of chivalry.

For the merchants of Europe, the Crusaders' con-tacts with the Middle East brought an enormously expanded demand for Middle Eastern goods. Frank-ish and Norman soldiers carried home with them a taste for sesame seeds and carob beans, maize and rice, lemons and melons, apricots and shallots, and soon these foodstuffs enlivened the Western diet. Muslins from Mosul, baldachins from Baghdad and damasks from Damascus introduced Europeans to a whole new range of clothing materials; even the word cotton comes from the Arabic *(kutn)*. Life in the West was also brightened by Persian tapestries and carpets, toilet articles such as glass mirrors and face powder, and brilliant dyes such as lilac and carmine. Cleanliness was reintroduced to a dubious Europe by Crusaders who had sampled the Arabian bath, and were unwilling to forgo its pleasures—long frowned on by Christians as pagan. Even the Church itself benefited materially from its contact with the East. St. Dominic's invention of the rosary was inspired by the chain of beads on which faithful Muslims told off the names of God.

But if Europe was captivated by its contacts with Islam, so too were Islam's neighbors to the East. On the broad and barren plains of central Asia, the Prophet's faith found ready followers among a series of Turkish-speaking tribes that were destined to refurbish the military tradition of Islam. At first, these Turks were military slaves in the service of the Umayyads and the Abbasids, but later they invaded Islam with armies of their own. Under such leaders as Ibn Tulun—the Turkish slave who became Egypt's governor—and under such dynasties as the Seljuks, the Ottomans and the Mughals, Turkish Muslims were to influence vast areas of the earth.

The Seljuks, who took over the Abbasid empire, expanded that empire into Byzantium, laying the foundation for the modern state of Turkey. The Ottomans, who followed the Seljuks, carried Islam across the Bosporus into Europe. Far to the East, the Mughals introduced Islam into India and left behind a flourishing Muslim civilization that became the basis for modern Pakistan.

But the Turks were not only great soldiers, they were also great builders, and they invigorated Islamic architecture by combining it with the architecture of the people they conquered. Ibn Tulun built Egypt's first hospital and a royal palace whose walls were covered in gold. But he is best known for the Great Mosque in Cairo that bears his name—a mosque designed for him by a Christian architect. Similarly, the Seljuks, who founded the first *madrasas*, or mosque-colleges, originated a new cruciform plan for these buildings—created for them by Persian craftsmen. As for the Ottomans, when they took over Byzantium they also took over Justinian's famous Church of Hagia Sophia and subsequently used it as a model for their own Turkish mosques.

But it was the Mughals of India who probably fused Muslim architecture with the style of another culture most effectively. Like the early mosque-builders of Cairo and Persia, who turned the columns of Greek temples and Coptic Christian churches to a Muslim purpose, the mosque-builders of India incorporated elements of Hindu architecture into their Muslim buildings. Later, under the Mughals, Indian Muslims developed one particular kind of building to new heights of grace and refinement. Perhaps the Turkish conquerors of India were recalling some contact with the ancestor-worshiping Chinese, who memorialized their dead with gracious buildings in lovely gardens. Whatever the reason, the Mughals became great builders of tombs.

The Indian mausoleum was designed to reflect the pleasures of this world and to foreshadow the pleasures of the world to come. They were set in elaborate gardens embellished with flowers and splashing fountains, and were used by their owners as places of entertainment. As the architectural historian James Fergusson points out, Indian Muslims "built their sepulchres of such a character as to serve for places of enjoyment for themselves and their friends during their lifetime, and only when they could enjoy them no longer, they became the solemn resting places of their mortal remains." This was often quite literally true. Under the building's central dome, where eventually he would be buried, the owner held decorous picnics. One of the loveliest buildings on earth, the Taj Mahal at Agra, is built upon this dual-purpose premise. Erected between 1630 and 1648 by Shah Jahan for a wife who died while she was still young, the Taj Mahal was intended as a tomb for Mumtaz Mahal and as a pleasure garden for the Shah who loved her.

The Seljuks, the Ottomans and the Mughals carried Islam far afield mostly by means of the sword. But equally great victories for Islam in distant places were achieved by nonviolent means. As merchants and teachers, Muslims were even more persuasive than they were as soldiers. Islam had originated in a country where trading was an honored profession —Muhammad himself had been in commerce before receiving his call to become a prophet. And the religion of Islam had from the beginning honored the scholar's pen as much as it respected the soldier's sword. In two great areas of the world—Africa and Indonesia—Islam took root largely through the contacts made by Muslim traders and teachers.

Throughout the Middle Ages, from Muslim cities all along the North African coast, caravans plodded south across the Sahara in quest of the gold and ivory of Negro Africa. The traders practiced and preached a religion that had the same attraction for nomadic Negro tribes that it had formerly had for the nomadic tribes of Arabia. The traders were followed by Muslim scholars who established academies in such places as Timbuktu, schools whose reputations were often as great as those in Morocco and Tunisia and Cairo. The Muslim school at Timbuktu had a library, for example, that attracted many eminent Muslim scholars to study there. Gradually, over the centuries, Islam became one of the major cultural forces in Negro Africa.

A similar result was accomplished by similar means in the Far East. As early as the 13th Century, Muslim trading ships from Persia, Arabia and India were putting into the ports of Java and the other islands of Indonesia, carrying the seeds of Islamic culture. Marco Polo, on his way back from the court of Kublai Khan, found a Muslim kingdom on Sumatra in 1292, and in 1345 an Arabian traveler named Ibn Battuta reported that the kingdom's Malayan ruler was a man deeply interested in Islamic learning. By the 15th Century, partly through the intermarriage of Muslim sailors and Indonesian women, and partly through the proselytizing zeal of Muslim traders among the islands' princes and leading men, the whole Malayan archipelago with the exception of Bali had been converted to Islam. Indonesian scholars, like all the other peoples absorbed by Islam— Turks, Berbers, Persians and Somalis—traveled to the great Muslim universities such as al-Azhar in Cairo, to study the Koran and carry Islamic learning back to their homeland.

Thus Islam used religion to hold together a far-flung empire, much as Alexander the Great had tried to do many centuries before. But where Alexander's method had been to make himself a divinity, Islam's method was to make every Muslim a messenger for what it called the House of Peace. Soldiers, sailors, merchants and scholars impressed Islam's modes of being on Indians and Africans, Spaniards and Indonesians. In a world whose ultimate destiny it was to grow smaller and more united, Islam managed to fit many varied peoples into one mold. The Don Quixote who tilted against windmills in Spain, the Crusader who returned to Europe with new habits of thought and new styles of dress, the Turk who battled across eastern Europe to the very walls of Vienna, the patient cameleer who bedded down his camels in some African caravanserai, the Sinbad who beached his ship on a coral shore—each had been affected by a society that at its zenith straddled most of the known world.

SLENDER COLUMNS, *reflected in a floor splashed by fountains, surround the Alhambra's Court of Lions.*

PATTERNS OF AN ENCHANTED PALACE

In their genius for ornamentation, the architects and craftsmen of Islam had no peers in the medieval world. Their mosques and palaces abounded in rich interior views carefully framed by patterns of columns and arches *(above)*, and walls and ceilings were everywhere surfaced with intricate configurations in plaster and ceramic tile. The most dazzling single example of this virtuosity is the Alhambra, the fairy-tale palace in Granada from which the Nasrid sultans ruled southern Spain until Christian armies expelled them in 1492. In its halls and chambers can be seen the whole range of basic Islamic motifs, drawn from geometry, writing and vegetation, and woven into an endless variety of enchanting forms.

Photographs by David Lees

A Bright Play
of Geometrical Design

Prohibited by religious strictures from creating representational art, Muslim artists relied heavily on abstract patterns. Geometry, in particular, provided craftsmen with a fertile source of designs. The Muslims were the greatest mathematicians of the medieval world, and they delighted in logical, coherent systems of lines like that of the tile mosaic shown here. The artist started with the 12-pointed star in the center of the panel, which is about five inches in diameter and is made of white tile inlaid with one continuous, delicately carved piece of black tile; it is regarded as the finest example of inlaid ceramic art in the Alhambra. By extending patterns from the star, the artist was able to generate the rest of his design, and by a careful arrangement of straight lines, he created figures that give the brilliant illusion of star shapes, circles and curves.

The Divine Language of Script

Of all the arts, Muslims respected calligraphy the most. Writing was considered the invention of God, and the use of the pen one of the major skills He passed on to man. So exalted was calligraphy that Muslim architects used it both as writing and as pure decoration in their buildings. The walls of the Alhambra abound with Arabic inscriptions, written in two styles. The style known as Kufic *(left)* was made up of characters so angular and ornamented that only a practiced eye could read it. The more cursive style, called Naskhi, was equally elaborate but somewhat easier to understand. The poem in the medallion below, like many Islamic inscriptions, praises the surrounding architecture—while doing much to contribute to the beauty it celebrates.

Stylized Gardens
of Plaster Flowers

Plant motifs were the most widely used designs in Islamic art and architecture, but in their treatment of plants, as in their rendering of all aspects of the natural world, Muslim artists sought to give them an abstract and unrealistic appearance.

One way to stylize vegetation was to render it with a minimum of depth; another was to picture imaginary plants that were made up of elements borrowed from different kinds of vegetation. In the stucco panel at left, for example, a curling acanthus vine is attached to highly simplified leaves, flowers and pineapplelike shapes—a fanciful combination that never grew in any garden. Finally, artists departed from nature by isolating single parts of plants. Thus, they took palm fronds and made them into a background for the acanthus vine shown at left, or arranged detached leaves, cones and blossoms (right) into purely decorative assemblages.

Richly Interwoven Forms

Although Muslim motifs—geometric, calligraphic and floral—occasionally appeared separately, they were more often woven together. In the panel at left above, octagons and stars, script and acorn forms are combined. In the friezes below, designers introduced ribbons of calligraphy *(far left)*, and superimposed a raised grillwork over a background floral pattern *(left)*.

As with all decorative Muslim script, the writing in the octagons above relates to the surroundings; it says "Honor and glory to the Lord Sultan Abu'l-Hajjaj," and is inscribed in the Sultan's throne room. Similarly, references to water were written around niches where jugs were stored. The phrase "Only Allah is the most powerful" was placed beside the massive entrance to the palace—a reminder to its proud rulers that protection lay not in wooden doors but only in almighty God.

A Fantastic Fusion of Design

"The women of Granada are carrying the magnificence of their attire and adornment to the brink of fantasy," wrote a 14th Century chronicler of the court ladies who inhabited the Alhambra. The description could have applied equally well to the palace itself. Its builders concealed almost all the solid

functional components—walls, arches, ceilings—behind ethe-real webs of decorative plaster and tile. Even the capitals of columns, like the one pictured at left below, were elaborately carved with a profusion of plant forms and capped by hori-zontal bands of Arabic script. The Alhambra's residents usually sat or reclined on the floor; looking up, they could fully enjoy what their architects had wrought: scalloped arches and walls, and ceilings exquisitely patterned with honey-comb vaulting that hung like stalactites, bathed in light filtering down from jewel-like domes (below and overleaf).

A SUNBURST OF ORNAMENT, *the dome of a chamber in the Alhambra is composed of thousands of carved plaster "stalactites." The ceiling is generally considered*

to be the finest of its kind in the Islamic world. A Muslim poet once claimed that at the sight of its beautiful proportions "all other cupolas vanish and disappear."

8

A DURABLE RELIGION

During the Middle Ages, Islam had justifiably regarded the West as a civilization less advanced than its own; to the Muslims, the Crusades had been not so much a challenge from equals as an incursion of barbarians. But from the late Renaissance onward, the roles began to reverse. Despite the rise of a new and powerful Islamic state —the Ottoman empire—the lead in scientific and cultural matters was to pass to the West. The threat would no longer be from Islam to Christendom, but from a resurgent Europe to the Muslim world. Western civilization forged ahead, and Islam fell behind. For those who believed that Muhammad had been God's final messenger to man, and that the Koran contained God's last and most complete revelation, the future would be a time of sternest challenge.

The beginning of Arab Islam's decline dates from the 11th Century. When the Seljuk Turks invaded Baghdad in 1055, they briefly revived a disintegrating Abbasid empire, but they also signaled the end of that empire's rule by an Arab dynasty. Although the Abbasid Caliph remained on his throne, he was little more than a figurehead. The Seljuk commander was acknowledged by the Caliph as Sultan and King of the East and the West and held the actual power. Thereafter, while the Turkish empire expanded, the power of its traditional ruler declined. In the 13th Century, the caliph's role was eliminated altogether by another wave of invading Turks, the Mongols.

In 1219, Genghis Khan crossed into Islam from the Mongol lands in central Asia, and by 1221 had reached Persia. Six years later Genghis himself was stopped by death, but the Mongol hordes swept onward under his grandson Hulagu, destroying everything in their path. In 1258 they laid siege to Baghdad, and took it almost without a fight. Tens of thousands of its peoples were massacred, the Caliph's palace was reduced to smoking ruins, and the Caliph himself, along with most of his family, was killed (the few who escaped found refuge in Egypt, where one eventually became the puppet Caliph for another Turkish dynasty, the Mamluks, who reigned for almost 250 years).

The Mongol destruction of Baghdad ended an important phase in Islamic and world history. No

CONQUEROR OF CONSTANTINOPLE, *the 15th Century Turkish sultan Muhammad II, shown here in a conventional pose, greatly increased Ottoman power by taking the Byzantine city, as well as Serbia, Greece and Albania.*

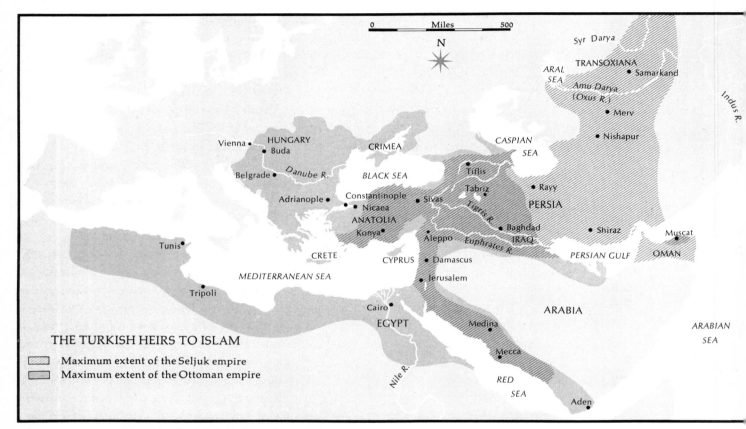

THE TURKISH HEIRS TO ISLAM

░ Maximum extent of the Seljuk empire
▓ Maximum extent of the Ottoman empire

A UNITED ISLAM *was achieved by the Seljuk Turks in the 11th Century, after the empire's political breakup under the Arabs. The Ottomans, heirs to the Seljuks, marched into Africa and Europe and dominated the areas shown in green until 1683, when they suffered a major setback at the Siege of Vienna.*

longer would an Arabic-speaking caliph, claiming descent from the Prophet's tribe, preside with charismatic authority over the world's most powerful state and complex culture. After the Mongols, and partly because of them, the Muslim states were to rearrange themselves into new patterns and new empires; Islam was to change its perspectives. The fall of Baghdad had shown the debility of Islam as a state—but it was a state that was far more than a body of political rules and customs. Islam was also

a society. As a society, it had strengths and weaknesses. The latter brought about its defeat at the hands of pagan conquerors; the former, in a very short time, turned the conquerors into ardent Muslims. The same strengths and weaknesses were to determine how Islam confronted the future.

Islam's most durable strength had always been its religion. For a variety of reasons this religion appealed to a variety of people. Its warnings and promises spurred its faithful followers to selfless action, while its sense of brotherhood, transcending race and class, created a human solidarity in which the slave and the sultan were equal in the eyes of God. Its personal approach to God, worked out in the various Sufi movements, aroused an ardor in its followers that made it more effective as a social force than any system of legal obligations. Thanks to its religion, Islam continued to expand long after the caliphate had ceased, in any real sense, to exist. In every succeeding century it would advance, offering honor especially to those dishonored by history or society.

But Islam's strength was also its weakness. Muslims were convinced that they possessed in the Koran the final and incontrovertible statement of truth. To this conviction was added the doctrine that the Koran was eternal and uncreated. Together, these led to a basic conservatism. In the Ninth Century this attitude became dominant when the doctrines of the rationalist Greek-inspired Mu'tazilites were rejected by the conservative members of the *ulama*, Islam's intellectual elite—the scholar-jurists who interpreted Koranic law and formed the backbone of Islam. The Mu'tazilites were replaced by orthodox Muslims, who used their power and prestige in later centuries to oppose innovation and experiment.

As the administrators of Islam's educational system—from the primary-school *kuttabs* where little boys swayed back and forth, memorizing the Koran, to the great mosque-universities like Cairo's al-Azhar—this orthodox *ulama* controlled the minds of generations of Muslims. Believing that all that was worth knowing was already known, and that the ideas of non-Muslims were of no account, they instilled in Muslims a mood of complacency that lasted for centuries. When tyrants governed Islam, the *ulama*—the one force strong enough to oppose them—instead urged Muslims to accept bad rulers along with good ones, since it was far more essential to preserve the stability of Muslim society.

Under the leadership of this reactionary elite the adventurous spirit that had once characterized Islam yielded to one of self-satisfied certainty. Every attempt at change or renovation, no matter what its point of origin—inside or outside Islam—was stubbornly resisted. Only when religious conformity had so enfeebled Islam that every Muslim state stood in danger of being dominated by infidels did this pattern begin to crumble. And nowhere did the effects of the pattern—and its break-up—show more clearly than in the rise and fall of the last great Islamic state: the Ottoman empire.

In the wake of the Mongol invasion, the Muslim lands in Asia Minor were overrun by a variety of Turkish tribes. Most of them from time to time encroached upon the border lands of the empire of Byzantium, none more successfully than the people who came to be known as the Ottomans. Under the leadership of Osman, the man for whom they were named, the Ottomans (from the Turkish *Osmanli*) gradually pushed back the borders between Islam and Byzantium and by the time of Osman's death in 1326 had reached the western coast of Anatolia. Osman's son inherited his empire, ruling as Sultan and "Hero of the World," and his sons and grandsons carried on the dynastic tradition. At the time of its collapse in 1922, the Ottoman empire was still ruled by a descendant of Osman, the 36th of his line.

Shortly after it was begun, however, Osman's empire very nearly expired. In 1379, another wave of Mongols from central Asia swept into the Middle East. They were lead by Timur the Lame, sometimes called Tamerlane, who ruled an Asian empire from his fabled capital of Samarkand. Timur, who claimed to be descended from Genghis Khan, outdid his forebear in the extent of his conquests and in his brutal treatment of those he conquered. Timur's exploits took him twice into Russia, once to spend a year in Moscow. His sojourn in India took him east to the Ganges, and left much of the subcontinent in ruins. (Like Genghis, Timur indulged in wholesale massacres, and made a practice of piling up the heads of his victims into enormous pyramids; one such, outside the city of Delhi, numbered 80,000 skulls.) In 1392, Timur's westward drive took him into the once-proud city of Baghdad. In 1400, Damascus fell to his troops. A year later his westward drive had taken him into the Ottoman lands of Anatolia.

By this time the Ottomans had absorbed most of the old Byzantine empire except for its capital city of Constantinople, and their armies had reached the shores of the Adriatic and the borders of Hungary. Much of their military success was due to a newly formed infantry corps, the *yeni cheri* (New Troops), or Janissaries. Conscripted from among Christian boys in the Balkans and raised as Muslims, the Janissaries were not only trained as soldiers but were encouraged to think of themselves as an elite brotherhood. A century later their courage and prowess on the battlefield were to make them the scourge of Europe—but against Timur they were helpless. By 1402 the Ottoman army was crushed and the Sultan was Timur's prisoner. For seven months, until his death, the hapless monarch accompanied the Mongol on his campaigns, locked, legend says, in an iron cage slung between two of Timur's horses.

Fortunately for the Ottoman empire, Timur's days too were numbered; in 1405 he died. While his heirs fought among themselves for possession of his vast holdings, most of his conquests reverted to their former owners. In Anatolia the Ottomans took back their lost lands and, after some family squabbles of their own, the empire finally fell to one ruler, the Sultan Muhammad I—who stabilized his sovereignty by the simple expedient of murdering all his brothers. This bloody practice was followed by subsequent sultans right down to the close of the 16th Century.

By 1453 the Ottomans had raised their banners above the walls of a conquered Constantinople, and the capital of Christian Byzantium was henceforth for many centuries to be the major city of Islam. The Ottoman Sultan now ruled an empire that included most of the Balkans and Asia Minor. To the south and east, however, lay two other powerful Islamic states, the Safavid dynasty in Persia and the Mamluks in Egypt. In 1512 Selim the Grim, newly come to the Ottoman throne, resolved to put an end to both of them. Within a year he had captured the Safavid capital of Tabriz, and might have moved eastward into the rest of Persia if it had not been for the appearance of a Mamluk army on his western flank.

In 1516, near the town of Aleppo in Syria, Selim destroyed this Mamluk army in a battle that foreshadowed many another Ottoman success. All through its history the Ottoman army, unlike the other armies of Islam, welcomed the notion of technological improvement. At Aleppo it won because it used artillery while the Mamluks did not. Flushed by this victory, Selim pressed on through Syria and into the Nile valley. By 1517, he stood at the gates of Cairo, demanding that the Mamluk Sultan relinquish his authority. When the Mamluk Sultan refused, Selim had him hanged—and Egypt and most of North Africa became part of the Ottoman empire.

Selim carried back to Constantinople one important hostage. Living in Cairo as a shadowy religious puppet was the last survivor of the Abbasid dynasty, a purely nominal Caliph. Later Ottomans, attempting to shore up a sagging empire, argued that this Caliph had transferred his sacred rights to the Ottoman line—as perhaps he had. But the Ottomans were in no sense descendants of the Prophet's tribe, necessary for a true caliph, and in their heyday they ruled without resorting to any pretense of religious authority. The Ottoman empire was held together by military force, able administration and the sultans' ability to utilize Muslim ardor in propagation of the faith.

But though they ruled from the city that had once been Europe's headquarters in the East, and though they brought within their empire most of the southeastern sector of the European continent —and in fact reached the very walls of Vienna before being turned back—the Ottomans were never able to recapture for Islam its economic and cultural superiority to the West. With Vasco da Gama's circumnavigation of Africa at the end of the 15th Century, the Middle East was no longer the crossroads of world commerce: India and the Orient were accessible to Europe by sea. Neither were the Ottomans able to revive the intellectual vitality of the early days of the Abbasids, when scholars of many kinds—Christians, Jews, Greeks, Zoroastrians—made Baghdad the cultural capital of the medieval world.

By the middle of the 16th Century, the Ottoman empire was the major military power of Europe; by the end of the following century it had already begun its long period of decline. In 1683 a second attempt to take Vienna ended in a complete rout; in 1686 the Ottomans were driven from their 145-year occupation of the Hungarian city of Buda; in 1699, by the Treaty of Karlowitz, the Sultan was forced to relinquish to various European powers Ottoman territorial holdings in Hungary, Poland, Croatia, Slavonia, Dalmatia and the Greek Peloponnesus. Armies that the Ottomans had once despised were beginning to inflict upon them defeat after defeat and whittle away their empire.

For a long time the Ottomans thought that their troubles were purely military; they refused to concede that the origin of the problems might lie deep in Islamic life. As early as 1580, for instance, one adviser to the Sultan observed that Europe's growing maritime power might soon cause it to bypass the overland routes to the East—a threat to the empire's economy. Yet his advice to the Sultan was, in effect, an attempt to turn back the clock. He suggested sending an Ottoman fleet into the Indian Ocean to drive out infidel shipping, a recommendation the Sultan could not afford, since the empire no longer had the resources for such an offensive.

Finally, after a century of military defeats, Selim III, in 1793, decided on a policy of wholesale modernization and reform. He began with the army, proposing to reorganize it completely—new rules and regulations, new schools, new weapons and equipment, even new taxes to support it. Selim's plan was called, in fact, the New Order, and it was partly inspired by the New Order that had risen in France in the wake of the French Revolution. Almost immediately it landed Selim in conflict with the Janissaries. This once-great fighting force had deteriorated into a military caste that stood, like the Mamluks in 13th Century Egypt, as the power behind the throne. Corrupt, lethargic, opposed to all reform, the Janissaries saw the New Order as a threat to their own position. So deep were their fear and resistance that in 1808 they assassinated Selim—but not before Selim's modernization of the army had created a new, young officers' corps, Western in its outlook.

In 1798, despite his initial sympathy with the French Revolution, Selim had sent an army to Egypt to fight the invading French army of Napoleon. Western ideas were one thing, but the prospect of Western territorial holdings in Islam was another matter entirely. One of the officers in this Ottoman expeditionary force was a young Macedonian Muslim named Muhammad Ali, a man of no education but of vast ambition. Muhammad Ali was deeply impressed by the technological superiority of the French he had come to fight. When Napoleon left

Egypt for France—partly because a power struggle was brewing at home, partly because the British Mediterranean fleet had cut his lines of communication—the young Muslim stepped into the vacuum created by the French departure. By 1805 he was undisputed ruler of Egypt.

Muhammad Ali engineered this feat by first getting Selim to name him pasha, or governor. Then he disposed of the opposition, Egypt's old-guard Mamluk aristocracy, by cleverly inviting 300 of its leading members to a reception in Cairo and having them massacred. After that, he embarked on a series of reforms designed to make Egypt an independently powerful nation. He built technical schools and colleges and staffed them with teachers from the West. He encouraged Egyptians to study in Europe. He established the first Muslim printing press in Egypt and put it to work publishing translations of Western textbooks, as well as a newspaper and his official decrees. He modernized Egyptian agriculture and built the country's first large-scale irrigation system. He even tried, without much success, to establish Egyptian industry.

Most of this effort was directed at improving the Egyptian army and navy, with which Muhammad Ali hoped to advance his fortunes. With his army he added Nubia and the Sudan to his Egyptian holdings and then, at the behest of the Sultan, sent his forces across the Mediterranean to put down uprisings against the Ottomans in Greece and on Crete. For this service, he was awarded Crete and was promised Syria, but the promise was never fulfilled. Undeterred, Muhammad Ali again used his army, this time to take Syria. In fact, only the threatened intervention of the British prevented the Egyptian Pasha from attacking Constantinople itself and, in a palace coup, setting himself up as the Sultan of a new Islamic state.

The Sultan, a cousin and disciple of the murdered Selim III, could scarcely approve of his vas-

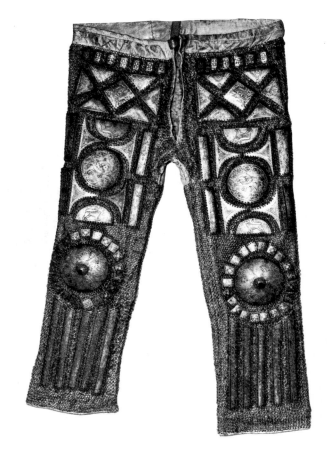

PROTECTION FOR A WARRIOR, *these chain-mail trousers from Persia were mounted on leather and fitted with steel plates. The Persians, famed for their weapons and armor, were the Ottomans' only serious rivals for power in the Middle East.*

sal's ambition, but he did admire his tactics. Mahmud II was quick to copy many of the Pasha's methods, and to initiate similar ones of his own.

He disposed of the Janissaries in a massacre that became known in reformist circles as the Auspicious Incident. He imported Western teachers and technology to create a new army, and founded new schools to teach Western ways to his officers and men. He even opened an Imperial Music School to provide his army with trumpeters and drummers. Like Peter the Great of Russia, with whom he is sometimes compared, Mahmud believed he could modernize his people's attitude by modernizing their dress. Over the violent objections of many Muslims, to whom the turban was sacrosanct (there is a popular saying that "two prostrations with the turban outweigh 70 without the turban"), Mahmud outlawed this traditional headgear as well as the long Eastern robe. He put the army in tunics and breeches, civilians in frock coats and fezzes.

But however effectively Muslim rulers adopted Western ways, they could not do so fast enough to keep abreast. Muhammad Ali was forced back into Egypt and out of the running as a Middle Eastern power by the British fleet's ability to knock out the military force behind which he had proposed to modernize his country. His grandson Isma'il, hoping to restore Egypt's strategic importance with the opening of the Suez Canal in 1869, instead invited disaster. Finding the Canal an irresistible lure to its imperial ambitions, Britain first bought a controlling interest in it in 1875, then occupied Egypt in 1882, and finally, at the outbreak of World War I, made Egypt a British protectorate.

Similarly, the Ottoman Sultan, despite his eager reorganization of his army, could not bind together the pieces of his rapidly disintegrating empire. As province after province was wrested from him—to become independent nations like Bulgaria and Greece, or the protectorates of England and France

—it became obvious that Western arms and Eastern dress were not enough. To meet the overwhelming power of the West, so attractive in some ways and so repulsive in others, Islam needed a profound spiritual renewal. In Egypt in the closing years of the 19th Century, two men did much to inspire this renewal—one a disciple of the other.

The earlier of the two was Jamal al-Din al-Afghani, who was born in 1839, probably in Persia, but who claimed to be an Afghan—as well as a descendant of the Prophet. Whatever his country of origin, Afghani spent most of his life as a wanderer. He lived for a while in Constantinople, then in Cairo, then in India, then in Paris and London. At the end of his life he returned again to Constantinople, where he was a virtual prisoner of the Sultan—who feared his outspoken anti-British sentiments. Afghani believed that what Islam needed was not to imitate Europe but to rediscover its own strengths and virtues. Islam, he said, was a civilization as well as a faith and Muslims should put aside their differences to unite against their foreign rulers.

At his corner in the teaching mosque of al-Azhar and in his favorite coffeehouse in Cairo, Afghani always drew a crowd of admiring students. One of them was the man who ultimately gave Afghani's ideas deeper meaning. His name was Muhammad Abduh, and he was the son of Egyptian fellahin, simple peasants who lived in a village of the Nile Delta. Abduh was destined to be the most influential thinker in modern Islam. Like Afghani, he traveled in the West, but unlike Afghani, he was willing to accept whatever he found good there—spiritual and intellectual, as well as material. He was quick to call attention to the contrast between Europe's ebullience and tolerance and Islam's bigoted conservatism. In fact, he was so critical of the Islam of his day that he was often taken by Westerners to be an agnostic: they found it impossible to believe that a Muslim could find Christian attitudes in some ways superior to his own.

Abduh, however, was not an unbeliever. On the contrary, he thought that the religion of Islam, rightly understood, could inspire an approach to life that would combine both personal piety and public-spirited action. The Prophet, he pointed out, had preached the need for a virtuous society as well as virtuous individuals; consequently, the quality of Muslim society was a proper concern for good and pious Muslims. But a society, Abduh argued, was only as successful as its laws—and these in turn must grow out of a society's particular values and circumstances. To return to the laws of a former society was to invite a kind of inner decay; "Laws vary as the conditions of nations vary," he wrote, and urged Muslims to know themselves.

In pursuit of this goal Abduh demanded and worked for two basic reforms: the modernization of Muslim schools and colleges, which still taught much the same subjects that they had in the Middle Ages, and the purification of the Arabic language, a once pithy and subtle tongue grown flowery and diffuse. Neither reform was wholly achieved in Abduh's lifetime. Despite the fact that he rose to the post of Mufti of Egypt, the highest judicial position in the land, Abduh was never able to use his influence to gain the cooperation of Egypt's ruler, the Khedive. It remained for his disciples to carry out his reforms, eventually altering every aspect of 20th Century Islamic life.

One of these disciples, Qasim Amin, advocated the emancipation of women. Amin put his thesis into a book, published in 1899. In it he argued that Islam's decline was caused by its suppression of women. The basis of a sound society, he wrote, was the family—and when women were made mute and powerless, family life deteriorated. Qasim Amin claimed that the harem and the veil were alien to Islam's true spirit. Islam, he pointed out, had once allowed women to play vigorous roles, and Koranic law even allowed them to control their own property—long before such an idea occurred to Europe.

The distinctions made by men like Abduh and Amin, between what Islam had become and what it had once been and might be again, played an important part in the crisis of soul that troubled 20th Century Islam. For some, it led to a decision to discard the old concept of a unified Islam in favor of new secular states. For others, it meant the rebirth of a spiritual force strong enough not only to create a new Islam but to include within it alien modes of thought and action.

In the heartland of the defeated Ottoman empire, Kemal Ataturk tried to build a modern Turkish nation, entirely divorced from Islam. He abolished traditional Muslim modes of dress, outlawed the Arabic alphabet so that Arabic and Ottoman texts could no longer be read, replaced Islam law with Western law, did away with such traditional institutions as the caliphate and sultanate, and announced that Friday would no longer be an official day of prayer. In short, his new Turkey turned its back on the entire Islamic past.

Elsewhere, however, modern Muslim leaders have found it possible to accept Western ideas without rejecting their own past, and in fact have revived this past and used it as a basis for establishing a new sense of cultural unity. Islam has proved to be not only as resilient as Christianity, the religion of the West, but as open as the West to new ideas. In the fields of education, science and philosophy, once cultivated so well and then neglected, it has shown promise of new harvests. It is even possible that educated Muslims might form a new consensus, restating for a changed world those ideas of piety, brotherhood and justice which the Prophet had so vigorously preached and humbly practiced. As the spokesmen for the Muslim world they might yet bring about a new golden age for Islam.

A FRAGMENT *of a 13th Century Turkish carpet, one of Islam's oldest surviving rugs, echoes the pointed shapes of early Arabic script.*

ISLAM'S MAGIC CARPETS

The most original and lasting expression of Islam's artistic genius is the so-called "Oriental" carpet, knotted on looms in the Middle East for more than a thousand years. Its brilliant colors and exquisite patterns have long set the standards of the art, and a Turkish or Persian rug is a prized possession today.

Perhaps more surprising is the basic, and pervasive, role that these carpets played, and still play, in the Islamic world. They covered not only floors, but walls as well; in a Muslim's tent, which lacked furniture, they also served as storage bags, cushions and blankets, and as prayer rugs they sanctified the ground on which he worshiped. Out of these magical coverings, in fact, was made everything from the saddle cover for a nomad to the throne for a king.

UNDER A CARPET CANOPY, *a Persian king receives his courtiers. Beneath his dais is spread a medallion rug.*

The Rugs of Royalty

Directed by a *salim*, or foreman, who monotonously chanted the sequence of colors, Muslim carpetmakers painstakingly tied some 900 knots an hour, averaging a weave as dense as 320 knots to the square inch. For the wealthy they produced carpets of stunning grandeur, sometimes using silk instead of wool and even silver and gold thread and semiprecious jewels; the Caliph Harun al-Rashid had no less than 22,000 fine rugs adorning his palace.

The carpets of royalty were generally of the "medallion" type, characterized by complex arabesque designs around a central motif, and sometimes extending over 25 feet in length. Russia's Peter the Great, it is said, gave Austria's Habsburgs a silk medallion Persian carpet of 783 knots per square inch that took several years to weave.

A UNIVERSAL PATTERN, *the medallion was*

woven throughout Islam. The carpet at left came from Ushak, Turkey. The one at right, which shows a fleet of Portuguese ships, was made in Persia.

The Paradise of a Persian Garden

LOVERS ON A CARPET, *a Persian prince and his princess exchange tender vows in their garden.*

A FORMAL GARDEN *is recreated in a 17th Century Persian rug. Pools, connected by channels in which fish can be seen swimming, are set off by trees, flower beds and borders of lilies.*

174

In accordance with the words of the Koran, Muslims envisioned Paradise as a verdant garden where the chosen reclined on beautiful carpets, delighting in the perfume of flowers, the ripple of water and the rustle of leaves. For the wealthy it was possible to strive for a near-duplicate on earth; Persian aristocrats in particular created lush gardens with pavilions and brimming pools, underlaid by lead pipes fitted with as many as 500 jets that rhythmically sprayed water into the air. Lacking garden furniture, they used carpets *(left)*. Gardens played an important role in daily life, and their owners spent many hours in them, relaxing, entertaining friends, playing chess.

Persians, in fact, so cherished gardens that they brought pictures of them into their homes in the form of patterned rugs like the one below, which reproduced in silk and wool a man-made oasis where trees, sheltering nightingales, spread over beds of stylized flowers.

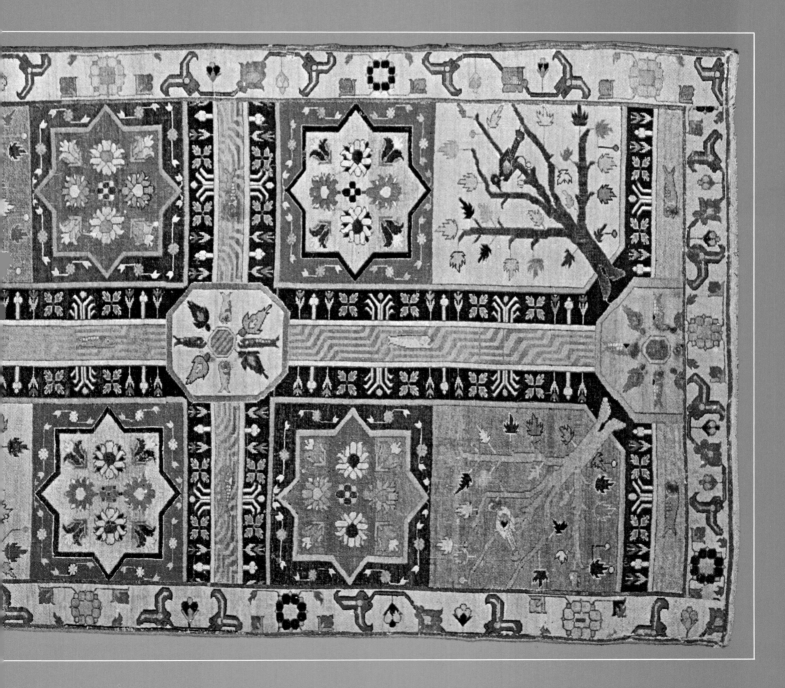

A MOSQUE LAMP *decorates the niche of a Ladik rug.*

TALL TULIPS *(top) are a characteristic Ladik motif.*

MUHAMMAD ON HIS PRAYER RUG *is depicted in a Persian miniature.*

Patterns For Prayer

Prayer, the single act most essential to a Muslim's faith, brought into use rugs unlike any others. Prayer rugs, generally large enough for one person, made sacred the area the worshiper used. Each had a central panel that contained at least one pointed niche resembling the *mihrab* or prayer niche in a mosque. Above it was a rectangle that the worshiper touched with his forehead. The decorations often included other mosque motifs: hanging lamps, elaborate archways, inscriptions from the Koran.

Five times daily the good Muslim spread his rug with its niche facing toward Mecca, prostrated himself, and intoned his devotions. A prayer rug, like the Turkish ones shown here, is to this day the one piece of property that all good Muslims must own.

FLOWERED COLUMNS *line the niche of a rug from Ghiordes in Turkey. Like many other prayer rugs, it is bordered with abstract floral motifs.*

ORNAMENTAL FRIEZES *made of narrow strips of carpeting are wound around the tops of Persian tents. Other rugs adorn the tent walls and floors.*

OCTAGONAL MOTIFS, *called "camels' hooves," woven into a 13th Century Konya carpet, resemble those on the tent frieze in the miniature above.*

A COLORFUL DONKEY BAG, *made of carpeting in Persia's*

Carpets for Traveling

Wandering was a way of life for many Muslims, and as they roamed their rugs traveled with them in special ways. Knotted pile carpets made like saddle bags *(below)* were laid across the backs of camels, horses and donkeys to carry the nomads' possessions. Inside their tents special carpet bags, stuffed with household items and clothing, functioned as bureaus and cupboards, and as cushions on which to rest. The nomads made this "furniture" for themselves on small portable looms, which they packed and took with them, like their carpets, when they moved.

Shiraz region, carried nomads' food, clothing and sometimes their little children. The weave usually was coarse and loose but sturdily utilitarian.

A Jewel Worthy of a King

The creation of the brilliant, many-faceted carpet below, once the property of the House of Habsburg, has been whimsically associated with a charming Persian fairy tale. Long ago, the story goes, a thief was running off with a king's

most precious diamond when, suddenly, it fell on a rock and shattered. The grieving monarch ordered a carpet woven that would look like a landscape strewn with the pieces from his favorite stone; such a medallion carpet was the result. Whatever its origins, experts consider this 16th Century Mamluk rug, made in Cairo of finely knotted silk in kaleidoscopic colors, a supreme achievement of Oriental carpet making, and one of the finest carpets in the world.

CROSSROAD CIVILIZATIONS BETWEEN EAST AND WEST

This chart is designed to show the duration of the Islamic and Ottoman Empires, and relate them to others in the "Crossroad" group of cultures considered in one major group of volumes of this series. The chart is excerpted from a comprehensive world chronology which appears in the introductory booklet to the series. Comparison of the chart seen here with the world chronology will enable the reader to relate the crossroad civilizations to important cultures in other parts of the world.

On the following pages is a chronological listing of important events that took place in the period covered by this book.

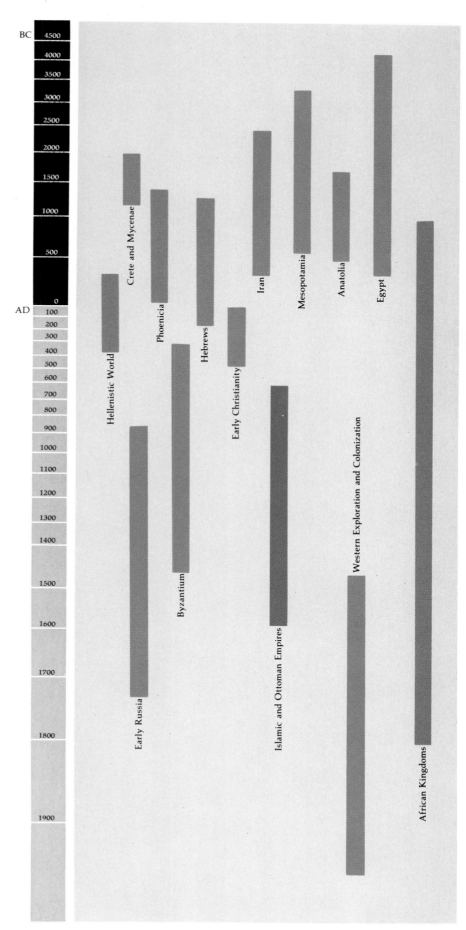

CHRONOLOGY: A listing of significant events during the Islamic era.

Muhammad and the Caliphate

THE BIRTH OF ISLAM

570 Muhammad is born in Mecca
595 Muhammad marries Khadija, a wealthy widow
610 In seclusion on Mount Hira, Muhammad has his first revelation through the angel Gabriel, telling him he is the Prophet of God
622 Muslims migrate to Medina in the famed Hijra or Hegira
624 The Muslims defeat the Meccans at Badr
630 Mecca is conquered and becomes the spiritual center of Islam
632 After conducting the "Farewell Pilgrimage" to Mecca, Muhammad dies in the house of his wife A'isha in Medina

THE FIRST FOUR CALIPHS

632 Abu Bakr, A'isha's father, becomes the first caliph
634 On the death of Abu Bakr, Umar is named caliph
644 Umar is murdered and Uthman comes to power
656 Uthman is murdered and is succeeded by Ali; civil war begins
657 Mu'awiya, governor of Syria, challenges Ali's rule and they fight an indecisive battle near Siffin
661 A Kharijite zealot murders Ali at the mosque in Kufa

THE UMAYYAD CALIPHATE

661 Mu'awiya becomes caliph, establishing his capital at Damascus
680 Death of Mu'awiya and accession of his son Yazid; massacre of Ali's son Husayn and his tiny force at Kerbela
717 Umar II begins his rule and initiates internal reforms
747 The Abbasids overthrow the Umayyad governor of Persia
750 Abbas defeats Marwan II, ending Umayyad rule

THE ABBASID CALIPHATE

750 Abbas becomes caliph and makes Hashimiya his capital
754 Abbas is succeeded by his brother Mansur
762 Mansur founds Baghdad as the new capital
786 Accession of Harun al-Rashid to the caliphate
803 Harun murders the Barmakid Ja'far, deposing the family whose members had been viziers for generations
809 Harun dies and war breaks out between his two sons
813 Harun's son Ma'mun defeats his brother and becomes caliph
827 Mu'tazilite teachings become state doctrine for 22 years
833 Mu'tasim becomes caliph and guards himself with Turkish slaves

The Course of Empire

633 The Muslims conquer Syria and Iraq
639 The Muslims begin their conquest of Egypt
640 Persia comes under Muslim rule

670 Qayrawan is made the capital of the province of North Africa

711 Muslims invade the Iberian Peninsula and the Indus valley
732 Charles Martel, Frankish ruler, halts Muslims near Poitiers
738 Existence of Arab merchant colony reported at Canton, China
740 Muslims establish colony at Kilwa, in East Africa

756 The Umayyad Abd al-Rahman founds the Emirate of Cordoba

788 Morocco becomes independent under the Idrisid dynasty
799 Tunisia reaches independence during Aghlabid rule

825 The Aghlabids start the conquest of Sicily

The Islamic Culture

500 Pre-Islamic poetry flourishes in Arabia
600
608 The Kaaba in Mecca is built as the main shrine in Arabia
622 In Medina, Muhammad builds his house, which serves as a gathering place for his followers and as a model for future mosques

650 Uthman establishes an official version of the Koran

670 The Great Mosque of Qayrawan is founded by Uqba ibn Nafi'
691 Caliph Abd al-Malik erects Dome of the Rock in Jerusalem
696 Arab coinage is introduced and Arabic becomes the official administrative language of Islam
705 Caliph Walid begins to build the Great Mosque of Damascus

744 The Umayyads construct the palace of Mshatta

751 The Arabs learn paper-making from captured Chinese prisoners

765 Jurjis ibn Bakhtishu' founds a school of medicine in Baghdad
767 Abu Hanifa, creator of Hanafi school of law, dies in jail
785 Abd al-Rahman builds the Great Mosque of Cordoba
795 Malik ibn Anas, creator of the Maliki-school of law, dies

813 Caliph Ma'mun's reign marks flourishing of the mathematician Khwarizmi, the translator Hunayn and the philosopher Kindi
814 Shafi'i, founder of the Shafi'i school of law, goes to Egypt, where he writes his important treatise, the Risala
815 Death of Abu Nuwas, renowned poet at the Abbasid court

830 Caliph Ma'mun founds the "House of Wisdom" in Baghdad
833 Ahmad ibn Hanbal, leader of the Traditionist movement, is imprisoned for refusing to accept Mu'tazilite doctrine

851 Earliest Arabic description of China and the Indian coast
870 Death of Bukhari, famed for his collection of Traditions
876 In Cairo, Ibn Tulun builds a mosque bearing his name

921 Earliest Arabic description of Russia by Ibn Fadlan
922 Hallaj, Sufi mystic and martyr, is executed for heresy
925 Death of Razi (Rhazes), famed medieval physician, author of the first medical treatise on smallpox
948 The poet Mutanabbi named panegyrist to the ruler of Aleppo
970 Fatimids build the mosque-university of al-Azhar in Cairo
1010 The Persian poet Firdawsi completes his *Epic of Kings*
1030 Biruni writes his *Description of India*
1037 Death of Ibn Sina (Avicenna), philosopher and physician
1067 Vizier Nizam al-Mulk establishes the Nizamiyya Madrasa in Baghdad, and Ash'arism becomes the orthodox theology
1090 Chinese text makes first mention of Arabs using compass
1096 Ghazali, mystic and theologian, begins his greatest work, *The Revival of the Religious Sciences*
1123 Omar Khayyam, poet and astronomer, dies
1154 The geographer Idrisi compiles *The Pleasure of the Ardent Enquirer* which includes his circular map of the world
1171 Ibn Rushd (Averroes) writes *Middle Commentary on Aristotle*

1259 Hulagu Khan sets up an observatory at Maragha, Persia
1273 Jalal al-Din Rumi, Persian mystic and poet, dies
1325 Ibn Battuta sets out on his famous travels from Tangiers
1353 Most of the Alhambra is completed in Granada, Spain
1375 Ibn Khaldun, great Muslim historian, begins the *Muqaddima*
1390 Death of Hafiz, the great Persian lyric poet

1522 The Persian miniature painter Bizhad heads Safavid Library

1611 Shah Abbas I lays out a new capital at Isfahan, Persia
1648 Taj Mahal is completed as mausoleum for Shah Jahan's wife

1901 Muhammad Iqbal, an Indian Muslim poet, publishes in Lahore

1926 The Egyptian Taha Husein writes his autobiography, *The Days*
1928 The Latin alphabet is adopted in Turkey

868 Ibn Tulun founds the dynasty of the Tulunids in Egypt
892 Samarra is abandoned and Baghdad again becomes the capital
910 The Shi'ite Fatimids seize North Africa and reign as caliphs
912 Islam well-established among Bulgars on the Volga
929 The Emirate of Cordoba becomes a third caliphate
945 The Persian Buyids take Baghdad and control the empire
969 Fatimids conquer Egypt and Cairo is built as their capital
970 The Seljuk Turks become Muslims and occupy most of Persia
998 Mahmud of Ghazna annexes parts of Persia and Northern India
1010 The ruler of Gao, on the Middle Niger, converts to Islam
1030 The Umayyad caliphate of Spain breaks up into small kingdoms
1055 The Seljuks seize Baghdad, retaining the Abbasids as rulers
1071 Battle of Manzikert; Seljuks take Asia Minor from the Byzantines
1085 Christians take Toledo and begin reconquest of Spain
1087 Mulsims build Timbuktu as a center of commerce and learning
1096 Crusaders reach Constantinople and advance southward
1099 Crusaders capture Jerusalem
1171 Saladin overthrows Fatimids and re-establishes orthodoxy
1187 Saladin defeats the Crusaders at Hittin and takes Jerusalem
1211 The Turk Iletmish establishes the Delhi sultanate

1221 On orders of the Great Khan, the Mongols ravage Persia
1258 The Mongol Hulagu Khan takes Baghdad, ending Abbasid rule

1260 The Mamluk sultanate controls Egypt and Syria
1292 Marco Polo discovers a Muslim kingdom on Sumatra
1345 Ibn Battuta discloses Islam's progress in Malaya

1492 Granada falls to the Christians; Ferdinand and Isabella burn Muslim libraries and expel Muslims and Jews

1526 At the battle of Panipat, Babur conquers the Delhi sultanate and founds the Mughal empire
1556 Akbar becomes emperor and expands the Mughal empire
1583 Expansion of Islam to Philippines, Celebes and New Guinea
1757 Robert Clive defeats the Nawab of Bengal, initiating British rule in India
1803 The British occupy Delhi but retain puppet Mughal emperors

1906 Revolution in Persia leads to a constitutional monarchy

ISLAM AFTER 1258

1260 Mamluks halt Mongols at Goliath's Well
1295 Ghazan Khan, Mongol ruler of Persia, is converted to Islam
1379 Timur the Lame (Tamerlane) invades Persia from the North
1453 The Ottoman Turks take Constantinople from the Byzantines
1498 Vasco da Gama sails to India via the Cape of Good Hope
1502 Isma'il the Safavid creates a Persian empire, takes the title of Shah and imposes Shi'ism as state religion
1520 Suleyman the Magnificent begins his 46-year reign
1535 Special trading rights are granted to France by Suleyman
1683 Ottoman siege of Vienna fails
1699 Treaty of Karlowitz: Ottomans lose territories in Europe
1798 Napoleon occupies Egypt, bringing scientific expedition there
1805 Muhammad Ali becomes undisputed ruler of Egypt
1826 Mahmud massacres the Janissaries and begins reforms
1881 The British occupy Egypt, French occupy Tunisia
1908 Young Turks revolt and create parliamentary rule
1922 Mustapha Kemal (Ataturk) begins reform programs leading to the creation of the Republic of Turkey

BIBLIOGRAPHY

These books were selected during the preparation of this volume for their interest and authority, and for their usefulness to readers seeking additional information on specific points.

An asterisk (*) marks works available in both hard-cover and paperback editions; a dagger (†) indicates availability only in paperback.

GENERAL HISTORY

Arnold, Thomas W., and Alfred Guillaume, eds., *The Legacy of Islam.* Oxford University Press, 1931.
Bovill, E. W., *The Golden Trade of the Moors.* Oxford University Press, 1958.
Brockelmann, Carl, *History of the Islamic Peoples.*† Capricorn Books, 1960.
The Encyclopaedia of Islam:
   Vols. I-IV. 1st ed. Leiden, E. J. Brill, 1913-1942.
   Vols. I-II, and Fascicles 41-46. New ed. Leiden, E. J. Brill, 1960-1966.
Esin, Emel, *Mecca the Blessed, Madinah the Radiant.* London, Elek Books, 1963.
Gibb, H.A.R., and Harold Bowen, *Islamic Society and the West.* Vol. 1. Oxford University Press, 1950 (pt. 1) and 1957 (pt. 2).
Glubb, John B., *The Great Arab Conquests.* Prentice-Hall, 1963.
Hitti, Philip K., *History of the Arabs.** 8th ed. Macmillan, 1964.
Ikram, S. M., *Muslim Civilization in India.* Ed. by A. T. Embree. Columbia University Press, 1964.
Landau, Rom, *Islam and the Arabs.* Macmillan, 1959.
Lane, Edward W., *Arabian Society in the Middle Ages.* London, Chatto, 1883.
Levy, Reuben, *The Social Structure of Islam.** Cambridge University Press, 1957.
Lewis, Bernard:
   *The Arabs in History.** Harper Torchbooks, 1960.
   The Emergence of Modern Turkey. Oxford University Press, 1961.
Mez, Adam, *The Renaissance of Islam.* Transl. by Salahuddin Khuda Bakhsh and D. S. Margoliouth. Patna, India, Jubilee Printing and Publishing House, 1937.
Rauf, M. A., *A Brief History of Islam.*† Oxford University Press, 1964.
Roolvink, Roelof, ed., *Historical Atlas of the Muslim Peoples.* Harvard University Press, 1958.
Schroeder, Eric, *Muhammad's People: An Anthology of Muslim Civilization.* Bond Wheelwright Co., 1955.
Sordo, Enrique, *Moorish Spain: Cordoba, Seville, Granada.* London, Elek Books, 1963.
Spuler, Bertold, *The Muslim World.* Transl. by F.R.C. Bagley. 2 vols. Leiden, E. J. Brill, 1960.
Stewart-Robinson, J., ed., *The Traditional Near East.*† Prentice-Hall, 1966.
Von Grunebaum, Gustave E., *Medieval Islam.** University of Chicago Press, 1953.
Von Grunebaum, Gustave E., ed., *Unity and Variety in Muslim Civilization.* University of Chicago Press, 1955.
Watt, W. Montgomery, and Pierre Cachia, *A History of Islamic Spain.* Edinburgh University Press, 1965.

ART AND ARCHITECTURE

Arnold, Thomas W., *Painting in Islam.*† Dover Publications, 1965.
Creswell, K.A.C., *A Short Account of Early Muslim Architecture.*† Penguin Books, 1958.
Dilley, Arthur U., *Oriental Rugs and Carpets.* Rev. ed. by Maurice S. Dimand. J. B. Lippincott, 1959.
Dimand, Maurice S., *A Handbook of Muhammadan Art.* 3rd ed. Metropolitan Museum of Art, 1958.
Erdmann, Kurt, *Oriental Carpets.* Transl. by Charles G. Ellis. Universe Books, 1962.
Ettinghausen, Richard:
   Arab Painting. Skira, World Publishing Co., 1962.
   Turkish Miniatures from the 13th to the 18th Century. New American Library, 1965.
Gray, Basil, *Persian Painting.* Skira, World Publishing Co., 1961.
Grube, Ernst J., *The World of Islam.* McGraw-Hill, 1967.
Hill, Derek, and Oleg Grabar, *Islamic Architecture and Its Decoration.* University of Chicago Press, 1964.
Kühnel, Ernst, *Islamic Art and Architecture.* Transl. by Katherine Watson. Cornell University Press, 1966.

Liebetrau, Preben, *Oriental Rugs in Colour.* Macmillan, 1962.
Luken, Marie G., *Islamic Art.*† The Metropolitan Museum of Art, 1965.
Pope, Arthur Upham:
   Masterpieces of Persian Art. Dryden Press, 1945.
   Persian Architecture. George Braziller, 1965.
Sebag, Paul, *The Great Mosque of Kairouan.* Transl. by Richard Howard. Macmillan, 1965.
Wilkinson, Charles K., ed., *Iranian Ceramics.* Harry N. Abrams, 1963.

LITERATURE, SCIENCE AND THOUGHT

Arberry, Arthur J., *Classical Persian Literature.* Macmillan, 1958.
Browne, E. G., *Arabian Medicine.* Cambridge University Press, 1962.
Campbell, Donald, *Arabian Medicine and its Influence on the Middle Ages.* 2 vols. London, Kegan Paul, Trench, Trubner & Co., 1926.
Campbell, Joseph, ed., *The Arabian Nights.** Viking Press, 1962.
De Boer, T. J., *The History of Philosophy in Islam.*† Dover Paperback, 1965.
Dunlop, D. M., *Arabic Science in the West.* Karachi, Pakistan Historical Society, 1967.
Gibb, H.A.R., *Arabic Literature.* 2nd ed. Oxford University Press, 1963.
Gibb, H.A.R., ed., *The Travels of Ibn Battuta, A.D. 1325-1354.* Cambridge University Press, 1958-1962.
Hourani, Albert, *Arabic Thought in the Liberal Age, 1798-1939.* Oxford University Press, 1962.
Hourani, George, *Arab Seafaring.* Verry, Lawrence Inc., 1963.
Ibn Khaldun, *The Muqaddimah.* Transl. by Franz Rosenthal. 3 vols. Pantheon Books, 1958.
Khayyam, Omar, *Rubaiyat.* Transl. by Edward Fitzgerald.* Peter Pauper Press, 1949.
Kritzeck, James, ed., *Anthology of Islamic Literature.** Holt, Rinehart & Winston, 1964.
Nicholson, Reynold A., *A Literary History of the Arabs.* Cambridge University Press, 1962.
Rosenthal, E.I.J., *Political Thought in Medieval Islam.** Cambridge University Press, 1958.
Sarton, George, *Introduction to the History of Science.* 3 vols. William & Wilkins, 1927, 1931, 1947.

RELIGION

Andrae, Tor, *Mohammed, the Man and his Faith.** Harper & Row, 1960.
Arberry, Arthur J., transl., *The Koran Interpreted.** Macmillan, 1955.
Arberry, Arthur J., *Sufism.* London, G. Allen & Unwin, 1950.
Coulson, N. J., *A History of Islamic Law.* Edinburgh University Press, 1964.
Gaudefroy-Demombynes, Maurice, *Muslim Institutions.* Barnes & Noble, 1961.
Gibb, H.A.R.:
   Modern Trends in Islam. University of Chicago Press, 1947.
   *Mohammedanism: An Historical Survey.** Oxford University Press, 1953.
Guillaume, Alfred, *Islam.** Barnes & Noble, 1964.
Guillaume, Alfred, transl., *The Life of Muhammad.* Oxford University Press, 1955.
Jeffery, Arthur, ed., *Reader on Islam.* The Hague, Mouton & Co., 1962.
Nicholson, Reynold A., *The Mystics of Islam.* London, Routledge & Kegan Paul, 1914.
Pickthall, Mohammed M., ed., *The Meaning of the Glorious Koran.*† New American Library, 1954.
Schacht, Joseph, *An Introduction to Islamic Law.* Oxford University Press, 1964.
Von Grunebaum, Gustave E., *Muhammadan Festivals.* Henry Schuman, 1951.
Watt, W. Montgomery:
   Islamic Philosophy and Theology. Edinburgh University Press, 1962.
   *Muhammad, Prophet and Statesman.** Oxford University Press, 1961.
   Muslim Intellectual: A Study of Al-Ghazali. Edinburgh University Press, 1963.

ACKNOWLEDGMENTS

For the help given in the preparation of this book, the editors are particularly indebted to R. Bayly Winder, Chairman, Department of Near Eastern Languages and Literatures, New York University; Jeanette Wakin, Committee on Oriental Studies, Columbia University; Richard Ettinghausen, Professor of Fine Arts, New York University; and Muhammad Abdul Rauf, Director, Islamic Foundation of New York. The editors also express their gratitude to the following advisers: Frederick G. Kilgour, Yale University Library; Richard Van Gelder, Chairman, Department of Mammalogy, The American Museum of Natural History; John Plummer, Curator, Medieval and Renaissance Manuscripts, The Pierpont Morgan Library; George C. Miles, Director, The American Numismatic Society; Jeremiah F. O'Sullivan, Professor of Medieval History, Fordham University; Ernst J. Grube, Curator, Islamic Art, The Metropolitan Museum of Art; Richard E. Fuller, Seattle Art Museum; Raffaello Causa, Superintendent, Soprintendenza Alle Gallerie della Campania, Naples; Umberto Scerrato, Università Degli Studi, Naples; Francesco Gabrielli, Università Degli Studi, Rome; Luciano Berti, Director, Museo Nazionale del Bargello, Florence; Enrico Pistolesi, Opera del Primaziale, Pisa; Antonio Gallego Morell, Delegación Provincial de Información y Turismo, Granada; Jesús Bermudez, Director, Museo de la Alhambra, Granada; Angustias Moreno Olmedo, Biblioteca de la Alhambra, Granada; Fray Dario Cabanelas Rodriguez, O.F.M., Universidad de Granada; Amor Msadek, Directeur de L'Information, Secrétariat D'État aux Affaires Culturelles et à

L'Information, Tunis; Riccardo Gizdulich, La Grande Mosquée, Kairouan; Abdel Rahman Abdel Tawab, Director of Inspectorate and Excavations for Islamic and Coptic Monuments, Cairo; Ahmed Abdel Razik, Department of Antiquities, Cairo; Abdel-Raouf Ali Yousuf, Curator, Museum of Islamic Art, Cairo; Tawfig Suleyman, Director General of Antiquities, National Museum, Damascus; Bachir Zouhdi, National Museum, Damascus; Hayrullah Ors, Director, Topkapi Museum, Istanbul; Kemal Cig, Deputy Director, Topkapi Museum, Istanbul; Can Kerametli, Director, Turkish Islamic Art Museum, Istanbul; Filiz Ogutmen, Director, Topkapi Museum Library; Yusuf Durul, Deputy Director, Turkish Islamic Art Museum; Tulay Reyhanli, Chief, Ceramic Division, Turkish Islamic Art Museum; Department of Oriental Printed Books and Manuscripts, The British Museum; The Chester Beatty Library, Dublin; The Department of Oriental Antiquities, The British Museum; Department of Manuscripts, Edinburgh University Library; Bodleian Library, Oxford; Royal Scottish Museum, Edinburgh; Henriette Bessis, Chargée de Mission à L'Atelier Delacroix, Paris; Arlette Calvet, Assistante au Cabinet des Dessins, Musée du Louvre, Paris; Jean David-Weill, Conservateur aux Antiquités Musulmanes, Musée du Louvre, Paris; Monique Ricour, Chef du Service de Presse au Musée des Arts Décoratifs, Paris; Johanna Zick, Staatliche Museen zu Berlin; Friedrich Rauch, Munich; Bayerische Staatsbibliothek, Munich; Victor Griessmaier, Director, and Gerhard Egger, Oesterreichisches Museum für Angewandte Kunst, Vienna.

ART INFORMATION AND PICTURE CREDITS

The sources for the illustrations in this book are set forth below. Descriptive notes on the works of art are included. Credits for pictures positioned from left to right are separated by semicolons, from top to bottom by dashes. Photographers' names that follow a descriptive note appear in parentheses. Abbreviations include "c." for century and "ca." for circa.

Cover—Title page from the *Kamseh* by Nizami, Persian, Herat School, ca. 1450, The Metropolitan Museum of Art, Gift of Alexander Smith Cochran, 1913. 8-9—Map by Murray Tinkelman.

CHAPTER 1: 10—Photograph by Roloff Beny. 13—Map by Rafael D. Palacios. 16—Detail of pilgrim scroll, Ms. Add. 27566, British Museum, London (Derek Bayes). 21 through 29—All illustrations from Turkish version of the *Siyar-i-Nabi* (Progress of the Prophet), 16th c. 21—Ms. Hazine 1222, folio 151, courtesy Topkapi Museum, Istanbul (Ara Güler). 22—Ms. Hazine 1221, folios 196; 200; 216b; 214-223, courtesy Topkapi Museum, Istanbul (Ara Güler). 23—Ms. Hazine 1222, folios 30; 158, courtesy Topkapi Museum, Istanbul (Ara Güler). 24-25—Ms. Hazine 1222, folio 382, courtesy Topkapi Museum (Ara Güler)—folios 3 recto; 5 recto—6 verso, courtesy The New York Public Library, The Spencer Collection (Lee Boltin). 26—Ms. Hazine 1222, folio 189a, courtesy Topkapi Museum, Istanbul (Ara Güler); folios 190 verso; 161 verso—136 recto, courtesy The New York Public Library, The Spencer Collection (Lee Boltin). 27—Folios 303 recto—309 recto; 319 recto, courtesy The New York Public Library, The Spencer Collection (Lee Boltin). 28—Folios 343 verso—350 recto; 356 verso, courtesy The New York Public Library, The Spencer Collection (Lee Boltin). 29—Folios 348 recto; 448 verso, courtesy The New York Public Library, The Spencer Collection (Lee Boltin)—Ms. Hazine 1223, folio 408, courtesy Topkapi Museum, Istanbul (Ara Güler).

CHAPTER 2: 30—Page from a Koran, Persian, 11th-12th c., Iran Bastan Museum, Teheran (Fernand Bourges). 32—Illustration from the *Qisas-al-Anbiya*, Persian, probably late 16th c., folio 225, courtesy The Chester Beatty Library, Dublin. 34—Diagram drawing by Gamal El-Zoghby. 39—Ceramic dish from Nishapur, Persia, 9th c., Collection Foroughi, Teheran (Photo Bulloz). 41 through 51—All photographs by Roloff Beny except p. 46, bottom (Anderson, Rome).

CHAPTER 3: 52—Photograph by Roloff Beny. 54-55—Map by Rafael D. Palacios. 59—Illustration from the *Zubdat al-Tawarikh* (Cream of Chronologies), Turkish, ca. 1600, Ms. 423, folio 21b, courtesy The Chester Beatty Library, Dublin. 62—*Dirham*, silver coin, from Cordoba, Spain, 722-723, courtesy The American Numismatic Society. 65—Photograph by John Lewis Stage. 66-67—Photograph by Dmitri Kessel; photograph by Larry Sherman from Black Star. 68-69—Photograph by Elmar Schneiwind from Rapho Guillumette; photograph by Tor Eigeland from Black Star. 70-71—Photograph by Eliot Elisofon; photograph by Sabine Weiss from Rapho Guillumette. 72-73—Photograph by Bruce Davidson from Magnum. 74-75—Photograph by Elliott Erwitt from Magnum; photograph by James Burke. 76-77—Photograph by James Burke.

CHAPTER 4: 78—Ceramic bowl from Kashan or Rayy, Persia, 13th c., courtesy of the Smithsonian Institution, Freer Gallery of Art, Washington, D.C. (Fernand Bourges). 83—Chessman, ivory, Persian, 11th-12th c., The Metropolitan Museum of Art, Purchase 1965, Gustavus A. Pfeiffer Fund. 84-85—Page from *Kitab Suwar al-Kawakib ath-Thabita* (Treatise on the Fixed Stars) by as-Sufi, from Ceuta, Morocco, 1224, Ms. Ross. 1033 folio 64 verso, Vatican Library. 86—Koran stand, from Persia or West Turkestan, wood, 1360, The Metropolitan Museum of Art, Rogers Fund, 1910. 89 through 99—Illustrations from the *Maqamat* of al-Hariri, painted by Yahya ibn Mahmud al-Wasiti, from Baghdad, Iraq, 1237, Ms. Arabe 5847 (Schefer Hariri), folios 120 verso, 152 recto, 5 verso, 4 verso, 105 recto, 125 recto, 19 recto, 33, 11 verso, 94 verso, 29 verso, Bibliothèque Nationale, Paris.

CHAPTER 5: 100—Griffin, bronze, Egyptian, Fatimid period, 12th c., courtesy of the Opera del Primaziale, Pisa (Erich Lessing from Magnum). 105—Hawk and duck, fragment from stucco wall decoration, from Rayy, Persia, 11th c., courtesy of Museum of Fine Arts, Boston. 106-107—Coronation cloak of Roger II of Sicily, silk with gold, pearls and gems, made by Egyptian artists, Fatimid period, in Palermo, 1133-1134, Schatzkammer, Kunsthistorisches Museum, Vienna (Erich Lessing from Magnum). 109—Detail of page from a Koran, Egypt, 8th-9th c.—detail of page from a Koran, Egypt, 9th-10th c.—detail of page from a Koran, Arabic, 14th c., courtesy of the Smithsonian Institution, Freer Gallery of Art, Washington, D.C. 111—Doorknocker, bronze, Northern Iraq, ca. 1300, Staatliche Museen zu Berlin, Islamische Abteilung. 112—Rose-water sprinkler, silver-gilt, height about 10 inches, Persian, 12th c., courtesy of the Smithsonian Institution, Freer Gallery of Art, Washington, D.C.; jar from Raqqa, Syria, 12th-13th c., height about 9 inches, The Metropolitan Museum of Art, Bequest of Horace Havemeyer, 1956, The H. O. Havemeyer Collection. 113—Gilded bronze object, possibly a buckle, about 2½ inches high, Persian, 11th-12th c., Musée Guimet, Paris (Giraudon, Paris)—incense burner, bronze with turquoise, height about 10 inches, Egypt, 15th c., Louvre, Paris (Eddy Van Der Veen); plate, from Nishapur, Persia, 10th c., courtesy of the Smithsonian Institution, Freer Gallery of Art, Washington, D.C. 114—Box, ivory with silver filigree hinges and paste glass gems, about 2½ inches high, Museo Nazionale del Bargello, Florence, Carrand Collection (Paolo Tosi)—knife, bronze, about 10 inches long, probably Egyptian, 14th c., Museo e Gallerie Nazionali di Capodimonte (Aldo Durazzi)—bracelet, gold, Persian, 11th-12th c., courtesy of the Smithsonian Institution, Freer Gallery of Art, Washington, D.C. 115—necklace pendant, gold with filigree work, height about 2 inches, Egypt, Fatimid period, 12th c., Museo Nazionale del Bargello, Florence, Carrand Collection (Paolo Tosi)—ceramic bowl from Rayy, Persia, early 13th c., courtesy of the Smithsonian Institution, Freer Gallery of Art, Washington, D.C. 116-117—Ewer, bronze, about 15½ inches high, Persian, 8th c., The Metropolitan Museum of Art, Samuel D. Lee Fund, 1941; bottle, glass, blown and carved, about 4½ inches high, from Gurgan, Persia, ca. 1200, Seattle Art Museum, Eugene Fuller Memorial Collection; ceremonial knife or saw, bronze, about 14 inches long, from Gurgan, Persia, 12th c., Seattle Art Museum, Gift of Mrs. John C. Atwood, Jr.—ceramic bowl from Kashan, Persia, early 13th c., courtesy of the Smithsonian Institution, Freer Gallery of Art, Washington, D.C.; inkpot, brass, inlaid with silver, about 2½ inches high, from Mosul, Iraq, mid-13th c., Museo e Gallerie Nazionali di Capodimonte (Aldo Durazzi). 118-119—Coffer, bronze with applied gilt figures, height, 7½ inches, Persian, 1197, Museum of Fine Arts, Boston, The Holmes Collection (Ken Kay); lamp, glass with enamel colors and gilding, height about 8¼ inches, Syrian, 13th c., by courtesy of the Victoria and Albert Museum, London—key, bronze with gold inlay, Egypt, 15th c., Louvre, Paris (Eddy Van Der Veen); ceramic ewer, height, 13¾ inches, from Gurgan, Persia, early 13th c., Museum of Fine Arts, Boston, The Holmes Collection (Ken Kay).

CHAPTER 6: 120—Illustration from Ms. of *Automata* (Treatise of Abu'l Izz Isma'il al-Jazari), Egypto-Arabic, Mamluk School, probably from Cairo, ca. 1315, The Metropolitan Museum of Art, Rogers Fund, 1955. 126—Astrolabe, brass, Yemenite, ca. 1296, The Metropolitan Museum of Art, Bequest of Edward C. Moore, 1891. 131 through 139—Illustrations from the *Manafi' al-Hayawan (The Advantages Derived from Animals)* by Ibn Bakhtishu', Persian, ca. 1295, Ms. 500, folios 55, 19, 11, 13, 18, 24, 16 verso, 37 verso, 14 verso, courtesy of The Pierpont Morgan Library (Hans Lippmann).

CHAPTER 7: 140—Illustration from the *Aja'ib ul-Makhlukat (The Marvels of Creation)* by Qasvini, Turkish, probably 16th c., Ms. Add. 7894, folio 59b, The British Museum, London, (John Freeman). 146—Map by Rafael D. Palacios. 149 through 161—Photographs by David Lees.

CHAPTER 8: 162—Portrait of Sultan Muhammad II, the Conqueror, by Sinan Bey, Turkish, late 15th c., Topkapi Museum, Istanbul (photo by Dudley, Hardin and Yang from exhibition "Art Treasures of Turkey" circulated by the Smithsonian Institution, at Seattle Art Museum). 164—Map by Rafael D. Palacios. 168—Trousers, riveted mail, with plates of steel inlaid with gold, on base of leather and linen, Persian, 18th c., by the courtesy of the Royal Scottish Museum, Edinburgh (Tom Scott). 171—Detail of carpet border, wool, from Konya, Turkey, 13th c., Turkish Islamic Art Museum, Istanbul (Giraudon, Paris). 172-173—Illustration from the *Kamseh* by Nizami, from Herat, Persia, 16th c., Ms. 8, folio 64a, The Metropolitan Museum of Art, Gift of Alexander Smith Cochran (Lee Boltin); medallion carpet from Uschak, Turkey, wool, about 9 x 14 feet, ca. 1600, Oesterreichisches Museum für Angewandte Kunst, Vienna (Erich Lessing from Magnum); "Portuguese" carpet, wool, about 22½ x 12½ feet, Persian, 17th c., Oesterreichisches Museum für Angewandte Kunst, Vienna (Erich Lessing from Magnum). 174-175—Illustration from the *Shah-Nameh* by Firdausi, from Isfahan, Persia, 17th c., Ms. 3, folio 475b, The Metropolitan Museum of Art, Gift of Alexander Smith Cochran (Lee Boltin); "Garden" carpet, wool, about 8½ x 4½ feet, Persian, 17th c., Musée des Arts Décoratifs, Paris (Sabine Weiss from Rapho Guillumette). 176—Prayer carpet, wool, from Ladik, Turkey, 17th c., Private Collection, Munich (Robert Braunmüller)—prayer carpet, wool, about 4 x 6 feet, from Ladik, Turkey, 18th c., Musée des Arts Décoratifs, Paris (Sabine Weiss from Rapho Guillumette); Illustration from Ms. Or. 8755, folio 4, Persian, 1453, courtesy of the Trustees of the British Museum, London. 177—Prayer carpet, wool, from Ghiordes, Turkey, 18th c., Oesterreichisches Museum für Angewandte Kunst, Vienna (Erich Lessing from Magnum). 178-179—Illustration from Ms. Elliott 149, folio 226a, from Shiraz, Persia, 16th c., Bodleian Library, Oxford—carpet fragment, wool, from Konya, Turkey, 13th c., Turkish Islamic Museum, Istanbul (Ara Güler); camel and driver, Persian, Herat School, late 15th c., courtesy of the Smithsonian Institution, Freer Gallery of Art, Washington, D.C.; donkey bag, wool, from Shiraz, Persia, 18th c., Oesterreichisches Museum für Angewandte Kunst, Vienna (Erich Lessing from Magnum). 180-181—Mamluk carpet, silk, about 17 feet, 9 inches by 9 feet, 6 inches, from Cairo, Egypt, early 16th c., Oesterreichisches Museum für Angewandte Kunst, Vienna (Erich Lessing from Magnum).

INDEX

This symbol in front of a page number indicates an illustration of the subject mentioned.

MAPS IN THIS VOLUME

A View of the Islamic World (632-1258)	8-9
Pre-Islamic Trade Routes	13
The Expansion of Islam to 750	54-55
Crusader States	146
The Turkish Heirs to Islam	164

A

Abbasid party, 63-64
Abbas, Caliph, leads Abbasid party, 63; moves capital of Islam, 79, 103; proclaimed caliph, 64
Abbasid dynasty, 53, 64, 79, 142, 147; allows Christians access to Palestine, 145; architectural development under, 103; autocratic rule of, 81; brief revival of empire, 164; end of rule, 87-88; last ruler of, 166; moves Islam's capital to Iraq, 79, 103; palaces of, 104; prosperity under, 83; revenge on the Umayyads, 64
Abd al-Rahman ("the Falcon of the Quraysh"), 64, 87; establishes Umayyad state in Cordoba, 142
Abdullah (father of Muhammad), 14
Abdullah (Persian general), 64
Abdullah ibn Masud, *26
Abraham (prophet), 25, 32
Abu Ayyub, *28
Abu Bakr (*Khalifat Rasul Allah*), 20, *26, *27, *28, 33, *59; becomes one of Muhammad's first converts, 16; character, 54; death of, 57; as first caliph, 54; generals of, 56; military conquests of, 56; names successor, 57; physical appearance, 54; and the *ridda* wars, 54; suppresses rebellion of Arab tribes, 54
Abulcasis (physician), 125
Abu Jahl, *26
Abu Muslim, 64
Abu Nuwas (poet), 108
Abu Talib (uncle of Muhammad), 14, 17, 59
Abu Yaqub Yusuf, 125
Abu'l-Hajjaj, Sultan, 157
Abyssinia, 14; attacks Mecca, *22; King of, 14; *map* 13; as a refuge for persecuted Muslims, 17
Acre, *maps* 13, 146
Adam (prophet), 32
Aden, *maps* 13, 164
Adrianople, *map* 164
Afghani. *See* Jamal al-Din al-Afghani
Afghanistan, *75
Africa, 130; circumnavigation of, 167; invaded by the Ottomans, 165; Islam as a major cultural force in, 148; Islamic empire in, 11; trade with Islam, 83, 97; influence of Muslim traders and teachers, 148; Muslim university established, 141; trade routes to, *map* 13. *See also* North Africa
Aghlabids, 144
Agra, India, 148
A'isha (daughter of Abu Bakr and wife of Muhammad), 20, 54, 105; enmity with Ali, 60
Ajnadain, 56
Al-Andalus. *See* Spain
Al-Azhar (Muslim university in Cairo), 148, 165, 169
Albania, conquered by Muhammad II, 163
Alchemy, 126, 127-128

Alcohol. *See* Drinking habits
Aleppo, Syria, *68, 166; *maps* 8, 13, 55, 146, 165
Alexander the Great, 141-142, 148
Alexandria, Egypt, 103; captured by Amr, 70; falls to Islam, 58; *maps* 8, 13, 55
Alf Layla wa Layla. See Arabian Nights
Algebra, 128-129; developed in Islam, 12; origin of term derived from Arabic, 123
Alhambra, palace of, *149-161; Arabic inscriptions, *152-153, 157; splendor of, *158-159; women of the court, 158
Alhazen, 129
Ali, Caliph (cousin of Muhammad), *59, 63; assassination of, 61; becomes one of Muhammad's first converts, 16; defeats Kharijites in battle, 61; enmity with A'isha, 60; rebellion against, 60; rule of, 59-60; submits dispute with Mu'awiya to arbitration, 60-61; and Syrian revolt, 60-61
Allah, as chief deity of Meccans, 14. *See also* Koran, Muhammadanism
Almagest (Ptolemy), translated into Arabic, 129
Almsgiving, 36, 39
Alvaro, Bishop, quoted, 143
Amin. *See* Qasim Amin
Amina (mother of Muhammad), *22
Amr ibn al-As (Arab commander), 57, 60, 61, 70
Amu Darya, *maps* 9, 55, 164
Amusements. *See* Games and pastimes
Anatolia, 165; invaded by Mongols, 166; recaptured by Ottomans, 166; *maps* 13, 164
Anesthesia. *See* Medicine
Animals, in fact and fiction, *131-139
Antioch, 145; *maps* 55, 146
Aqaba, Gulf of, 145; *map* 146
Aquinas, Thomas, Saint, 86, 144, 145
Arabesque, 12, 105-106, 107
Arabia, 55; as an ancient trading link between the Mediterranean and the Far East, *map* 13; beginnings of Islam in, 11; as cradle of Islamic empire, 65; cultural barrenness of, 101; desert area, *65; end of tribal faction, 19; lack of public buildings, 102; lack of resources as cause of migration, 54; *maps* 9, 13, 55, 164; poverty of, 65, 66; religious influences in, 14; slavery in, 20; trade with Far East, 148; trading commodities, 97; unification of under Muhammad, 19; warriors of, 56
Arabian Nights, The, 12, 84; compilation of, 110
Arabian Sea, *maps* 13, 55
Arabic figures. *See* Numerals
Arabic language: alphabet outlawed by Kemal Ataturk, 170; Arabic words in Spanish common usage, 143; becomes the common language of Islam, 11; denounced in Spain, 143; development of, 108, 110; as the language of the Koran,

11; as the language of scholarship during the Middle Ages, 124; as the official language of the Islamic empire, 61, 110; as one of the official languages of Sicily, 145; purification of, 170; replaces Greek and Persian languages, 61; as the sacred language of the Muslims, 106
Arabs: conquer Egypt, 55; eating habits, 83, 116; expansion of empire, *map* 55; history of, 130; loss of power in Islam, 81; poetry of, 108; and political breakup of Islamic empire, 165; rebellion of tribes after Muhammad's death, 54; rustic style of life, 102; withdrawal of some tribes from Muslim state, 54. *See also* Arabia
Arafa, 38
Aral Sea, *maps* 13, 55, 164
Archimedes, 121
Architecture: achievements in, 101, 108; building materials, 102, 103, 104; concealment of functional components by decoration, 158-159; decoration considered more important than structural form, 104; decoration in, 153, 155; evolution of form, 102; evolution of Islamic style, 102; Muslim, in India, 147; religious influence in, 101; under the Seljuks, 147; trend toward ostentation under the Umayyads, 102; Turkish, 147. *See also* Decoration; Mosques; Palaces
Arioso, 143
Aristotle: Averroes' commentaries on, 125, 144; works translated into Arabic, 121, 125
Armenians, 69
Armor: chain-mail trousers, *168
Army: reorganization of, 169. *See also* Warfare
Art, 101-110; animal symbols in Islamic art, 105, 114; the arabesque, 12, 105-106, 107; bronze griffin, *100; carved ivory chessman, *83; contributions of foreign artists and craftsmen, 102; domestic articles, 83, 106-107, *111-119; embossed leaf from the Koran, *30; embroidered cape, *106-107; of India, 141-142; Islam's contributions to, 101-110; Koran stand, *86; painting of the Nativity, *32; Persian, *78, 105, 108, *176, *178; religious background of, 101, 105; representation of humans or animals forbidden, 105, 106, 111; stucco reliefs, *105, *154. *See also* Ceramics; Decoration; Miniatures; Painting
Asceticism, 86-87
Ash'ari, 86
Asia, Central, 56, 88, 147; conquered by Arabs, 75; invaded by Islam under the Umayyad dynasty, 62; Islamic empire in, 11; Mongols in, 163, 165; trade with Islam, 83, 97
Asia Minor, 165, 166
Astrolabe, use of, 129; Yemini, *126
Astrology, 80; use of astrolabe in casting horoscopes, 126
Astronomy, 105, 122; Arabic names of stars, 129; the astrolabe, *126, 129; importance of to religion, 123; Muslim researches in, 129-130; views of Sagittarius, *84
Ataturk. *See* Kemal Ataturk
Atlantic Ocean, 62, 70; *map* 54
Atlas Mountains, *70-71
Auspicious Incident, the (the massacre of the Janissaries), 169
Averroes. *See* Ibn Rushd
Avicenna, "Prince of Philosophers," *Canon of Medicine,* 124-125; invents precision device for measuring instruments, 125; investigations in physics, 125; life and work, 124-125
Aydhab, *map* 13
Ayla, *maps* 13, 146

B

Babylon, *map* 13; surrender of, 57
Backgammon, 83
Badr, 18, 36; *map* 13
Baghdad (Madinat al-Salam, "The City of Peace"), 50, 53, 87, 107, 124, 147; as administrative center of the empire, 80; building of, 80-81; caliphate returns to, 88; as capital of Islam, 53, 64, 79-80, 101; as a center of culture and science, 121, 122; cultural background of, 84; hospital, 124, 127; invaded by Seljuks, 163; *maps* 9, 164; nicknamed "the round city," 80; observatory, 129; original city lost in subsequent rebuilding, 103; pharmacies, 126-127; plan of, 80-81; poetry in, 108; sacked by Mongols, 11, 163-164, 166; splendor of, 83; as a trading center, 83, 97
Baldwin of Boulogne, crowned King of Jerusalem, 146
Balkans, the, 141, 166
Balkh, *maps* 13, 55
Banking, development of in Islam, 84; origin of word "check," 84
Barmakids, rule of, 82-83
Barqa, *map* 55
Basra (Iraq), 60; *maps* 9, 55
Battle of the Camel, 60
Bazaars, profusion of wares in, 111. *See also* Trade
Bedouins: *asabiyya* (clan spirit), 12; dynasties, 88; life of, 12; poetry of, 108; poverty of, 66; religion of, 12; shelter Muhammad, *27; victory at Yarmuk, 69; wars, 56, 63
Berbers, 75, 125, 148; Berber states; as converts to Islam, 77; invade Spain, 142
Bestiaries, *Manafi' al-Hayawan* ("The Uses of Animals"), *131-139; illumination of, 107; popularity of in Arabic world, 131
Bible: stories found in the Koran, 32
Bilal (first muezzin), 18
Biruni (scientist and traveler), 130
Birth: celebration of, 89
Black Sea, *maps* 13, 55, 146, 164
Black Stone of the Kaaba. *See* Kaaba; *Book of the Secret of Secrets* (Razi), 128
Books: Arabic books burned in Spain by Christians, 143; bookmaking, 12; guide books, 130; page from religious work, *140; possession of as a status symbol, 143; printing press established in Egypt, 168; as a treasured household possession, 107; Turkish chronology, *59. *See also* Bestiaries; Koran
Buda, Hungary, 167; *map* 164
Bukhara, *maps* 9, 13, 55
Bukhara, Sultan of, 124
Bulgaria, 169
Buyids (Persian dynasty), 88
Byzantium: attacked by Islam under Abu Bakr, 54; challenged by Islam, 11; classical ornament of, 105; conquered by Ottomans, 146, 147, 165, 166; decay of, 65; defeat at Damascus, 57; defeats Persia, 54; defeated at Yarmuk, 69; as enemy of Persia, 54; imports food from Egypt, 70; Muslim conquest of, 101, 121; as part of Islamic empire, 102; religious orthodoxy of, 84; sells slaves to Islam, 83; trading routes threatened, 13; wars with Islam, 62

C

Caesarea, 57; *map* 146
Cairo, 57, 70, 103, 145, 147, 169, 181; Guyushi Mosque, *41, *47; *maps* 8, 146, 164; massacre of Mamluks, 168;

Mosque of Ibn Tulun, *42-43, *45, *46-47, *48, *49, 103, 147; threatened by Selim the Grim, 166; university (al-Azhar), 148, 165, 169
Calendar (Islamic), 27
Caliphate: abolished by Kemal Ataturk, 170; arbitration, 60-61; duties of, 81-82; end of, 164; governors of Islam, 53; origin of designation, "Commander of the Faithful," 57; "rightly guided," 53-54. See also Abbasids; Fatimid dynasty; Kharijites; Umayyad dynasty; and names of individual caliphs throughout
Calligraphy, 12, 117, 157; as decoration on Ibn Tulun Mosque, 103; "gliding Kufic," *109; Kufic script, *39, *109, *152-153; Naskhi script, *153; revered by Muslims, 106, 153; "thuluth," *109; used as decoration on textiles, 107
Canals, use of in irrigation, 62. See also Irrigation
Canon of Medicine (Avicenna), 124-125
Caravans, 97. See also Trade
Carpets, 106, *171-181; camel cover, *178; "camels' hooves" motif, *178; garden, *174-175; Ghiordes, *177; knotting, 172; Konya, *178; Ladik, *176; lamp motif, *176; making of, 172; Mamluk, *180-181; medallion, *172-173, *180-181; in myth and legend, 180-181; octagonal motifs, *178; Persian, *173, *174-175, *178-179; prayer rugs, 171, *176, *177; role of in Islamic world, 171; royal, 172; saddle bags, *178-179; Shiraz, *178-179; silk, 172, *174-175, *180-181; supreme art of, 12; tulip motif, *176; Turkish, *171, *172-173, *176, *177; use of as tent coverings, *178; use of by nomads, 179; Ushak, *172-173
Caspian Sea, 88; maps 13, 55, 164
Castles. See Palaces
Catholic Church. See Roman Catholic Church
Central Asia. See Asia
Ceramics, 12, *117; art of, 107; Kashan, 116, *117, *119; lusterware, 107; mosaic tile, *150-151; Persian, *39, *78, *112, 113, *115; Syrian, *112
Cervantes, Miguel de, 144
Ceuta, map 54
Ceylon, trade with Islam, 83
Chanson de Roland, 143
Charlemagne, 143
Chemistry: chemical apparatus, 128; debt of modern chemistry to Islam, 127; Muslim contributions to, 12
Chess: carved ivory chessman, *83; imported from India, 83; introduced by Persians, 83; popularity in Islam, 83
China, 55, 141; earliest Islamic description of, 130; map 55; trade routes to, map 13; trade with Islam, 83, 97
Chivalry, 146; possible origin of in Muslim Cordoba, 144
Christ. See Jesus
Christianity and Christians, in Arabia, 14; assimilation of Islamic culture in Spain, 142, 143; in Byzantium, 54; Christian churches in Syria, 103; conflict with Zoroastrianism in Seventh Century, 54; Greek manuscripts translated into Syriac by Christians, 85; in Islamic Spain, map 146; in Mecca, 14; Muslim-Christian struggle in Spain, 142-143; religious activity suppressed by Islam, 58; religious practices permitted in Islam, 19; treated with restraint by Umar, 57. See also Crusades
Church of the Holy Sepulcher, Jerusalem: destruction ordered by Hakim, 145; visited by Umar, 57
Church of Hagia Sophia, 147
Coinage. See Currency
Columbus, Christopher, 145
"Commander of the Faithful." See Caliphate
Commerce. See Trade
Communications systems, 62
Constantinople, 54, 102, 122, 168, 169; captured by Ottomans, 166; conquered by Muhammad II, 163; maps 13, 146, 164; threatened by Muslims, 62

Cordoba, Spain, 125; cultural advancement under Islam, 142; Great Mosque, *46-47; maps 8, 54; taken by Muslims, 142
Crete, map 164
Crimea, map 164
Croatia, 167
Crusades, 148; accelerate flow of Eastern ideas to the West, 145; Chanson de Roland, 143; conquests of the First Crusade, map 146; Crusader states, map 146; establish pockets of Christianity, 145; impact on Islam, 145; Muslim view of, 163; purposes of, 145-146; results of, 146; targets of, 141
Ctesiphon, 54, 79, 80; maps 13, 55
Currency, 84; first Islamic, 61-62; Spanish Muslim coin, *62
Customs. See Manners
Cyprus, maps 55, 146, 164

D

Dalmatia, 167
Damascus, 60, 63, 102, 122, 147; besieged by Khalid ibn al-Walid, 56; as capital of Islam, 53, 79, 101; captured by Mongols, 166; falls to Arabs, 57; as focal point of Islam, 61; Great Mosque of, 62, 103; maps 8, 13, 55, 146, 164
Dante Alighieri, Muslim influence on, 144
Danube River, maps 55, 164
Dark Ages in Europe, 142
Daybul, map 55
Dead Sea, map 146
Decoration: abstract patterns in, 105; the arabesque, 12, 105-106, 107; considered more important than structural form by Muslims, 104; of houses, 106; motifs in, *157, 158; Muslim genius for, 104, 149; plant motifs in, 105, *154, *155, *157; profusion of decoration, 158-159; stylization of natural forms, 155, 157; traditional forms in, 110. See also Art
Delhi, India, 166; map 9
Dhofar, map 13
Dioscorides, 121
Divine Comedy (Dante), 144
Divorce, 33, 40, 92, 93
Dome of the Rock, Jerusalem, 102
Domestic life: household articles, 83, 106-107, *111-119
Dominic, Saint, 147
Don Quixote, 144, 148
Dress: Arab, 83; court dress at the Alhambra, 158; elegance of, 101; modernization of, 169; popularization of trousers, 169; traditional Muslim clothing abolished, 170; the turban, 169
Drinking habits: proscription of alcohol, 20, 40, 95; enjoyment of wine, 79; tavern scene, *95. See also Eating habits; Food and Cooking.
Drugs, use of in medicine, 126-127
Du'a (private prayer), 35

E

East Indies, trade with Islam, 83
Eating habits, 83, 116. See also Drinking habits; Food and Cooking
Edessa, 146; map 146
Education: of boys, *90-91; educational system, 165; in Egypt under Muhammad Ali, 168; modernization of schools and colleges, 170. See also Jundishapur; Madrasas; Universities
Egypt, 12, 75, 80, 88, 122; adversely affected by Umar's tax reforms, 63; conquered by Amr ibn al-As, 57-58, 70; controlled by Mu'awiya, 61; conquered by Islam, 55, 56, 103; 11th Century bronze, *100; grievances against Uthman, 59; invaded by Napoleon, 167-168; Mamluk dynasty, 166; maps 8, 55, 164; in the 19th Century, 169; opens the Suez Canal, 169; relations with Great Britain, 169; under Muhammad Ali, 168; occupied by Persia, 54; pyramids of, *70; trade with Islam, 83, 97. See also

Cairo; Ibn Tulun Mosque
Entertainments. See Games and pastimes
Ethiopia. See Abyssinia
Euclid, 121
Euphrates River, 13, 54, 60, 79, 80; maps 13, 55, 146, 164
Europe: astrolabe introduced into Europe by Muslims, 129; challenge to Muslim ascendency, 163-169; contrasted with Islam, 169; importation of Middle Eastern goods following the Crusades, 146-147; invaded by Ottomans, 147, 148, 165, 167; influenced by Islam, 11, 141-146, 147, 148; mathematical knowledge derived from Islam, 129; technique of paper making learned from Muslims, 12; trade routes to, map 13; Western ideas and teachers imported by Turkey, 169
Expansionism: 54-64, 65-77, map 54-55

F

Fadl, son of Yahya, 82
Fakir (Muslim holy man), 143-144
Falconry, 145
Falsafa (knowledge of the universe), 122-123
Far East, Muslim trade with, 13, 148
Faraj, Sultan, 119
Fatima (daughter of Muhammad), 15, *29, 59
Fatimid dynasty, prevents Christian access to Palestine, 145; map 146
Fergusson, James, quoted, 147-148
Financial system, 84
Fitzgerald, Edward, 110
"Five Pillars of Islam," 31-40, 141
Folklore: animal tales in bestiaries, 131-139; Arabic, 12
Food and Cooking: exotic cuisine of Islam, 83; post-Ramadan feast, 39; Middle Eastern foods introduced to Europe by returning Crusaders, 146-147; religious law, 40. See also Drinking habits; Eating habits
Fortresses, desert, 104
France: inspires Ottoman New Order, 167; invaded by Muslims, 55, 65, 77; protectorates of, 169
Friday Mosque (Samarra), 88
Funeral customs, *98-99
Furniture, 83; simplicity of, 106
Fustat, Egypt, 103; map 55

G

Gabriel (angel), *23, *24, *29, 34
Galen, 121, 122, 125, 126
Gama, Vasco da, 167
Games and pastimes, 83. See also Chess; Food and Cooking; Gardens; Holidays; Music; Poetry
Ganges River, 166
Gardens: laid out by the Abbasids, 104; Persian, 174, 175
Gaza, 56; maps 55, 146
Genghis Khan, 163, 165, 166
Genoa, 145
Geographers, 130
Geometry, 129; developed in Islam, 12
Ghandara sculpture, 142
Ghazali (theologian), 87
Gibraltar, 62
Glass, 107, *116, *118-119; manufacture of, 80, 128
Granada, Spain, 149, 158; Arabic books burnt, 143; culture of under Islam, 142; map 54
Great Britain: challenges Ottoman power, 168; defeats Muhammad Ali, 169; policy toward Egypt, 169
Greece: 128, 169; art of introduced to India by Alexander the Great, 141; conquered by Muhammad II, 163; heritage of returned to Western world through Islam, 12; influence of Hellenistic thought upon Islamic science and philosophy, 84-85, 86, 107, 108, 122, 141;

influence of Greek naturalism upon Islamic representational painting, 106; uprisings against the Ottomans, 168
Guadalquivir River, 143
Guyushi Mosque, Cairo, *41, *47

H

Habsburg family, 172, 180
Hadhramaut, the, 13; maps 13, 55
Hadi, Caliph, succession of, 82
Hadith (Traditions), 38-39
Hakim, Caliph, orders destruction of the Church of the Holy Sepulcher, 145
Hallaj (mystic), 87
Hanifs (religious sect), 14
Harems, 106, 145, 170; establishment of in Spain, 143
Hasan (son of Ali), 61
Hashimiya, Iraq, 79
Heraclius, 54; attempts to regain Damascus, 57; defeated by Islam, 56
Herat, maps 9, 55
Hidalgo (Spanish concept of the ideal man), 143-144
Hijaz, the, 13
Hindu Kush (mountain range), *76-77
Hindus, 128
Hippocrates, 121, 125
Hira, Persia, 15, 122
Hisab al-Jabr wa'l Muqabala (Khwarizmi), 129
Historians, Muslim, 130
Holidays: "Great Festival," 38, *94. See also Ramadan
Holy Land, access to as a purpose of the Crusades, 145
Holy Sepulcher Shrine, Jerusalem. See Church of the Holy Sepulcher
Homer, 85
Horoscopes. See Astrology
Hospitals, 124, 127, 147. See also Medicine
"House of Wisdom," the, 121, 122, 129
Household articles, 83, 106-107, *111-119
Hulagu (grandson of Genghis Khan), 163
Hunayn ibn Ishaq (physician), achievements of, 122; textbook on ophthalmology, 122
Hungary, 166, 167; map 164
Husayn (son of Ali), 63

I

Ibn Arabi (Spanish mystic), 144
Ibn Bakhtishu', 131
Ibn Bakhtishu', Jurjis, 124
Ibn Battuta, 148
Ibn Hazm, treatise on love, 144
Ibn Ishaq (first biographer of Muhammad), 15
Ibn Khaldun (philosopher and historian), 130
Ibn Maymun. See Maimonides
Ibn Rushd (Averroes) (physician), achievements of, 125; commentaries on Aristotle, 125, 144; as translator of Aristotle, 125
Ibn Sina. See Avicenna
Ibn Tulun, Governor of Egypt, annexes Syria, 88; builds Egypt's first hospital, 147; rule of, 103
Ibn Tulun Mosque, *42-43, *45, *46-47, *48, *49, 147; style of, 103
Idrisi (Arab cartographer), 145
Id al-Fitr (post-Ramadan feast), 39
Imam, 43, 50
India, 12, 55, 58, 62, 85, 128, 141, 169; art of, 141-142; Biruni's book on, 130; earliest Islamic description of, 130; invaded by Mongols, 166; maps 9, 55; Muslim architecture in, 147; origins of chess in, 83; as part of Islamic empire, 65; scientific works translated into Arabic, 121; tombs, 147-148; trade with Far East, 148; trade with Islam, 83, 97; under the Mughals, 147; under Muslim rule, 76, 77
Indian Ocean, 141, 167

189

Indonesia: influence of Muslim traders and teachers, 148; trade with Islam, 148
Indus River, 62, 142; maps 13, 55, 164
Infanticide, 66
Insane, treatment of, 127
Iraq, 13, 61, 64, 67, 80; conquered by Islam, 55, 56; held by the Persians, 69; irrigation in, 121; maps 9, 13, 55, 164; technique of making lusterware developed in, 107; trading commodities, 97
Irrigation: in Iraq, 121; irrigating machine, *120; use of canals in, 62
Isfahan, map 55
Ishma'il (son of Abraham), 32
Islamic empire: absorption of various cultures, 123, 141; adopts Western ways, 169; beginnings of, 11-20; boundaries of, 65; contrasted with Europe, 169; after the death of Muhammad, map 55; decline of power, 87-88, 163-166; emergence of great military leaders, 56; era of change and conquest, 53-64; expansion of, 11, 53-64, 65-77, map 54-55; future of, 170; Golden Age of, 12, 53, 64, 79-88; government of, 81; guide books to, 130; heritage of, 163-170; influence of, 141-148; intellectual awakening, 84-85; need for spiritual renewal, 169; prosperity of, 89, 97; religious wars, 141-142; resources of, 83; respect for scholarship, 122, 148; map 8-9; in the 20th Century, 170; uniting of achieved by Seljuk Turks, 165; unifying role of, 12
Isma'il I, Khedive of Egypt, 169
Israfil (angel), 34
Isra'il (angel), 34
Ivory carving, 12; Persian chessman, *83

J

Jabir ibn Hayyan (alchemist), 127-128
Ja'far, son of Yahya, 82-83
Jaffa, map 146
Jalal al-Din Rumi (Sufi poet), 110
Jamal al-Din al-Afghani, 169
Janissaries, 166, 167; massacre of, 169
Jawsaq palace, 104
Java, 148; Muslim trade with, 141
Jaxartes River, maps 13, 55
Jazari (engineer), 147
Jahan, Shah, 148
Jerusalem, 56; Dome of the Rock (mosque), 102; falls to Crusaders, 145; invaded by Persia, 54; King of, 145; maps 8, 55, 146, 164; remains undefeated by Islam, 57; surrenders to Umar, 57. See also Church of the Holy Sepulcher
Jesus Christ, honored in Islam, 25, 32
Jewelry: customs regarding, 114; Egyptian pendant, *114; Persian bracelet, *114
John of the Cross, Saint, 143
Jordan River, maps 55, 146
Jordan, Umayyad fortresses in, 104
Judaism and the Jews: 167; in Arabia, 14; disaffection of Jews in Spain aids Muslims, 142; harsh treatment of by Muhammad, 19; massacred by Crusaders, 146; Muslim political superiority over, 102; reject Muhammad, 17-18; religious activity suppressed by Muslims, 58; religious practices permitted in Islam, 19; sacred shrine in Jerusalem, 102; translate Greek manuscripts into Syriac, 85; treated with restraint by Umar, 57
Jundishapur, Persia, medical school, 122, 123, 124, 127
Jurjis ibn Bakhtishu'. See Ibn Bakhtishu', Jurjis
Justinian, 147

K

Kaaba (shrine at Mecca), 14, 18, 19, *26, 32, 36, 37, 38, 119; architectural form of, 102; attacked by Abyssinian army, *22; Muhammad prays before (painting), *21; plan of, *16; purification of, 19; Zamzam well, *16, 45, 98
Kandahar, Afghanistan, *75

Karlowitz, Treaty of, 167
Kashan, pottery of, 116, *117, *119
Kemal Ataturk, 170
Kerbela, map 55
Kerman, map 55
Khadija (first wife of Muhammad), 14, 15, 16, 17, 20; marriage of, *23
Khalid ibn Barmak, appointed governor of Persian provinces, 82
Khalid ibn al-Walid: attacks Syria, 56; captures Damascus, 56, 57; nickname, 56
Khalifat Rasul Allah (Successor of the Messenger of God). See Abu Bakr
Kharijites (Seceders), 61; form anti-Umayyad party, 63
Kindi, 85
Khosrau I, King of Persia, 59
Khurasan, 87-88; map 55
Khwarizmi (mathematician), 129
Konya, maps 8, 164
Koran, 31-40, 111; on Abraham, 32; on adultery, 20; battlefield prayers, 36; Bible stories in the, 32; carved stand for, *86; contains few details of Muhammad's life, 15; contents of, 11; on the Day of Judgment, 34; delivered by Muhammad, 11; embossed leaf from, *30; on fasting, 36; as the first great prose work of Islam, 109-110; on the giving of plunder, 31; on the goodness of God, 32; on Heaven, 34; on Jesus and the Virgin Mary, 17; Muslim belief in its infallibility, 33, 165; preparation of single text, 33; on the providence of God, 66, 70-71; read at funerals, 98; revelations challenged, 84; standardization of, 58-59; suras, 33; on taxation, 58; Traditionists vs. Mu'tazilites controversy, 85-86; teaching of, 90; on the treatment of women, 40; on warfare, 40, 141; as the Word of God, 11
Kublai Khan, 148
Kufa, Iraq, 60, 61, 63, 79, 128; maps 9, 55

L

Language. See Arabic; Persian
Law: Islamic law replaced by Western law, 170. See also Koran
Lebanon, *67
Levant, the, 145; influence of Islam on, 141
Literature: development of prose, 109-110; flourishes in Ninth Century Islam, 85; greatness of Islam's, 12; Islamic achievement in, 101; as Islam's most original creative art form, 108; Maqamat (collection of anecdotes), 89, 110; Persian court literature, 108, 110; teaching of, 90; translation of Arabic manuscripts from Spain into European languages, 144. See also Koran; Poetry
Little Armenia, 146; map 146
London, 169

M

Ma'arri (poet), 109
Madinat al-Salam ("The City of Peace"). See Baghdad
Madinat al-Nabi. See Medina
Madrasas (mosque-colleges), 103-104; founded by the Seljuks, 147
Mahmud II, Sultan of Ottomans, 168-169
Maimonides, Guide for the Perplexed, 125; life and work, 125
Malaya: converted to Islam, 148; Muslim trade with, 141
Mamluks, 163, 166, 167; massacre of, 168; rug, *181
Ma'mun, Caliph, 85, 122; builds observatory, 129; creates the "House of Wisdom," 121
Manners and Customs: behavior of gentlemen, 90; at court, 159; funeral customs, *98-99; legislation regulating behavior, 38; present giving, 111; use of perfume, 112; the wearing of jewelry, 114

Mansur, Caliph, autocratic rule of, 81; builds Baghdad, 80; cured of illness by Jurjis ibn Bakhtishu', 124; death of, 82; early rule of, 79
Manufacturing: production of consumer goods, 83
Manuscripts, illumination of, 107-108
Maps, early Muslim, 130
Maqamat (Arabian tales), 110; illustration from, 89
Marriage, 40, 94, 95; formalities, 92. See also Divorce
Martel, Charles, defeats Muslims at Poitiers, 55
Marwan I, Caliph, deposed and murdered by Abbasids, 64
Masnavi, the (religious poem by Rumi), 110
Mathematics: Arabic system of numerals becomes standard mathematical symbols, 12, 128; algebra, 12, 128-129; concept of zero, 128; decimal system, 128; geometry, 12, 129; influence on abstract design patterns, 105; Muslim contributions to, 12, 128-129; Muslims as the greatest mathematicians of the medieval world, 150-151; practical applications of, 123; trigonometry, 12, 129
Mawali (converts to Islam), 58; discrimination against, 63
Maysun (wife of Mu'awiya), poetry quoted, 108
Mecca: attacks Medina, 18-19; becomes important trading center, 13; Christians in, 14; clashes with Muslims, 18; at the crossroads of the caravan trade, 13; falls to Muhammad, 19; importance of, 13; key to Great Mosque, *118-119; maps 9, 13, 55, 164; pilgrimage to, 37-38, 94, *98; as site of Arabia's holiest pagan shrine, 13-14; as spiritual center of Islam, 19. See also Kaaba
Medicine: achievements in, 124-127; anesthesia, 125-126; debt of modern medicine to Islam, 122; development of surgery, 125-126; drugs, 126-127; hospitals, 124, 127, 147; influence of Islamic scholarship on European medicine, 124-125; medical school at Jundishapur, 122, 123, 124, 127; Muslim contributions to, 123; Muslim enhancement of Greek theory, 12; ophthalmology, 126; primitive medical knowledge of Arabs, 123; psychological disorders diagnosed, 125; training and examinations, 126, 127; traveling clinics, 127; treatment of cancer, 125; treatment of the insane, 127; treatment of smallpox, 124; tuberculosis diagnosed, 125. See also Hunayn ibn Ishaq
Medina (Yathrib), 13, 17, 19, 36, 43, 57, 59, 60, 63, 101; attacked by Mecca, 18-19; building of the mosque, *28, 29; as capital of Islam, 19; maps 9, 13, 55, 164; Muhammad's stay in, 26, *28; as political capital of Islam, 19
Mediterranean Sea, 58, 83, 145; maps 13, 55, 146, 164
Mehmet. See Muhammad
Men: life of, 95. See also Women
Merchants. See Trade
Merv, map 55
Mesopotamia, 80, 88, 122
Metalwork, 107
Mevlevi (Whirling Dervishes), 110
Michael (angel), 34
Military skills, during the Crusades, 146
Mina, 38
Miniatures, 107-108, *172; Persian, 107, *176, *178; Turkish, *21-29, *140. See also Art; Painting
Mohammed. See Muhammad
Monetary system, 84
Mongols: invade Islam, 163-164, 165, 166; sack Baghdad, 11, 163-164, 166; second invasion of Middle East, 165
Morgan Library, New York, 131
Morocco, 87; Muslim university in, 148
Mosaics, 106; tile, *150-151
Moscow, 166
Moses (prophet), 25, 32
Mosques, *41-51; arcades, *46-47; architecture of, 12, 41-51; building of, 62; building of the mosque at Medina,

*28, 29; calligraphy as a form of decoration, 106; decoration, *48, 49, 149; development of, 101; distinctive features of, 41; Dome of the Rock (Jerusalem), 102; form of, 36, 101-102, 103; fountains of, 45; Friday Mosque (Samarra), 88; Great Mosque of Cordoba, Spain, *46-47; Great Mosque of Damascus, 62, 103; Great Mosque at Qayrawan, Tunisia, *44-45, *50-51; Guyushi Mosque (Cairo), *41, *47; Ibn Tulun (Cairo), *42-43, *45, *46-47, *48, *49, 147; iwan, 103-104; key to Great Mosque of Mecca, *118-119; maqsura, 50; mihrab, 49, *50-51; minaret, *10, *42, 103; minbar, 49, *50; in Persia, 147; plan of, *34; qibla wall, 49; resplendence of, 102; ruins of largest mosque in Islam, *10; the sanctuary, 49; school, *90-91; in Spain, 143; staff of, 43; tombs of, 147; translations of Arabic word, 49. See also Madrasas
Mosul, 147; map 13
Mourning customs. See Funeral customs
Mu'awiya, Caliph, 108; becomes caliph, 61; death of, 63; dispute with Ali, 60, 61; efficient rule of, 61
Muezzin, 18, 37, *42, 43, 103; duties of, 35
Mughals: architecture of, 147; dynasty of, 147; introduce Islam into India, 147
Muhammad (Mohammed) (Mehmet), Prophet: achieves unification of Arabia, 19; ascension to Heaven, 102; assumes role of prophet, 15; becomes aware of lack of faith in his people, 14; birth of, 14, *22; birthplace of, 98; childhood and youth of, 15; children of, 107; death of, 20, *29, 53, 54, 55; delivers the Koran, 11; depicted in miniature, *176; desire to carry Word of God to northern peoples, 54; dream of, 76-77; early followers of, 16; first vision of, 15; flight from Mecca, 17, *26; harsh measures against Jews, 19; Hijra (Hegira), 17; home of, 36; humanitarian laws of, 19-20; increasing power of, 17; instructions of worship, 41; as the last prophet, 41; legends of, 21; life of, *21-29; lineage of, *59; marriage of, 15, *23; meaning of name in Arabic, 14; neglects to name a successor, 53; nickname of, 14; personality, 14, 19-20; physical appearance, 14-15; pilgrimage to Mecca, 19; prays before the Kaaba (painting), *21; Progress of the Prophet, *21-29; raids against Meccan caravans, 18; rejected by Jews, 17-18; revelations of, 15, *23, *24-25, 31, 33, 36; stay in Yathrib, 17; takes Mecca, 19; teachings of, 15-16; trading journey to Syria, 14; victory at Badr, 18; on water, 44; wives of, 20. See also A'isha; Khadija; Koran
Muhammad I, Sultan of the Ottomans, 166
Muhammad II, Sultan of the Ottomans, *162
Muhammad Abduh, Mufti of Egypt, 169-170
Muhammad Ali, Governor of Egypt, 167-168; defeated by British sea power, 169
Muhammadanism. See Religion
Mumtaz Mahal, 148
Muqaddima (Ibn Khaldun), 130
Muqtadir, Caliph, 127
Muscat, maps 13, 164
Music: enjoyment of, 79; Imperial Music School founded by Mahmud II, 169
Muslims. See Muhammadanism
Mu'ta, map 55
Mu'tadid, Caliph, 88
Mutanabbi (poet), 108
Mu'tasim, Caliph, 88; builds Jawsaq palace, 104
Mukawakkil, Caliph (son of Mu'tasim), 86, 88
Mu'tazilites (school of theology), 85-86, 165
Muzdalifa, 38
Mysticism, 86-87; influence on Dante, 144; passes into the Spanish Christian tradition, 143; poetry of, 110

N

Nabidh (fermented beverage), 95
Napoleon, invades Egypt, 167-168
Nasrid sultans, 149
Negus, the (King of Abyssinia), 17
Nehawand, Persia, battle at, 72
New Troops, the. See Janissaries
Newspaper, first Islamic, 168
Nile River, 13, 57, 166, 169; maps 13, 55, 146, 164
Nippur, Iraq, *69
Nishapur, maps 13, 55
Noah (prophet), 32, 59
Nomads, use of carpets as household objects, 179
Normandy, dynasty of Norman kings in Sicily, 144-145
North Africa: becomes part of the Ottoman empire, 166; conquered by Islam, 55, 56, 57, 62; map 55; trade with Islam, 83. See also Africa
Nubia, 168
Numerals, Arabic, transmitted to the Western world, 12, 128

O

Observatory of Caliph Ma'mun, 129
Oman, maps 55, 164
Omar Khayyam, Rubaiyat, 12, 110
Oriental rugs. See Carpets
Orlando Furioso (Ariosto), 143
Ophthalmology, 126
Optics, 129
Ornamentation. See Decoration
Orontes River, map 146
Osman, leader of the Ottomans, 165
Osman II, 165
Ottomans: besiege Vienna, 148, 165, 167; challenge Persia's power in the Middle East, 168; conquer Byzantium, 166; decline of empire, 165, 167, 169; defeated by Timur, 166; dynasty of, 147, 165; efficient army of, 166; empire of, map 164; expansion of empire, 166; fight French in Egypt, 167-168; invasion of Europe, 147, 148, 165; as major military power of Europe, 167; march into Africa and Europe, 165; modern Turkish nation, 170; mosque architecture of, 147; the New Order, 167; origin of name, 165; power of, 163; recapture Anatolia, 166; rise of, 163, 165; take Constantinople, 166. See also Seljuks; Turkey and the Turks
Oxus River, maps 13, 55

P

Painting: Eastern influence in, 106; Muslim scene of the Nativity, *32; representational painting, 106; stylized and symbolic, 106. See also Art; Miniatures
Pakistan, 147
Palaces: of the Abbasids, 104; the Alhambra, *149-161; Baghdad palace sacked by Mongols, 163; building materials, 104; built in cities, 104; caliph's palace at Baghdad, 80; desert fortresses of the Umayyads, 104; fortress-palace of Ukhaydir, 53; of Ibn Tulun, 147; Jawsaq palace, Samarra, 104; modeled on Roman frontier forts, 104; ornamentation of, 149
Palermo, Sicily, 107; as center of Arabic culture, 144-145; map 9
Palestine, 14, 54, 122; Christian access to as a purpose of the Crusades, 145; Christian states established in, 146; conquered by Islam, 55, 56, 57; map 55
Paper, brought from Far East to Islam, 12, 83
Paris, 169
Peloponnesus, 167
Perfume, use of, 112

Persia, 80, 82, 85, 148, 169; armor, *168; art, *78, 105, 108, *176, *178; attacked by Islam under Abu Bakr, 54; as center of Abbasid movement, 64; conquered by Muslims, 55, 56, 58, 72, 101, 121-122; court literature, 108, 110; culture of as a major element of Muslim civilization, 72, 80; decay of empire, 65; defeated at Qadasiya, 69; empire of, map 55; as enemy of Byzantine empire, 54; entertainments in, 79; falls under control of local leaders, 87-88; invaded by Mongols, 163; invades Middle East and captures "True Cross," 54; love of gardens in, 174, 175; maps 9, 13, 164; mosque-builders of, 147; occupies Egypt, 54; ominipotent kings of, 81; as part of Islamic empire, 11, 102; plains of, *72-73; poetry, 12, 110; Safavid dynasty, 166; scientific works translated into Arabic, 121; trade with Far East, 148; trading commodities, 97; trading routes threatened, 13
Persian Gulf, 13, 54, 60, 83; maps 55, 164
Persian language, 110
Peter the Great, Czar of Russia, 169, 172
Petra, map 13
Pharmacies, 126-127
Pharos (lighthouse at Alexandria), 103
Philippines, the, Muslim trade with, 141
Philosophy, 122; flourishes in Ninth Century Islam, 85
Physics: Avicenna's investigations in, 125; Muslim contributions to 12
Plato, 121
Poetry: Arabic, 12-13, 62, 101; in Baghdad, 108; Bedouin, 108; development of, 108-110; enjoyment of, 79; epic poem, 110; European, influenced by Islam, 144; lyrical, 101; mystical, 110; Persian, 108, 110; qasida (ode), 108; reflects transformation of Arabic society, 108; style of, 108-109
Poitiers, France, besieged by Muslims, 55, 65; map 55
Poland, 167
Polo, 83
Polo, Marco, 148
Polygamy, 40
Porcelain, brought from China to Islam in Ninth Century, 83, 107, 116. See also Ceramics
Postal routes, 62
Pottery. See Ceramics
Prayer, angels at, *140; form of, 18; importance of, 176
Predestination, theories of, 32
Printing press, first Muslim, 168
Progress of the Prophet, The, *21-29
Prose: replaces poetry in recording history and traditions of Islam, 110
Provence, troubadours of, 144
Ptolemy, 121
Pyramids, Egyptian, *70
Pyrenees, 142

Q

Qadasia, battle at, 69
Qadi (judge), *93
Qasim Amin, 170
Qayrawan, Tunisia: Great Mosque, *44-45, *50-51; maps 8, 55
Qazvin, map 55
Qudama (critic), 108
Quraysh (tribe): as chief citizens of Mecca, 14; defeat at Badr, 18, 36; opposition to Muhammad, 16; persecution of Muslims, 16-17

R

Rabi'a (Sufi), 87
Ramadan (holy month), 18, 36-37, 123; post-Ramadan feast, 39
Raqqa, map 13

Rayy, maps 13, 164
Razi (Rhazes): treatise on smallpox, 124; Book of the Secret of Secrets, 128; encyclopedia of medicine, 124; medical discoveries of, 124; work in alchemy, 128
Red Sea, 13, 14, 83; maps 13, 55, 146, 164
Religion: alms giving, 36, 39; Arabian characteristics of, 19; articles of faith, 31-40; beginnings of in Arabia, 11; belief in angels, 34; belief in the oneness of Allah, 32; belief in the prophets, 32; and caliphate, 81-82; conservatism in, 85-86, 165; converts, 58, 76, 77; Day of Judgment, 34; dietary laws, 40; early persecution of Muslims, 16-17; fasting, 36-37; "Five Pillars of Islam," 31-40, 141; "Great Festival," 38; hadith (Traditions), 38-39; hajj (pilgrimage), 37-38; importance of prayer, 34-35, 35-36; as Islam's most durable strength, 164-165; jihad (holy war), 40, 141-142; Judaeo-Christian concepts in, 32, 141; legislation regulating behavior, 38; mawali, 58; need for spiritual renewal, 169; not forced on subject peoples, 58; no organized priesthood, 31; pilgrimages to Mecca, 13-14, 37-38; plays dominant role in Muslim art, 101; ramadan, 18, 36-37, 39, 123; religious war, 141-142; ritual ablution, *22, 35, 37-38, *45; sacrifice, 38, shahada (declaration of belief), 31; shari'a, 38-39; simplicity of, 31; state control of religious life, 82; theories of predestination, 32; ulama (religious scholars), 31, 165; unchanging beliefs, 31; unique customs, 18. See also Christianity; Judaism
Rhazes. See Razi
Ridda (apostasy) wars, 54
Ring of the Dove, The (Ibn Hazm), 144
Roger de Hauteville, 144-145
Roger II (Roger the Pagan), 107, 145
Roland, Song of, 143
Roman Catholic Church: conflict with Muslims in Spain, 142-143; and the Crusades, 145; See also Christians and Christianity
Rome, 56
Rosary, Islamic origins of, 147
Rubaiyat of Omar Khayyam, 12, 110
Rugs. See Carpets
Russia: invaded by Timur the Lame, 165-166; Muslim travelers in, 130; trade with Islam, 84

S

Sadaqa (alms), 36
Safavid dynasty, 166
Sahara Desert, trading caravans, 148
St. Symeon, map 146
Saladin, Sultan of Egypt, 125
Salat (ritual prayer), 35
Samarkand, 12, 75, 165; maps 13, 55, 164
Samarra, 11, 103; as capital of Islam, 88, 103; Friday Mosque, 88; Jawsaq palace, 104; map 9; palaces of, 104
San'a, map 13
Saracens: routed at Jerusalem, 145
Scandinavia: trade with Islam, 84, 97
Science, 121-130; basis of Islamic scientific thought, 122; debt of modern science to Islam, 121, 122; flourishes in Islam, 85, 107, 121; influence of Greek scientific theory, 85; Muslim ascendancy is challenged by the West, 163; terminology derived from Arabic, 121, 123, 128
Scripts. See Calligraphy
Sea of Galilee, 57, *66-67; map 146
Seceders. See Kharijites
Selim the Grim, 166
Selim III, Sultan of Turkey, 167, 168
Seljuks, 88; architecture under, 147; dynasty of, 147; empire of, map 164; expansion of empire, 147; found the first madrasas, 147; invade Baghdad, 163; unite Islam, 165; use of ornamental tiles, 107. See also

Ottomans; Turkey and the Turks
Serbia, conquered by Muhammad II, 163
Seville, Spain, 125; culture of under Islam, 142; falls to Muslims, 142; map 54; reconquest of, 143
Sexual mores, 40
Shari'a, 38-39
Shi'a ("the party") (militant reform group), 63
Shi'ites, persecuted by Abbasids, 64; rebellion of Shi'ites, 79
Shiraz, maps 9, 55, 164
Sicily, 122; captured by Islam, 144; and cultural legacy of Islam, 144-145; influence of Islam on, 141; reconquest of, 144-145; taken from Islam by Normans, 107; under Norman Kings, 145
Sidon, map 146
Siffin, 60; map 55
Siraf, map 13
Sivas, map 164
Slavery: modified by Muhammad, 20; importation of slaves from Africa and Byzantium, 83, 97; slave market, *94-95
Slavonia, 167
Somalis, 148
Sophocles, 85
Sophronius, Patriarch of Jerusalem, 57
Spain, 55, 62, 64, *74-75, 107, 122, 130, 149; art of Moorish, *114; and cultural legacy of Islam, 142-144; hidalgo concept and influence of Islam, 143-144; Islamic dynasties in, 142; Islamic influence in, 141; maps 8, 54; Muslim conquest of, 62, 75, 77, 142, 149; as part of Islamic empire, 65; trade with Islam, 83
Sports. See Games and pastimes
Sudan, the, 168
Suez Canal, opening of, 169
Sufism, 86-87, 165; doctrine of the concept of God, 143; influence on Spanish Christians, 143; poetry of, 110
Sumatra, 148
Summa Theologica (St. Thomas Aquinas), 144
Surgery. See Medicine
Syr Darya, maps 55, 164
Syria, 13, 14, 54, 67, 70, 74, 80, 85, 122, 145; annexed by Ibn Tulun, 88; Christian churches in, 103; conquered by Islam, 55, 56, 57, 62, 69; conquered by the Ottomans, 166; held by Umayyads, 64; influence of culture, 102; lamp from, *118-119; maps 8, 13, 55; Muhammad's trip to, 14; as part of Byzantine empire, 14; pottery of, *112; promised to Muhammad Ali, 168; revolt against Ali, 60-61; trade with Islam, 83; trading commodities, 97; Umayyad fortresses in, 104

T

Tabriz, 166; map 164
Taif (Arabia), 13, 17; maps 13, 55
Taj Mahal, 148
Tamerlane. See Timur the Lame
Taxation: of conquered territories, 58; of Christians and Jews, 19; reforms under Umar II, 63; refusal of Arab tribes to pay Islamic tax, 54; as stated in the Koran, 58
Teresa of Avila, Saint, 143
Textiles, 83, 107; embroidered cape, *106-107; making of, 101; Muslim factory at Palermo, 107
Theodorus (Byzantine commander), 57
Theology: flourishes in Ninth Century Islam, 85; Traditionists vs. Mu'tazilites controversy, 85-86. See also Koran; Religion
Thousand and One Nights, A. See Arabian Nights
Tigris River, 13, 54, 61, 64, 79, 80, 88; maps 13, 15, 146, 164
Tiles, ornamental, 107
Timbuktu, establishment of Muslim university in, 141, 148
Timur the Lame (Tamerlane), 165-166
Toledo, Spain, falls to Muslims, 142
Tournaments, Muslim origin of, 146

Trade: Baghdad as a center of, 79-80; camel caravans, 97; expansion of, 83; with the Far East, 148; as an honored profession, 148; importance of Mecca to, 13; opportunities for during the Crusades, 145, 146-147; pre-Islamic trade routes, *map* 13; trading routes, *map* 13; sea-going, 141; widespread trade of Islam, 97

Traditionists vs. Mu'tazilites controversy, 85-86

Traditions (*hadith*), 38-39, 102

Transoxiana, *map* 164

Traveling, as a way of life, 179

Treaty of Karlowitz, 167

Trigonometry, 129; developed in Islam, 12

Tripoli (Libya); *maps* 8, 55, 164

Tripoli (Lebanon), *map* 146

Tulunid dynasty, 88

Tunisia, 87; conquered by Uqba, 70; Muslim university in, 148

Turkestan, 88, 124

Turkey and the Turks, 12; in Asia Minor, 165; conquer Byzantium, 146; empire of, *map* 164; invade Europe, 148; invade Islam, 147; as a major world power, 147; military conquests of, 147; miniatures, *21-29; modern state of, 170; routed at Jerusalem, 145; at siege of Vienna, 148, 165; Turkish guard of the Caliph, 88, 104. *See also* Ottomans; Seljuks

Tyre, *map* 146

U

Ukhaydir, *52

Umar, Caliph, *59; administrative policies of, 58; assassination of, 58; character of, 57; as greatest of the caliphs, 57; receives surrender of Jerusalem, 57

Umar II, Caliph, 64; tax reform of, 63

Umayyad dynasty, 58, 60, 61-62, 147; artistic and cultural development under, 102; autocratic rule of, 81; build Great Mosque of Damascus, 103; conquests of, *map* 54-55; desert fortresses of, 104; dynastic succession of, 61; end of power, 63-64; establishment of dynasty, 102; expansion to the east and west, 55; military conquests of, 62; in North Africa, 62; Spanish line, 87; systematic murder of, 64

Universe, knowledge of (*Falsafa*), 122-123

Universities: first official university chartered in Europe, 145; at Cairo (al-Azhar), 148, 165, 169; "House of Wisdom," 121, 122, 129; modernization of, 170; in Morocco, 148; at Naples, 145; at Timbuktu, 141, 148; in Tunisia, 148

Uqba, nephew of Amr, 70

Urban II, Pope, proclaims First Crusade, 145

"Uses of Animals, The," pages from, *131-139

Uthman, Caliph, *59; assassination of, 59; becomes caliph, 58; neoptism under, 59; standardizes the Koran, 33, 58-59

V

Venice, 145

Verse. *See* Poetry

Vienna, 180; besieged by Turks, 148, 165, 167

Vikings, 56

Visigoths, 142

Vizier, role of, 82

W

Walid, Caliph, builds Great Mosque of Damascus, 103

Warfare: desert, 56; emergence of great military leaders, 56; military skills learned during the Crusades, 146; Muslims use of carrier pigeons, 146; religious wars, 40, 141-142; standard terms of surrender, 56-57. *See also* Army

Water, importance of, 44-45. *See also* Irrigation

West. *See* Europe

Whirling Dervishes, 110

Women: care of young children, 90; as chess players, 83; emancipation of, 170; female poet, 108; Koranic law on control of women's property, 170; marriage rights, 92; on pilgrimage to Mecca, *98; seclusion of, 95; splendor of dress at Alhambra court, 158; subservience to men, 93; treatment of according to the Koran, 40. *See also* Divorce; Harems; Marriage; Men

Wood Carving, 12

World War I, 169

Writing, art of. *See* Calligraphy

X

Ximenes, Cardinal, 143

Y

Yahya (son of Khalid), becomes vizier, 82

Yahya al-Wasiti, 89

Yarmuk, battle of, 69

Yarmuk River, 57; *map* 55

Yathrib. *See* Medina

Yazid (son of Mu'awiya), 61; slays Husayn, 63

Yemen, 13; *maps* 13, 55

Yeni cheri (New Troops). *See* Janissaries

Yezdegerd, King of Persia, 54, 72

Z

Zakat (alms), 36

Zamzam (holy well in Mecca), *16, 45, 98

Zayd (slave freed by Muhammad), 16

Zoroastrianism, 167; conflict with Christianity in Seventh Century, 54; in Persia, 54

x

PRODUCTION STAFF FOR TIME INCORPORATED

John L. Hallenbeck (Vice President and Director of Production),
Robert E. Foy, Caroline Ferri and Robert E. Fraser
Text photocomposed under the direction of Albert J. Dunn and Arthur J. Dunn.